Build a Next-Generation Digital Workplace

Transform Legacy Intranets to Employee Experience Platforms

Shailesh Kumar Shivakumar

Apress®

Build a Next-Generation Digital Workplace: Transform Legacy Intranets to Employee Experience Platforms

Shailesh Kumar Shivakumar
Bangalore, India

ISBN-13 (pbk): 978-1-4842-5511-7   ISBN-13 (electronic): 978-1-4842-5512-4
https://doi.org/10.1007/978-1-4842-5512-4

Managing Director, Apress Media LLC: Welmoed Spahr
Acquisitions Editor: Shiva Ramachandran
Development Editor: Rita Fernando
Coordinating Editor: Rita Fernando

Cover designed by eStudioCalamar

Cover image designed by Pixabay

Distributed to the book trade worldwide by Springer Science+Business Media New York, 233 Spring Street, 6th Floor, New York, NY 10013. Phone 1-800-SPRINGER, fax (201) 348-4505, e-mail orders-ny@springer-sbm.com, or visit www.springeronline.com. Apress Media, LLC is a California LLC and the sole member (owner) is Springer Science + Business Media Finance Inc (SSBM Finance Inc). SSBM Finance Inc is a **Delaware** corporation.

For information on translations, please e-mail rights@apress.com, or visit www.apress.com/rights-permissions.

Apress titles may be purchased in bulk for academic, corporate, or promotional use. eBook versions and licenses are also available for most titles. For more information, reference our Print and eBook Bulk Sales web page at www.apress.com/bulk-sales.

Any source code or other supplementary material referenced by the author in this book is available to readers on GitHub via the book's product page, located at www.apress.com/9781484255117. For more detailed information, please visit www.apress.com/source-code.

Printed on acid-free paper

I would like to dedicate this book to:

my parents, Shivakumara Setty V and Anasuya T M,
from whom I borrowed love and strength,

my wife, Chaitra Prabhudeva and my son Shishir,
from whom I borrowed time and support,

my in-laws, Prabhudeva T M and Krishnaveni B,
from whom I borrowed help and courage,

and

to all my teachers, who bestowed lots of love and
knowledge upon me.

Table of Contents

About the Author

Dr. Shailesh Kumar Shivakumar is an inventor, author, and senior architect specializing in digital technologies. He is an award-winning digital technology practitioner with skills in technology and practice management and with experience in a wide spectrum of digital technologies, including enterprise portals, content systems, enterprise search, and other open source technologies. He has more than 18 years of industry experience and was the chief architect in building a digital platform, which won a "Best Web Support Site 2013" global award. He is a Guinness World Records holder for participating in successfully developing a mobile application in a coding marathon.

Shailesh has PhD in computer science from IGNOU, a central university of India, and has completed the executive program in business management at the Indian Institute of Management, Calcutta (IIMC). He is the author of seven technical books published by the world's top academic publishers. He also has published a dozen technical white papers and has authored eight textbook chapters for undergraduate programs. He has published more than ten research papers in international journals and is a member of the editorial boards for three international journals.

Dr. Shailesh is the sole inventor of the inventions related to web security and personalization and holds two granted U.S. patents. He also has five patent applications. Shailesh is a frequent speaker at events such as IEEE conferences and Oracle JavaOne. Shailesh is given invited talks and participated in panel discussions in international conferences. He was Conference Advisory Committee member of International Conference on Computational Intelligence and Communication (ICCIC-19).

Dr. Shailesh is a seasoned architect and is deeply focused on enterprise architecture, building alliance partnerships with product vendors, and has a proven track record of executing complex, large-scale programs. He has successfully architected and led many engagements for Fortune 500 clients of Infosys and built globally deployed enterprise applications. He also has headed up a center of excellence for digital practices and developed several digital solutions as well as intellectual property to accelerate digital solution development. He has led multiple thought leadership and productivity improvement initiatives and has been part of special interest groups related to emerging web technologies at his organization.

Dr. Shailesh was awarded the prestigious "Albert Nelson Marquis Lifetime Achievement Award 2018" for excellence in technology and has won multiple awards including the prestigious "Infosys Awards for Excellence 2013–14" for multitalented thought leader, brand ambassador for his MFG unit, and best employee, "Pinnacle Award" "Brand Ambassador Award 2013", "Unit Champion Award", "Best Employee Award 2015" as well as a delivery excellency award and multiple spot awards at Infosys for his exemplary performance and contribution. He also received an honor from the executive vice chairman of his organization. He is featured as an "Infy star" in the Infosys Hall of Fame and recently led a delivery team that won the "Best Project Team Award" at his organization. He was honored as Chief guest of honor of Presidency college IT Fest COMPUTANTRA-2018, and was the guest of honor at ISTE student chapters at BNMIT, Bangalore.

Dr. Shailesh holds numerous professional certifications such as TOGAF 9, Oracle Certified Master (OCM) in Java EE5 Enterprise Architect, IBM Certified SOA Solution Designer, and IBM Certified Solution Architect Cloud Computing Infrastructure.

Acknowledgments

I am deeply indebted to my wife Chaitra and son Shishir for their immense and unconditional support of all my initiatives.

I would like to convey my sincere and heartfelt thanks to T.P. Vasanth, my brother-in-law, for a constant stream of support and inspiration.

I would also like to recognize and thank Dr. P. V. Suresh for his constant encouragement and immense support.

Special thanks to the team at Apress consisting of Rita Fernando, Shivangi Ramachandran, and Laura Berendson for all their timely support and review help. The team is highly proactive and super responsive in planning and execution. I would also like to thank the editorial team and design team at Apress for the beautiful book design. I owe much of the book's success to the Apress team.

Introduction

Employees such as information workers are heavily dependent on intranet platforms.

Traditional intranet platforms have helped employees find relevant information, tools, and services. As employees have gotten used to highly engaging customer-centric platforms, naturally they expect a similar experience from intranet platforms. Legacy intranet platforms that lacked the dynamism and engagement features are giving way to modern digital workplaces that provide a more engaging, personalized experience that enhances employee productivity.

Digital workplaces/employee experience platforms (EXPs) are digital platforms where employees can collaborate, connect, and share information and use it for their day-to-day tasks, enabling them to work from anywhere. Unlike traditional intranet platforms, digital workplaces can be accessed anywhere, anytime, and on any device. Employee experience platforms cater to various crucial use case such as learning and training, information delivery, knowledge management, self-service, gamification, content management, personalization, and such. Digital workplaces aim to engage employees at all touchpoints and impact employees' daily lives.

Given the importance of digital workplaces, it is imperative for organizations to design and roll out a digital strategy that engages its workforce effectively, to design scalable platforms, and to optimize operations costs. Organizations need to lay out the vision, identify the needs of their employees, define the goals and success metrics of the program, implement the project, and provide continuous maintenance and support.

This book provides the end-to-end coverage needed to successfully design, implement, and maintain the next generation of digital workplace platforms. Starting from requirements elaboration for digital workplace platforms, the book discusses experience design, digital workplace strategy and transformation themes, development and rollout methods, testing best practices, automated maintenance, and support.

This book also discusses the main trends in digital workplaces—such as cloud transformation, mobile-first design, legacy intranet modernization, employee-centric design (such as persona-based design and employee journey mapping), collaboration (such as enterprise social tools), legacy modernization, and gamification—to motivate employees. The book provides proven methods for rolling out collaboration features, security features, process simplification, process optimization, and self-service. The book also elaborates on various automation and machine-led operations models and maintenance models for the continued success of the digital workplace platforms.

Personalized employee dashboards are one of the salient features of modern digital workplace platforms. The information and tools in the employee dashboard are based on employee roles, preferences, and previous interactions. The book discusses various design approaches to employee dashboards. The book also discusses proven best practices and methods such as transformation methods, migration steps, security design methods, and collaboration methods that can be leveraged for successfully building digital workplace platforms.

Finally, the book discusses various digital workplace case studies to provide insights into real-world implementation methodologies and rollout strategies.

The book will be useful for program managers, CIOs, digital enthusiasts, enterprise architects, and software developers to gain insights into the features and solution elements of modern digital workplace platforms.

Note   *Employee experience platform* and *digital workplace* are used synonymously in this book.

The products, tools, technologies, and cloud platforms used in the book are only for pedagogical purposes. The solutions can be built using alternative technologies as well.

CHAPTER 1

Introduction to Employee Experience Platforms

Superior experiences play a pivotal role in engaging end users. User-centric digital experience platforms (DXPs) engage end users and lead to long-term relationships with them. DXPs provide an omnichannel user experience that provides an optimal experience across various touch points in the user's journey.

An employee experience platform (EXP) is designed to engage employees throughout the employee lifecycle, providing productivity-boosting tools and features. Organizations use an EXP to retain talent and continuously improve the productivity of their employees. Intranet platforms provide access to unified information and provide collaboration among internal users.

Organizations should design and implement EXPs to enable their employees with the right set of tools and services. EXPs play a vital role in engaging, empowering, and retaining the employees of an organization. Next-generation workplaces demand constant innovation and responsiveness, which can be addressed effectively by EXPs.

In this chapter, I will go over the key features and latest trends of EXPs.

Brief Introduction to Intranet Platforms

Digital intranet platforms provide a holistic and personalized user experience for intranet users. Intranet platforms provide tools, content, and communication primarily for organization employees and internal users. Various flavors of intranet platforms are employee portals, colleague portals, sales portals, and such.

Employees expect their digital intranet experience to be similar to the most popular consumer-grade digital platforms. Digital features such as mobile-enabled user experiences, responsive user interfaces, hyper-personalization, and real-time content have become common needs of a digital user.

© Shailesh Kumar Shivakumar 2020
S. K. Shivakumar, *Build a Next-Generation Digital Workplace*, https://doi.org/10.1007/978-1-4842-5512-4_1

The intranet platform will be available to internal users in all geographic areas of the organization. The main features of intranet platforms are elaborated on in the subsequent sections.

Traditional Intranet Platforms vs. Employee Experience Platforms

Table 1-1 highlights the main differences between traditional intranet platforms and employee experience platforms.

Table 1-1. *Traditional Intranet Platform vs. Employee Experience Platform*

Category	Traditional Intranet Platform	Employee Experience Platform
Technology ecosystem	Product-based architecture Based on proprietary standards and integration plug-ins Involves multiple tools often with disjointed experience	Lean and web-oriented architecture Extensible with marketplace apps Open and web standards–based architecture
Integration ecosystem	Mainly service-oriented architecture (SOA) SOAP-based integration	Lightweight integration model REST-based integration Heavy usage of APIs and lightweight microservices
Deployment and hosting	Mainly on-premise model with license-based pricing	Mainly cloud based or cloud native
Implementation design	Implementation to primarily satisfy business requirements	Employee-centric design
User experience	Heavyweight web pages Mainly desktop-based user experience Nonintuitive information architecture	Rich response and single-page application (SPA) Minimalist design Omnichannel enabled

Key Challenges of Intranet Platforms for Employees

Though traditional intranet platforms are a popular choice for employees and internal users, traditional intranet platforms fall short of meeting modern employees' needs and expectations. Table 1-2 lists the main challenges of traditional intranet platforms.

Table 1-2. *Modern Employee Needs and Challenges with Legacy Intranet Platforms*

Category	Employees' Needs and Expectations	Challenges with Traditional Intranet Platforms
User experience	Modern employees expect seamless user experience across all services and information. Employees demand consumer-grade on-the-go mobile and omnichannel experiences. Single-page applications and minimalistic design are preferred. Dashboard experience provides a unified view of all information and transactions.	Mainly a desktop-driven user experience. Disjointed user experience across various tools and Intranet applications. Absence of single-stop-shop experience. Challenges with usability and accessibility. Inconsistent brand identity.
Information architecture	Personalized and contextualized information. Search-centered experience for faster information discovery. Easily findable information. Expanded footer and mega menus.	Difficult to find relevant information. Mainly driven by context menus. Unclear navigation. Nonintuitive navigation tools. Multiple clicks to reach required information.
Collaboration	Information should be easily shareable. Instantly collaborate with colleagues. Create interest-based groups and communities. Harness collective intelligence for increased productivity.	Challenges with cross-team collaboration. Lacks engagement and motivation for employees. Needs integration of multiple collaboration tools.

(*continued*)

Table 1-2. (*continued*)

Category	Employees' Needs and Expectations	Challenges with Traditional Intranet Platforms
Analytics	Employees expect analytics-based insights such as personalized content and information based on past transactions.	Minimal or absence of analytics. Absence of seamless analytics across various touch points.
Tools and features	Employees expect self-service and productivity improvement tools. Education, learning, and training tools. Usage of gamification features.	Minimal or absence of gamification features. Minimal self-service tools.
Artificial intelligence	Employees expect artificial intelligence (AI)–based continuous learning and improvement of the platform.	Minimal or absence of AI-based methods.
Information discovery	Organized information; provides contextualized and relevant personalized content.	Takes too much time to find relevant information. Duplicate and outdated information.
Ease of use and adoption	Should be easy to use and accessible to all. Should enable user participation.	Nonavailability of documentation; disjointed and desperate applications.
Content management	Easier authoring and publishing. Easier content discovery. Intuitive content workflows.	Lacks targeted and personalized content. Lacks localized content.
Governance	Clearly defined roles and responsibilities. Well-defined processes for business continuity, change management, and such.	Absence of success metrics. Absence of processes for content management, business continuity, and such.

Expectations of Next-Generation Digital Workplaces

We need to analyze the expectations of modern-day employees from a digital platform to understand the need for employee experience platforms. The key expectations of modern-day employees are as follows:

- **Self-service and empowerment**: Employees expect tools and services that empower them to do their activities quicker. Employees expect self-service features, automated tools, productivity improvement tools, a holistic view with a dashboard experience, a consumer-grade user experience, and such.

- **Work-life balance and work flexibility**: The digital platform should be available to the employees anywhere, anytime, and on any device. The tools and services should be available for "on-the-go" employees. To support work flexibility, the digital platform should provide collaboration tools, mobile apps, cloud-based secure applications, and such.

- **Instant recognition/rewards**: Modern employees are used to winning and expect an instant reward for a job well done. Hence, gamification features that reward employees through points and badges are expected in the digital platform. Organizations should foster a culture of recognition (recognition by leaders, peer recognition, 360-degree recognition).

- **Social and collaboration**: Modern employees are socially active and are heavy influencers. So, employees expect social and collaborative features in a modern digital platform. Modern digital platforms should also be integrated with external social media platforms such as LinkedIn, Facebook, and such.

- **Leveraging modern digital technologies**: Cloud, mobile apps, social media platforms, and analytics are mainstream digital technologies that have gained huge popularity. Digital platforms should leverage these technologies to meet the expectations of modern employees.

- **Automation:** The digital platform should leverage machine learning and artificial intelligence technologies to automate routine activities and to provide contextual and relevant recommendations and other features.

The expectations mentioned in this section cannot be fulfilled by traditional intranet platforms because of the challenges discussed earlier. An employee experience platform is a digital platform that is designed to meet the needs of modern-day digital employees.

In the next section, we will mainly look at drivers, features, and other details of EXPs.

Employee Experience Platform

EXPs are employee-centric intranet platforms that personalize the experience for all employees and that provide contextual content and services. EXPs offer next-generation digital workplaces that engage employees throughout the employment lifecycle and improve their productivity for their day-to-day activities. To meet the expectations of modern employees, EXPs provide a responsive and adaptive design. EXPs are built on a platform approach that is open and extensible. EXPs enable employees with the right set of self-service tools and content so that employees stay engaged with the organization.

EXPs will be the single most used application by the employees, and hence organizations must use EXPs to fully engage the employees.

Figure 1-1 shows a high-level view of an EXP.

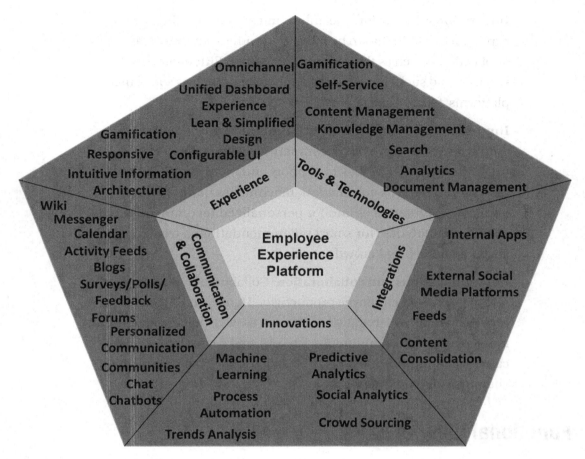

Figure 1-1. *High-level view of EXP*

EXP broadly covers five major areas.

- **Experience**: An EXP incorporates a minimalist design and modern user experience standards including a lean and omnichannel-enabled experience, responsive user interface (UI), adoption of gamification concepts, and intuitive information architecture (such as mega menus, an expanded footer, a search-centered experience, and such).

- **Tools and technologies**: An EXP is built using various tools and technologies such as content management (to manage web content, metadata), knowledge management tools, search (for information discovery), analytics, and document management (to manage documents, assets).

- **Integrations:** To provide a seamless, integrated, and single-view experience, an EXP has to be integrated with various internal applications (such as the enterprise database, ERP, enterprise services, and such) and external applications (such as social media platforms, feeds, external services, and such).

- **Innovations:** To meet the expectations of modern digital employees and to provide a competitive advantage to the organizations, an EXP has to support and incorporate modern innovations such as automation, machine learning (to learn employees' preferences and for personalized recommendations), predictive analytics (for smart recommendations), trend analysis, social analytics, and crowd sourcing.

- **Communications and collaboration:** Collaboration plays a pivotal role in improving employee productivity. Hence, an EXP has to provide various collaboration tools such as wiki, polls, calendar, chat, messenger, blogs, communities, surveys, and such. Organizations can use communication tools to establish a direct communication channel with employees.

Functional View of EXPs

EXP should provide various technical capabilities and prebuilt applications to meet the demands of modern employees.

Figure 1-2 shows a high-level functional view of an EXP.

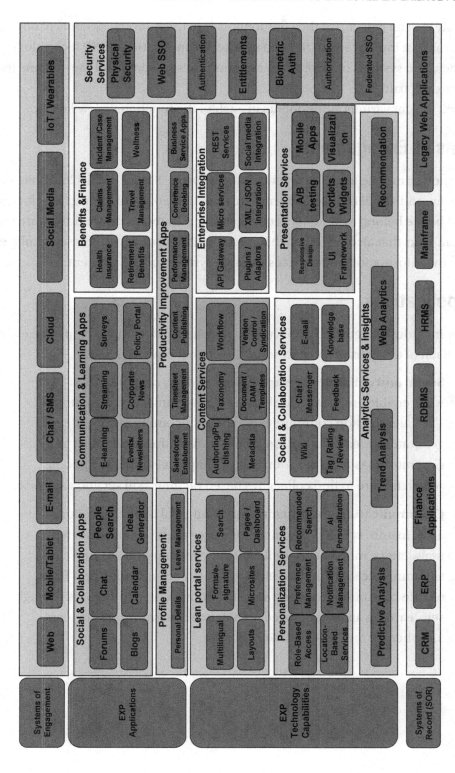

Figure 1-2. *Functional view of an EXP*

Broadly we can categorize the components into these layers: systems of engagement (the systems that interface with the end user), EXP applications, EXP technology capabilities, and systems of record (the systems that store data and the systems that are a single source of truth).

We will look at various components in each of the functional view layers.

Systems of Engagement

Systems such as mobile apps, browsers, chat platforms, SMS, e-mail, cloud-based applications, and social media platforms are the main points of interactions for end users and hence belong to systems of engagement. Chatbots and wearables are trending digital platforms that also belong to this category. End users (in this case, employees) consume the information and services through systems of engagement.

EXP Applications

This layer includes categorized applications that are specific to the employee experience domain. Each of the categories represents the main themes of EXPs.

- **Social and collaboration apps**: Apps such as chat, blog, and wikis enable employees to share and communicate information. The calendar app communicates about upcoming events. Idea generators/idea hubs are crowd-sourced platforms to solicit and generate ideas from the community. Employees need the people search feature to find colleagues based on their skill set and expertise.

- **Communication and learning apps**: Internal communication is a key feature of EXPs. Organizations use various features such as newsletters, mobile app notifications, streaming videos, and such, to communicate with their employees. Communication app EXPs enable continuous learning and skill improvement programs through self-learning apps. Employees can use self-learning apps to learn anywhere at any time at their own pace.

- **Benefits and finance apps**: EXPs should provide applications related to employee benefits such as health insurance, perks, leave, wellness, attendance, travel management, and such. Benefit applications enable employees to easily manage salary stubs, retirement benefits, employee stock management, and such. These applications provide reports and snapshot information. Other enterprise applications are claims management, incident/case/ticket management, software management, directory, performance management, asset management, and such.

- **Profile management**: Employees can manage their profile information, health information, and leave-related information.

- **Productivity improvement apps**: Based on the job roles and as required in daily activities, EXPs provide various applications to the employees. Regular employees can use applications for timesheet management, performance management, conference booking applications, software downloads, and such. The sales team can use applications such as opportunity management, contract management, deal management, order management, invoice management, budget management, and such. The content team can use content publishing–related applications. Besides these, EXPs provide various self-service applications such as account unlock/password reset, document management applications, and such.

EXP Technical Capabilities

EXP applications leverage the underlying technical capabilities of the platform. An EXP is built on a platform philosophy to provide modular services. The following are the key technical capabilities supported by EXPs:

- **Lean portal services**: An EXP provides built-in dashboards, forms equipped with multilingual features, and search features.

- **Content services**: In this category, an EXP provides various content-related functionality such as content authoring, content publishing, content workflow management, content versioning, content archival, metadata management, and such. Applications related to corporate communications and internal communications leverage content services for content needs.

- **Enterprise integration**: An EXP needs to be integrated with various internal and external systems of records (SORs). Various integration capabilities such as API-based integration, services-based integration, and extensible adapters are part of this category. The integration components enable EXP to have high-performing and scalable integrations.

- **Personalization services**: To provide role-based and context-sensitive content delivery, EXP should support a fine-grained permission model, preference management, notification management, and such.

- **Social and collaboration services**: The social and collaboration services enable the applications to manage the collaboration content and implement social features such as wiki, blog, communities, forums, and such. Internal social and collaboration services use content services for managing the social/collaboration content.

- **Presentation services**: An EXP provides various presentation services such as a responsive design, built-in widgets/portlets/modules, and visualizations for seamless dashboard experience across all devices and channels.

- **Analytics services and insights**: Web analytics and artificial intelligence (AI) methods will be used for understanding user behavior, doing trend analysis, and providing relevant recommendations.

Security services is a horizontal concern covering all layers. EXP security involves authentication, authorization, single-sign-on (SSO), a fine-grained permission model, and other services that secure EXP resources.

Systems of Records

Enterprises use a System of Record (SOR) as a single source of truth for managing enterprise data. Various ERP applications internally use the data managed by SORs. For instance, case management/incident management systems use customer relationship management for managing the incident data. Systems such as human resource management systems (HRMSs), enterprise resource planning (ERP), relational database management systems (RDBMSs), and legacy applications are used by EXP applications.

Drivers of EXPs

The main drivers and motivations for EXP are as follows:

- Enable employees with self-service features to improve their productivity

- Provide an enhanced collaboration platform for all employees

- Provide improved access to information through personalized content delivery

- Inspire and engage employee across all touch points

- Add value to the employees' daily activities and increase loyalty, brand affinity, and job satisfaction

- Improve the work-life balance for employees by providing various communication modes

- Realize the overall vision and objectives of the organization.

- Optimize the operational costs through self-service and automation

- Improve the overall agility and responsiveness of the organization

Key Features of EXPs

The following are the core attributes of EXP:

- An EXP provides rich and omnichannel-enabled user experiences.

- An EXP provides a dashboard view of relevant communication, content, functionality, and services personalized for the employee.

- An EXP should provide collaborative features for sharing content through a collaborative platform.

    - Integrate with external social media platforms such as LinkedIn or Facebook

    - Use surveys and feedback to gauge the effectiveness of tools and services

- An EXP should provide context-sensitive search.

- An EXP should provide self-service and productivity improvement tools.

- An EXP should provide integration with popular social media platforms.

- An EXP should provide a knowledge base for learning and training/ education content.

  - Technical and domain skills

  - Anytime, anywhere self-learning

  - Certifications

  - Interactive multimedia-based training material

- An EXP should enable the co-creation of content, productivity improvement through active engagement, and participation from various stakeholders.

- An EXP should provide business tools and services needed by the employees. The nature of the business tools and services mainly depends on the employee's role and job expectations. For example, a salesforce dashboard is needed for sales team and senior management, whereas regularly employees mainly use tools such as finances, employee benefits, claims, incident management, and such.

Figure 1-3 gives the key features of EXPs across the various lifecycle stages of the employee journey.

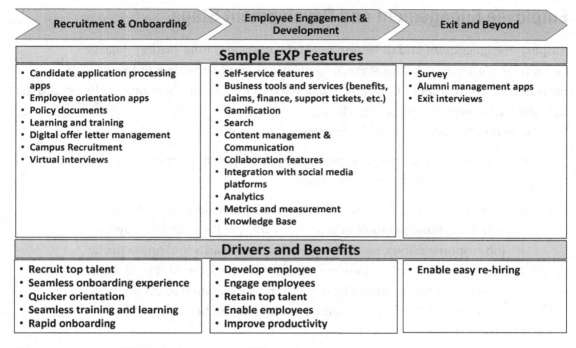

Figure 1-3. *An EXP across various lifecycle stages*

As depicted in Figure 1-3, an EXP provides apps to manage the entire lifecycle of an employee's association with the organization.

Recruitment and Onboarding Stage

The employee engagement lifecycle begins with the recruitment phase. Organizations aim to provide a seamless experience with application processing, screening and interviews, and overall recruitment process. EXPs enable corporate recruitment teams to manage recruitment events, process candidate applications, manage interviews, and manage digital offers.

During the employee onboarding stage, EXP provides applications for employee orientation and training and for managing the employee process and policy documents.

Employee Engagement and Development Stage

Employee engagement and development is the main and long-lasting stage in an employee's journey. In this stage, organizations aim to enable employees with productivity improvement tools and self-service tools. EXP applications are leveraged to develop and engage the employees in this stage.

The main EXP features used in this stage as follows:

- Self-service features such as auto approvals, people search, search-enabled knowledge base, and such.

- Business tools and services that an employee uses in day-to-day activities. Business tools and services are specific to an employee's job responsibilities; for instance, sales dashboards and opportunity management applications are mainly relevant for a sales workforce. There are a few common business applications such as for finance management and claims management that can be used by all employees.

- Collaboration features such as blogs, wikis, chat, and forums that enable employees to share information.

- Content management (content authoring and publishing) mainly used by communications applications.

- A searchable centralized knowledge base that stores how-to articles and process/policy documents to provide employees with much needed actionable and timely information.

- Integration with internal and external applications (such as external social media platforms) to provide a holistic view of information to employees.

- Analytics methods to track the employees' actions and information usage patterns to gain further insights.

Exit and Beyond Stage

An EXP provides features such as surveys and exit interview management in the exit stage. An EXP also provide alumni management features to enable the easy rehire of ex-employees.

Critical Success Criteria of EXPs

To measure the success of DXP, we can use the following critical success criteria. We need to devise the metrics for these critical success criteria to measure the overall success of the employee experience platform:

- **Employee engagement**: The principal aim of an EXP is to engage employees more effectively. So, the adoption of an EXP should increase the employee engagement in the EXP tools, collaboration features, knowledge management systems, and such.

- **Standards compliance**: An EXP should create uniformity in the user experience and should create a platform with open and consistent standards. This makes the EXP easy to extend and enhance.

- **Application consolidation**: An EXP should consolidate all internal tools and applications into a single platform to provide a unified view.

- **Return on investment (ROI)**: The self-service features, AI features, and productivity improvement tools should optimize the overall cost for the organization. EXP should reduce the employee tickets, reduce call center volume, reduce support resources, minimize infrastructure costs, and reduce other operational overheads.

- **Enhanced productivity**: Employees should utilize the self-service tools and collaboration tools to improve their overall productivity.

The metrics related to productivity, number of ideas generated, communication effectiveness, and employee satisfaction should increase, and the metrics related to employee onboarding time and the time to find relevant information should decrease.

Various Dimensions of EXPs

Figure 1-4 details the five key dimensions of EXPs.

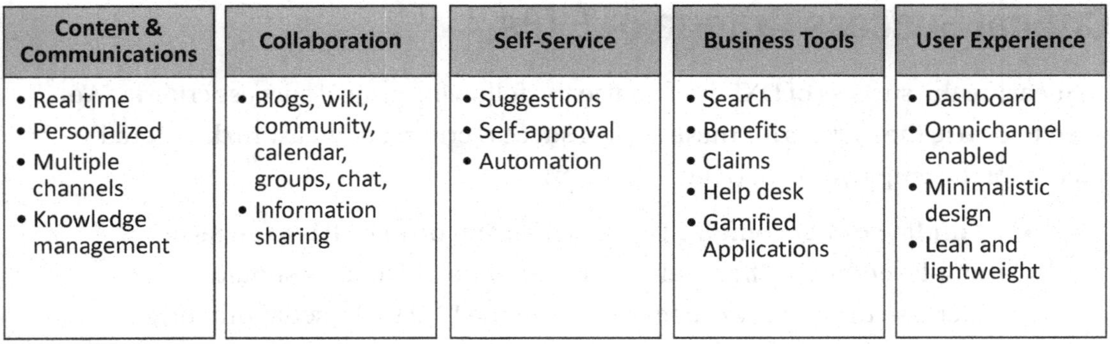

Content & Communications	Collaboration	Self-Service	Business Tools	User Experience
• Real time • Personalized • Multiple channels • Knowledge management	• Blogs, wiki, community, calendar, groups, chat, • Information sharing	• Suggestions • Self-approval • Automation	• Search • Benefits • Claims • Help desk • Gamified Applications	• Dashboard • Omnichannel enabled • Minimalistic design • Lean and lightweight

Figure 1-4. *EXP dimensions*

To effectively engage employees, an EXP has to provide features under these key dimensions:

- **Content and communications**: The applications should provide real-time and relevant/personalized content to all employees. The content and communications delivery should be enabled on all channels.

- **Collaboration**: EXPs should provide collaborative features such as chat, forums, and communities to enable information sharing.

- **Self-service**: EXP applications should enable self-service through search, automation, recommendations, and so on.

- **Business tools**: EXPs should provide role-based business tools and services such as search, claims management, gamified applications, and such.

- **User experience**: EXPs offers richer and engaging user experience across various channels.

Recent Trends in EXP

The following are some of the recent trends in EXP:

- Employee analytics to gain insights into actions and preferences.

- Predictive analytics to anticipate employee needs and future actions.

- AI-based chatbots and virtual assistants that provide quicker access to information.

- Self-service tools such as calculators, comparators, search, and such.

- Adoption of gamification concepts. Gamification is a concept that encourages, incentivizes, and rewards the participant/contributor, thereby enhancing the adoption and utility of the feature. Incentives are provided in the form of points, loyalty programs, badges, recognition, and such. For instance, ranking and rewarding top knowledge base contributors are classic examples of gamification.

- Co-creation of content with the complete involvement of employees in all stages of the product.

- Crowd-sourcing of ideas and using gamification concepts to select the most effective idea for implementation.

- Collaboration-specific microsites for blogging, interest-based communities, product marketing, and such.

- Leadership connected through direct communication channels.

End-to-End EXP Design Steps

Figure 1-5 depicts the high-level EXP design steps. We will elaborate on the EXP design in the coming chapters.

- **EXP strategy and high-level design**: As an initial step in the EXP design, you define the business benefits, objectives, and goals/KPIs for the EXP. You interview stakeholders to understand the priorities of all needed EXP features.

- **User experience design**: In the user experience design stage, you define the user experience design (such as wireframes, visual design) and information architecture design (such as navigation design, site map, menus, and such). You also define various user personas and develop the content.

- **Application design, build, and implementation**: During the application design and implementation stage, you prioritize the EXP features and select the best-fit technology option for the implementation. The low-level design and implementation follows technology stack selection. Iterative testing is carried out to identify issues in the early stages.

- **Adoption and change management**: Adoption and change management are ongoing activities once the EXP is in production. During this stage, you define business processes and standard operating procedures to maintain the new platform. You define the KPIs and metrics to continuously monitor and track the EXP. EXP-related communications and trainings are carried out to spread awareness about new platform and to enhance adoption.

- **Operations and community management**: During the operations and community management stage, the EXP support team provides the necessary technical and business support for the EXP. The operations team regularly monitors and maintains the EXP and conducts trainings for the EXP.

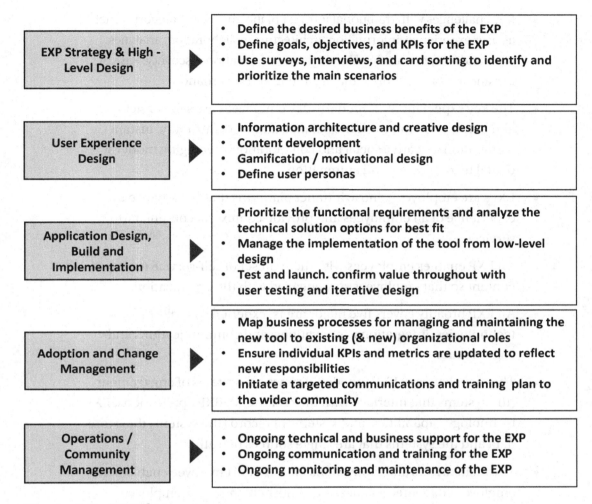

Figure 1-5. *EXP design steps*

Summary

I covered the following in this chapter:

- Digital intranet platforms provide a holistic and personalized user experience for intranet users.

- Traditional intranet platforms differ from EXP in categories such as the technology ecosystem, integration ecosystem, deployment and hosting, implementation design, and user experience.

- Key challenges with traditional intranet platforms are in categories such as user experience, information architecture, collaboration, analytics, tools and features, artificial intelligence, information discovery, ease of use and adoption, content management, and governance.

- The key expectations of modern-day employees are self-service and empowerment, work-life balance and work flexibility, instant recognition/rewards, social and collaboration, leveraging modern digital technologies, and automation.

- EXPs are employee-centric intranet platforms that personalize the experience of all employees and provide contextual content and services.

- An EXP enables employees with the right set of self-service tools and content so that employees stay engaged with the organization.

- An EXP broadly covers five major areas: experience, tools and technologies, integrations, innovations, and communications and collaboration.

- The main layers of EXP functional views are systems of engagement (the systems that interface with the end users), EXP applications, EXP technology capabilities, and systems of record (the systems that store data and the systems that are single sources of truth).

- The main drivers and motivations for EXPs are employee enablement, employee collaboration, increased information access, employee engagement and inspiration, and productivity improvement.

- EXP has to provide features to manage all the lifecycle stages of an employee in an organization including recruitment/onboarding, engagement/development, and exit.

- The critical success factors of EXPs are employee engagement, standards compliance, application consolidation, return on investment, and enhanced productivity.

- The end-to-end EXP design steps include EXP strategy and high-level design, user experience design, application design, build and implementation, adoption and change management, and operations and community management.

CHAPTER 2

Requirements Elaboration for EXP

Identifying the detailed requirements for an employee experience platform is the first step of building it. The requirements should capture the vision elements, user stories, and business objectives of the organization, and they should also capture the needs and expectations of the employees. The requirements captured will form the basis for future stages of employee experience platform development such as the design, development, and testing phases.

I'll discuss the requirements aspects of an employee experience platform in this chapter.

Employee Experience Requirements

In this section, I'll discuss the main tenets of an employee experience platform and the main requirement categories.

Key Employee Experience Tenets

The key tenets of the overall employee experience can be categorized into three broad categories.

- **Physical experience**: This category includes workplace norms, travel experience, accessibility-friendly features at the office, the office campus, help-desk accessibility, and such.

- **Digital experience**: This includes the intranet platform, mobile apps, and other online channels that engage employees.

© Shailesh Kumar Shivakumar 2020
S. K. Shivakumar, *Build a Next-Generation Digital Workplace*, https://doi.org/10.1007/978-1-4842-5512-4_2

- **Emotional experience**: An employee's emotional experience is shaped by various factors such as organization culture, values, physical/digital experience, and such. Flexible work hours, belief in leadership, meaningful work and autonomy, timely recognition of employees, and a fair and inclusive work environment all enhance the emotional connection with the organization.

In this book, I'll cover the digital experience topics. As such, the physical experience and emotional experience are outside the scope of this book.

The employee experience requirements can be categorized into these main themes:

- **Engagement**: The employee platform should actively engage and inspire the employees. Collaboration tools, effective communication channels, and surveys are effective means for active engagement.

- **Usability**: The employee platform should be easy to use and accessible by all. Localization, responsive user interface, intuitive information architecture, and implementation of accessibility features are some of the ways to improve the usability.

- **Adoption**: Executive management and the leadership team should support, communicate, and create awareness about the employee platform. Gamification concepts can be used to promote and encourage employee collaboration and contribution. The employee platform should be scalable and have maximum availability.

- **Relevancy**: The information and functionality should be relevant for the employees. The search function should provide contextual results. The platform should provide a personalized experience.

- **Self-service**: The employee platform should provide tools and services to improve the employee productivity.

Key Employee Experience Requirements

In this section, I'll briefly discuss the main requirement categories in the employee experience domain.

- **Profile management**: Employees need to manage and administrate their profile information. Profile information includes employee full name, address, contact numbers, address, skill set, education qualification, bank information (for crediting salary and reimbursements), and such.

- **Employee benefits**: In this category, employees like to manage their benefits such as health insurance details, retirement benefit details, nominee details, entitlements, and such.

- **Work-related details**: This is a broad category that includes all work-related aspects based on an employee's job role and responsibilities. This includes skill sets, roles and responsibilities, experience, tool details, organization units, and such.

- **Applications and tools**: Employees use various tools in their daily lives to complete their tasks. Tools such as incident management systems, e-mails, messengers, asset management systems, mobile apps, schedulers, performance management apps, survey tools, calendars, travel management application, claims application, leave management, attendance management application, and learning management are in this category.

- **Content and communication**: Employees are the major consumers of internal communication. The key requirements in this category are the delivery of personalized content, effective leadership communication, document management for managing policy documents, and crowd sourcing,

- **Collaboration**: Employees need various collaboration tools such as wikis, forums, blogs, communities, and groups for internal collaboration.

- **User experience**: Employee dashboards that provide a holistic view of employee profiles, employee performance, and job-related data are key requirements in the user experience category. Mobile-enabled experience and localization are other key requirements of an effective user experience. Mega menus, notifications, and expanded footer are others.

- **Search**: People search, content search, and search analytics are key things in information discovery. Search features such as filtering, faceted navigation, and secured search should be supported.

- **Security**: The employee platform should enforce the security rules such as authentication, role-based access, and authorized access to resources. When the employee platform acts as a gateway to enterprise applications, single sign-on (SSO) should be supported.

- **Integration**: The employee platform needs to be integrated with multiple enterprise applications such as databases, ERPs, services, payroll systems, and such.

- **Other miscellaneous requirements**: Other requirements are analytics, SEO, reports/dashboards, feeds, workflows, mobile apps, and alerts/notifications.

Employee Experience Requirements Gathering and Modeling

To identify and model employee experience requirements, you can do as-is system studies, employee surveys, and interviews. In addition to these proven methods of requirements gathering, I'll discuss voice of employee (VoE) and employee persona modeling methods in this section. I'll also briefly discuss the common challenges you'll face while implementing an employee experience platform and the best practices to address those challenges.

Voice of Employee

Organizations need to build the employee experience based on the implicit and explicit feedback of its employees. VoE involves collecting employee feedback and analyzing the explicit and implicit feedback. VoE acts as a pulse check for employee engagement initiatives, and it can be used to assess the effectiveness of an employee experience platform.

Organizations need to use the following methods to frequently collect employee feedback:

- Managers have one-on-one discussions with their team members on a monthly basis.

- Employee engagement surveys assess the overall employee satisfaction across the organization.

- Social listening tools monitor the employee sentiment on external social media platforms.

- Regularly monitor internal enterprise collaboration platforms such as blogs, wikis, and discussion groups to assess the employee sentiment.

- Analyze employee tickets to understand the problem patterns and gain insights into employee feedback.

Employee Persona

Organizations need to model employee personas to satisfy the various needs of employees. Employee personas depict the needs, motivations, and interests for a group of employees. You need to conduct exhaustive interviews to identify the main employee personas covering the following points:

- Nature of work

  - Skill sets and technologies required

  - Individual contributor versus collaborative work

- Key access devices (laptop, mobile)

- Desired career plan

- Key motivations at work

- Key needs and expectations

- Attitude toward change management and learning

You can understand these data points through various communication channels. You can conduct employee surveys and interview a select set of employees to understand these factors.

Employee Journey Map

Once you identify the key employee personas based on the previous factors, you need to map the employee journey across all stages of employee involvement (pre-hiring, development, engagement, and exit). Once you model the journey, you need to identify the key pain points in the employee journey. Once you identify the pain points, prioritize them based on business impact and address them.

By modeling employee journey maps, you can identify the challenges faced by employees and potential opportunities to improve the employee experience. You can understand the following from the employee journey map:

- Most commonly used intranet features and journey paths used by employees.

- Most common tasks for which employees use the intranet

  - Average time taken to complete the task

  - Existing challenges in completing the task

- Opportunities to improve the overall employee experience and overall employee productivity

Common Challenges and Best Practices with Employee Experience Platforms

The employee journey map and persona analysis exercise reveals the common challenges faced by employees. The following are some of the common challenges and best practices found in employee platforms and intranet platforms.

Business Context

Next, I'll discuss the common challenges and best practices in the "business context" category.

Common Challenges

- The organization values and brand identity are not properly communicated.

- User adoption is minimal because of a lack of communication and leadership support.

- There are no defined success metrics to measure the effectiveness of the intranet portal.

- The intranet is not properly organized and has a poor information architecture (navigation, metadata, tagging, breadcrumbs, site structure, page hierarchy, controlled vocabulary, and such). Employees find it hard to find relevant information.

- There is an absence of a sharing culture and a lack of incentives and intrinsic rewards leading to challenges in collaboration.

- There is an absence of governance defining roles, responsibilities, and process ownership for managing the employee platform.

- There was a poor platform rollout, and there is a lack of executive communication leading to minimal employee adoption.

Best Practices

- Define a clear vision for the employee experience platform and communicate the vision and brand values across all channels. The corporate communications and leadership communications should be well articulated and communicated to the employees.

- Design and develop an employee-centric platform so that employees can quickly discover relevant information and complete tasks quickly.

- Adopt gamified concepts to promote collaboration features and encourage employee participation.

- Define and track the success metrics for the employee platform.

- Define a comprehensive governance plan and establish clearly defined roles, processes, and responsibilities. A well-defined process should be established for content authoring, content publishing, and platform maintenance.

Employee Experience

Now, let's go over the common challenges and best practices in the "employee experience" category.

Common Challenges

- Employee experience is not seamless on mobile devices.

- Employees lack motivation for using the digital platform features.

- Employees take lot of time to complete tasks.

- The absence of localization reduces the usability of intranet platforms for globally distributed sites.

- The visual design is not appealing and does not communicate the values and brand story. Inconsistent user design poses challenges in information discovery.

- The absence of a taxonomy and metadata strategy poses challenges for information discovery.

- There is an organization-centric or business-centric information architecture instead of employee-centric information architecture.

- The challenges in performance impact the overall user experience.

- There is no smart search, or the quality of search results is poor.

Best Practices

- Organizations need to provide learning and development opportunities through digital and online channels.

- The employee experience platform should provide personalized content and functionality.

- The performance management tools should capture the employee performance data iteratively and frequently against clearly defined goals and metrics.

- A culture of recognition should be implemented through reward and recognition tools to recognize high-performing employees.

- Define and implement a user-centric information architecture to increase the information usability and information manageability. Information architecture defines content, metadata, and site hierarchy and aids search, navigation, and personalization.

- Define consistent brand and visual design standards for the employee platform.

Requirements Elaboration Case Study

In this section, I will discuss a detailed case study and explain the requirements elaboration phase of EXP. The case study details the vision elements, scope, and categorized requirements. I will also discuss various elements of as-is system analysis as part of this case study.

Employee Portal Redesign Vision

The vision for the next-generation employee platform is to transform the legacy intranet web site from an organization-centric one based on one-way communication to an employee-centric, scalable platform that encourages innovative culture and connects employees to each other with relevant information, enabling each employee to have a voice and ultimately advancing productivity and growth. The overall aim of the project is to streamline the employee experience and content delivery system with cost-effective technology. The key features of the project include user experience (UX), responsive web design, document management, security, and integration with existing systems, collaboration features, and personalization.

Transformation Principles

The following are the key guiding principles for transforming a legacy intranet into an extensible employee experience platform:

- Improve productivity

  - Simplify and streamline to help drive productivity

- Enhance employee experience

  - Make it easier for employees to find other employees, information, and tools/sites and services

  - Make the new platform accessible on all devices and channels

  - Provide a rich and engaging user interface

  - Provide an intuitive information architecture

  - Provide access to relevant information securely delivered in one organized and controlled place

  - Provide easy navigation to locate desired content to troubleshoot/service the products

  - Create a simple, intuitive, and user-friendly UX solution

- Collaboration

  - Provide collaborative tools and services such as wikis, blogs, communities, chat, and such

  - Make it easier to share information and solve problems

  - Make an employee voice visible and reachable

- Self-service

  - Enable employees with self-service tools and services

  - Provide business self-service tools for administrators

Key Requirements

Next, we will go over the main requirements for the next-generation employee experience platform. Figure 2-1 shows the high-level requirements.

Figure 2-1. *Key requirements of an EXP*

The main requirements for a next-generation employee experience platform are as follows:

- **Improved productivity**: Make it easy for employees to find contextual information.

- **Improved collaboration**: This includes the following:

  - Share ideas

  - Blog, share, like, rate, and review for content

  - Connect with other employees

- **User experience**: This includes the following:

  - Employee-centric platform

  - Omnichannel-enabled experience to provide a seamless transition between the web and mobile channels to the employees

  - To enable each employee to customize the portal based on their interests and needs

  - Intuitive information architecture

- **Content, collaboration, and communication**: This includes the following:

  - Easy-to-find company communications and role-specific information

  - Place for employees to access key information that the company wants them to know and information in which they have an interest/need

  - Launching point to other items on the intranet and external sites related to organizational information

  - Features that can encourage employee interaction and exchange of knowledge and ideas

- **Information discovery**: This includes the following:

  - Create effective search tool for providing contextual and personal information

  - Provide intuitive navigation, saved links feature, saved search feature.

  - Based on standard taxonomy to enable employees to easily find the information they are looking for

- **Workflows**: Better workflows can enforce the review, rating, and approval process to enable content governance.

- **Security**: This enables easy and secure access to the portal for each employee.

- **Reports and analytics**: You want to gauge employee adoption and accordingly reward employees and also improve user experience.

- **Governance**: This provides proper processes for content management, content publishing, and application maintenance.

- **Next-generation platform features**: This means features such as the following:

  - Easier scalability to sustain expected performance at high user load.

  - High availability by ensuring that services and application has maximum availability.

I will now break down the requirements into categories, such as general requirements, content requirements, landing page requirements, mobility requirements, collaboration requirements, and technical requirements.

General Requirements

- Integrate the digital workplace with internal systems such as the payment system and Human Resources Management System (HRMS) ERP system.

- Design an engaging and omnichannel-enabled user experience.

- Define and establish a governance plan to provide fresh and relevant content to employees.

- Make content accessible on all mobile devices.

- Provide advanced search features such as faceted search, personalized search, and such.

- Provide personalization features such as personalized content delivery, favorite links, saved search, and configurable widgets/portlets.

- Define and implement site analytics such as site traffic rate, exit ratio, most visited links, popular downloads, and such.

- Implement real-time messenger, chat, and virtual assistants.

- Implement security features such as authentication, authorization, and single sign-on.

Content Management Requirements

- The system should provide easy-to-use steps for content authoring, publishing, and editing using what-you-see-is-what-you-get (WYSIWYG) tools.

- The system should provide inline editing of web pages.

- The system should support various content types (such as images, videos, multimedia files, audio files, and other binary files) and document types (such as PDF and Microsoft Office documents)

- The system should support various content features such as content archival, content retention, content publishing scheduling, and content expiry.

- The system should have the ability to review and rate content.

- The system should have the ability to manage content with metadata and taxonomy.

- The system should have the ability for approval workflows and security.

- The system should have the ability to address compliance requirements.

Landing Page Requirements

- The system should allow authorized users to publish news and marketing content.

- The system should display role-based content and information access.

- The system should display feeds for the configured topics.

- The system should allow employees to share content, rate content, like content, and review content.

- The system should enable content tagging and enable content search by tags.

- The system should provide content governance features such as content archival and content retention.

- The system should configure banner content and images.

- The system should have the ability to sort the news content based on popularity.

Collaboration Requirements

- The system should enable collaboration features such as discussion posts, wikis, forums, and ratings.

- The system should enable filtering and sorting of blog entries.

- The system should have the ability to archive information to a centralized knowledge base.

- The system should manage team/project workspaces.

- The system should share content with individuals, teams, and groups.

- The system should enable employees to share relevant information across teams, departments, and the enterprise.

- The system should share ideas on a social platform.

- The system should use feeds to keep up-to-date with activities across domains and teams.

Mobility Requirements

- The system should enable employees to access information from mobile devices.

- The system should provide inherent support for mobile devices for the employee platform.

- The system should allow users to view office documents in mobile browsers.

Technical Requirements

- Create a security model that provides the appropriate authority and access to employees.

- Define a taxonomy and an information architecture and metadata strategy for properly tagging content and classifying information and to provide relevant search results.

- Use gamification features to recognize and reward top contributors to the knowledge base.

- Define governance to keep employee data (profile details, skill details, trainings, certification, contact information, interests, responsibilities, photos, etc.) up-to-date.

- Provide an effective search tool to search by person's skillls and other information. The search feature should enable users to filter by various attributes such as skills, department, and such. The system should support the following search features:

  - Enable users to find information across the enterprise, structured and unstructured.

  - Enable users to find content from various enterprise applications.

  - The system should provide personalized search results.

  - Design and implement enterprise search to retrieve search results from external sites such as social platforms and external service providers.

  - Design and implement enterprise search to retrieve search results from external sites such as social platforms and external service providers.

  - Implement search features such as autosuggest, faceted browsing, filtering, sorting, synonym match, and auto correction.

- **Integration**

  - Integrate the employee platform with a messenger tool.

  - Integrate the employee platform with other systems such as SAP ERP, Oracle, or any custom applications.

As-Is System Analysis

As part of the requirements elaboration phase, you need to conduct a system study and pain point analysis. During this phase, you analyze the existing system that needs to be transformed and provide improvement suggestions and pain point analysis. You also must do benchmarking with competitor platforms. This section provides salient features of as-is system analysis and improvement suggestions for the existing intranet platform of this case study.

General Observations of the Existing Intranet Platform

The following are generic observations made during the as-is system study (see Figure 2-2 and Figure 2-3):

Overall User Experience

- Has a traditional look and feel with a heavy home page

- Scope for introducing an immersive, interactive, and responsive experience

- Scope for better branding and visual appeal

Information Architecture

- Traditional navigation features

- Scope for search improvements

- Lacks intuitive features such as product carousel, type-ahead search, and others

Social and Multichannel Access

- Can improve upon social features such as technical forums to promote self-service features

Site Organization

- Search can be positioned more effectively and enhanced to include features such as faceted browsing, saved search results, metadata-driven content aggregation, and so on.

- SEO can be improved by effectively using the metadata for web content.

Platform Improvement Suggestions

Based on the as-is system analysis, we can now come up with the platform improvement suggestions shown in Figures 2-2 and 2-3.

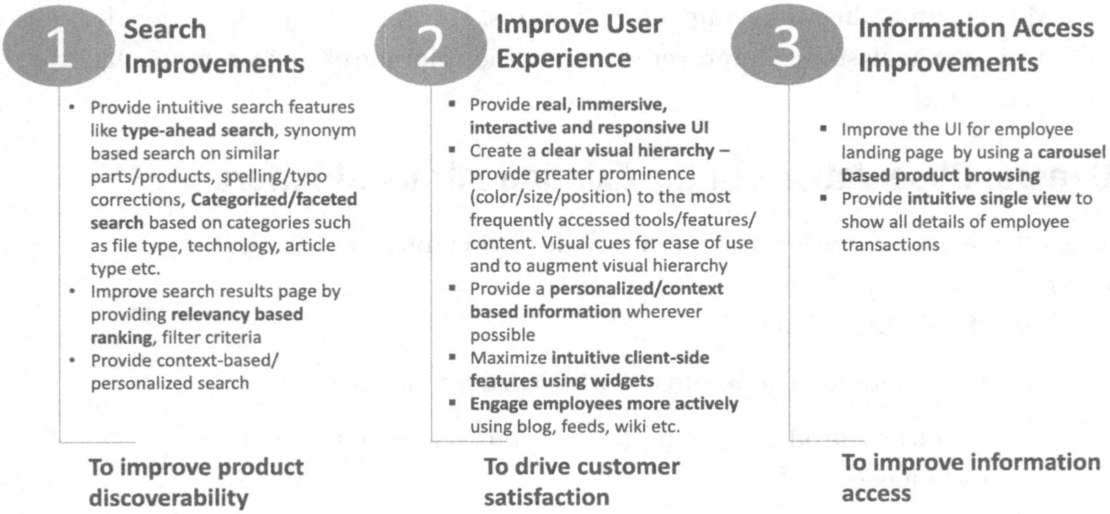

1 Search Improvements

- Provide intuitive search features like **type-ahead search**, synonym based search on similar parts/products, spelling/typo corrections, **Categorized/faceted search** based on categories such as file type, technology, article type etc.
- Improve search results page by providing **relevancy based ranking,** filter criteria
- Provide context-based/ personalized search

To improve product discoverability

2 Improve User Experience

- Provide **real, immersive, interactive and responsive UI**
- Create a **clear visual hierarchy** – provide greater prominence (color/size/position) to the most frequently accessed tools/features/ content. Visual cues for ease of use and to augment visual hierarchy
- Provide a **personalized/context based information** wherever possible
- Maximize **intuitive client-side features using widgets**
- **Engage employees more actively** using blog, feeds, wiki etc.

To drive customer satisfaction

3 Information Access Improvements

- Improve the UI for employee landing page by using a **carousel based product browsing**
- Provide **intuitive single view** to show all details of employee transactions

To improve information access

Figure 2-2. Platform improvement analysis, part 1

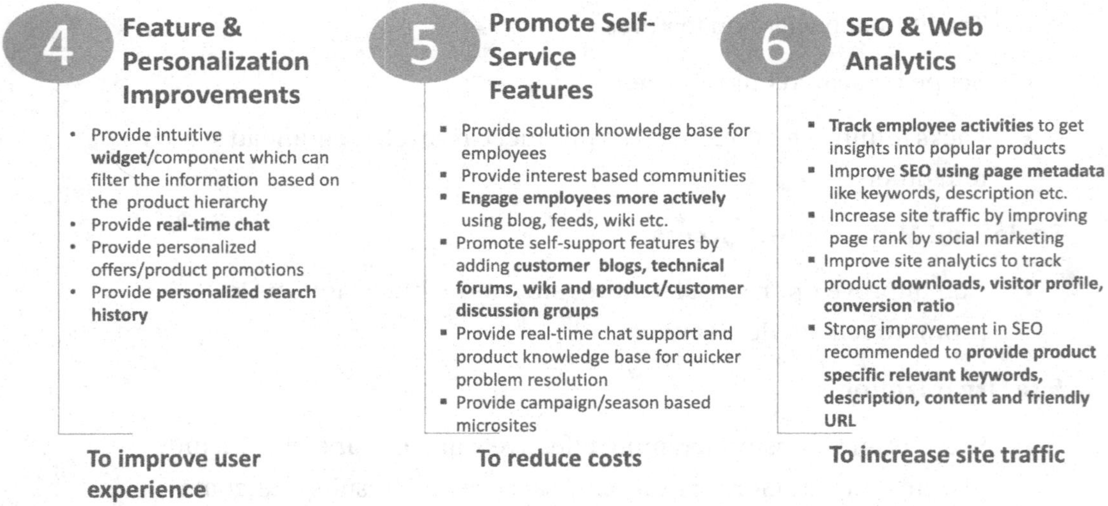

4 Feature & Personalization Improvements

- Provide intuitive **widget**/component which can filter the information based on the product hierarchy
- Provide **real-time chat**
- Provide personalized offers/product promotions
- Provide **personalized search history**

To improve user experience

5 Promote Self-Service Features

- Provide solution knowledge base for employees
- Provide interest based communities
- **Engage employees more actively** using blog, feeds, wiki etc.
- Promote self-support features by adding **customer blogs, technical forums, wiki and product/customer discussion groups**
- Provide real-time chat support and product knowledge base for quicker problem resolution
- Provide campaign/season based microsites

To reduce costs

6 SEO & Web Analytics

- **Track employee activities** to get insights into popular products
- Improve **SEO using page metadata** like keywords, description etc.
- Increase site traffic by improving page rank by social marketing
- Improve site analytics to track product **downloads, visitor profile, conversion ratio**
- Strong improvement in SEO recommended to **provide product specific relevant keywords, description, content and friendly URL**

To increase site traffic

Figure 2-3. Platform improvement analysis, part 2

High-Level Competitive Benchmarking

I have provided high-level competitive benchmarking for the current employee platform with two competitors, as shown in Figure 2-4.

Employee Platform Feature	Current Platform	Competitor 1	Competitor 2
Branding & Look and Feel → Uniform and consistent brand identity → Intuitive information architecture → Friendly navigation features → Search	▪Can provide contemporary, responsive UI ▪Need to improve search features like type-ahead, faceted browsing ▪Need to provide more intuitive client-side features	▪Slightly better landing page by providing immersive UI	▪Traditional look and feel
Search →Product Search →Faceted search	▪Provides no autocompletion and auto suggestion	▪Provides auto completion ▪Intuitive categorized search results	▪Provides basic product search ▪Product categorization, faceted browsing is not present
Personalization → Custom landing page → Role based access → Localization	▪Absence of localization	▪Provides language specific pages	
Social → Blogs, wiki, Forum → Social media marketing →Subscription	▪Absence of self support features and social features like blog, wiki, technical support forums	▪Absence of self support features and social features	▪Provides basic product locator with pre-defined filters
Others →Analytics & Reporting →Security →Performance	▪Web analytics using Google analytics ▪Decent page performance ▪Page level metadata on parts page is not present for SEO	▪Uses Omniture Analytics ▪Faster page performance ▪Better page metadata like keywords, content and description for SEO	▪ Uses Google analytics
Overall			

Legend   Poor ○ ◔ ◑ ◕ Excellent ●

Figure 2-4. Competitive benchmarking

Summary

This chapter covered the following:

- The key tenets of overall employee experience are physical experience, digital experience, and emotional experience.

- The requirements should satisfy these themes: engagement, usability, adoption, relevancy, and self-service.

- The main requirement categories of the employee experience are profile management, employee benefits, work-related details, applications and tools, content and communication, collaboration, user experience, search, security, integration, and other miscellaneous requirements.

- Voice of employee (VoE) involves collecting employee feedback and analyzing the explicit and implicit employee feedback.

- An employee persona depicts the needs, motivations, and interests for a group of employees.

- An employee journey map traces the employee journey across all stages of employee involvement (pre-hiring, development, engagement, and exit).

CHAPTER 3

EXP Experience Design

Experience design involves designing the user interface, brand elements, and navigational elements that impact the overall experience of the end users. The user experience in an EXP primarily impacts the employee engagement and satisfaction and hence plays a crucial role in the overall success of the EXP.

In this chapter, I'll discuss the key elements of experience design such as the experience design methodology, design best practices, design core attributes, and design principles. I'll also cover popular designs of employee platforms and elaborate on the key elements of the designs. Toward the end of the chapter, I'll discuss a detailed case study for the experience design of an employee platform.

Figure 3-1 depicts the threefold advantages of experience design.

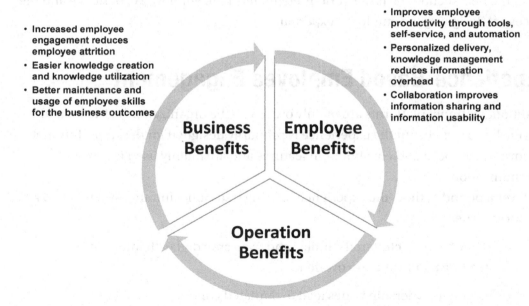

- Increased employee engagement reduces employee attrition
- Easier knowledge creation and knowledge utilization
- Better maintenance and usage of employee skills for the business outcomes

- Improves employee productivity through tools, self-service, and automation
- Personalized delivery, knowledge management reduces information overhead
- Collaboration improves information sharing and information usability

Business Benefits   **Employee Benefits**

Operation Benefits

- Automation and self-service features reduces support costs
- Consolidation and standardization reduces maintenance costs
- Search and personalization reduces information discovery costs

Figure 3-1. *Benefits of an effective experience design*

S. K. Shivakumar, *Build a Next-Generation Digital Workplace*, https://doi.org/10.1007/978-1-4842-5512-4_3

43

The benefits are as follows:

- **Business benefits**: A good experience engages employees and reduces employee attrition. The knowledge artifacts and collaborative features improve employee productivity. Employee skills are better utilized for the organization's goals and business outcomes.

- **Employee benefits**: A good experience enhances employee productivity through tools, services, and automation features. Personalized information reduces the overall information overhead for the employees. Employees can easily share the information and collaborate more effectively.

- **Operation benefits**: Support costs will be reduced because of the automation and self-service features of the experience. A uniform and consistent experience reduces the maintenance costs, and search and personalized delivery reduces the information discovery costs.

In the next section, I'll cover various elements of the employee experience and the process of designing the employee experience.

Experience-Based Employee Engagement

Traditional intranet platforms are mainly owned by the organization's IT team and provide basic search, but the experience is primarily designed for desktops. Intranet platforms lack social and collaboration features and are mainly used for top-down communication.

Over a period of time, the experience of using traditional intranet systems also runs into these issues:

- They become cluttered, clunky, and over-crowded with information, leading to information overload.

- Content ownership issues lead to outdated content.

- There's a lack of leadership commitment.

- Employees become frustrated, and there's a shrinking user base because of usability and performance issues.

- The organization values and brand identity are not reflected fully in the user interface.

- Employees find it difficult to find information and encounter accessibility issues.

- For global intranets, users may not be able to find information in their local languages.

By contrast, digital workplaces enable a collaborative and social enterprise network that enhances employee engagement. Though employees are the primary consumers, they also contribute through blogs, wikis, comments, and reviews via collaboration features. Figure 3-2 depicts the key elements of the experience layer in an employee experience platform.

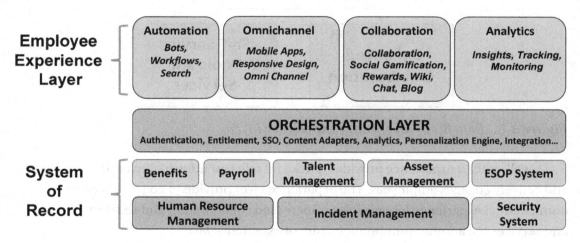

Figure 3-2. *Experience-based EXP architecture*

As depicted in Figure 3-2, the employee layer mainly consists of automation features (with bots, automated workflows, and search), omnichannel enablement (through mobile apps and responsive design), collaboration features (such as blog, wiki, chat, gamification, and such), and analytics (such as user tracking, monitoring, and reporting). The experience layer interacts with the system of record (SOR) layer through the orchestration layer (plug-ins, adapters, and services). The SOR layer includes systems such as benefits, payroll, talent management, human resource management, and incident management that maintain various aspects of employee data.

Benefits of the Employee Experience Layer

A well-designed experience layer provides the benefits mentioned in Figure 3-3.

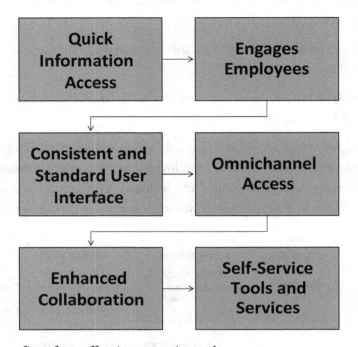

Figure 3-3. *Benefits of an effective experience layer*

A well-crafted experience provides quick and relevant information access and actively engages employees. The experience layer provides a consistent and omnichannel experience for employees. Increased collaboration and self-service tools and services are another prominent feature of experience layer.

In the next section, you will analyze the steps and overall process for experience design.

Experience Design

The initial success of an EXP depends on a well-designed user experience. The end-user experience is a result of a continuous and iteratively executed design process. This section covers the various steps involved in experience design, as shown in Figure 3-4.

	Discovery (Get business, brand, and user insights)	Design (Design experience and navigation)	Build, Test & Measure (Develop UI artefacts)
Activities	• Finalize scope • Stakeholder interviews • User research • Usability assessment • Industry & competitive insights • Standards definition • Initial brand explorations • UX goals • Task models • Requirement workshops • Voice of employee survey • Content audit	• UX strategy design • Information architecture • Personalization design • Localization design • Collaboration design • User experience design • Interaction design • Technical design • Quality control planning • Design co-creation • Design thinking workshops • Navigation taxonomy design	• UI prototype/production asset development • HTML development and integration • Test and validation of UI components • Usability assessment (Heuristic testing) • User feedback • Evaluation • UI Quality testing for W3C compliance, Accessibility and cross-browser compatibility • A/B testing
Deliverable	• UX plan • Heuristic & competitive assessment • User research results • Technical assessment • Release plan • User personas • Journey map • Content analysis report & inventory • UX KPIs and metrics • Features roadmap	• UX strategy document • Technology recommendation • Execution plan • Site Structure & navigation • Design comps/style guide • UI specification document • Technical design document • Test plan • Visual design • Low-fidelity and high-fidelity wireframe	• Use stories and spring plan • Executable code • Production assets • Page templates • Content matrix • KPI measurement and reporting • Test reports and summary • Live site

Figure 3-4. Experience design steps

47

Primarily, experience design is a three-step process. The *discovery* stage is the first stage during which you do discovery and requirements analysis. During the *design* stage, you design the experience elements, and during the *build, test, and measure* stage, you develop the experience artifacts and do the quality validation.

I'll cover each of the stages in detail next.

Discovery Stage

The primary activity in the discovery stage is requirements discovery, wherein you get a thorough understanding of the organization's needs and business goals and the employees' needs. This includes specifications of the projects, discussion of the aesthetics, and discussions of the user as well as the business goals and deliverables. During this stage you will also come to understand the brand values and the pain points of the user.

During the discovery phase, you will have focused group discussions and conduct voice of employee (VoE) surveys to understand and map the employee journey and task models. You conduct industry benchmarking and competitive analysis of the existing design with industry peers. You also analyze the brand elements that will be helpful for the visual design in subsequent stages. In addition, you audit the existing content guidelines, assets, and standards and create an inventory of existing content artifacts.

User Research and Analysis

User research exercises involve activities to understand the activities, goals, and motivations for various users.

- Interviews with organization users, stakeholders, or subject-matter (domain) experts

- Questionnaire surveys or user observation (using the application, performing their tasks, etc.)

User research aims to understand the tasks that users of the intranet perform, as well as understand the relevance of the tasks, the pain points in using the current site, and the wish lists of future features and functionality. User requirements are gathered in tandem with business analysts, paving the way for effective task analysis and helping balance, at times, conflicting business and user goals.

This activity also helps to understand user roles, demographics, preferences, capabilities, and skills (captured through a series of interview sessions with representative end users).

- Helps in building personas, key scenarios, and collating user inputs to make summarized findings/requirements

- Surveys, interviews, and focus groups used to understand user needs and desires

- Targets a larger audience with more accuracy

- Captures actual user issues in detail

UI Requirements Gathering

The following checklist is used to capture the UI requirements:

- Understand the business and technology drivers impacting the user interface

- Understand the user profiles, workflows, and user tasks

- Identify the visual design constraints and device capabilities

  - Use as-is evaluation or heuristic-based expert evaluation of current UI and usability

- Visually benchmark the visual design, tone and manner, information design, interaction design, and usability

The outcomes of this stage include the identification of gaps and challenges, user scenarios and user stories, well-defined user goals, heuristics, user research results and competitive assessment reports, release plan, and technical assessment. You'll analyze the user journey to come up with user personas and scenario/task analysis.

Usability Assessment

Here you perform a cycle of usability assessment of the current intranet and as-is analysis. The assessment findings are then combined with the requirements to reach a refined set of objectives. During the evaluation phase, the end-user study will be carried out using various methods to consolidate the user requirements. Subsequently, UI design requirements are captured by structured and unstructured means. This includes formal meetings with business and end users as well.

A usability review (*heuristic evaluation*) includes a systematic inspection of the intranet's user interface design to ascertain usability issues. The goal of heuristic evaluation is to find the usability problems/gaps in the design so that they can be addressed through an iterative design process. Heuristic evaluation involves having a small set of evaluators examine the user interface and judge its compliance with recognized usability principles (the *heuristics*). It is quick, and it does not involve actual users.

The final report highlights all the usability issues present in the interface, categorized according to severity such as showstoppers, major, and irritants.

Content Evaluation and Assessment

UX architects will evaluate all the existing content (or content types) to scope the universe of content and functionality. This will identify duplicate or redundant content. This is also a critical driver of the information architecture phase. The content inventory is a key deliverable of this activity.

Design Stage

Based on the insights gathered from the discovery stage, you know what employees care about, how they truly behave, what their needs are, and what influences them. In this stage, you mainly translate insights from the discovery phase to a design solution.

You can conduct design workshops to quickly prototype the ideas to arrive at the most suitable options. As part of this stage, you'll perform these activities:

- Card sorting as a rational approach to bring in the collective understanding of the user group.

- Clusters and affinity diagrams to infer the user's mental model.

- Information architecture that matches the user mental models to establish the overall system framework.

- Technical design for the overall user experience layer by shortlisting and identifying the right set of tools and technologies.

- Defining the plan for the overall quality of the experience layer.

- Navigational taxonomy that defines the site map and feature maps.

- Navigation model to understand and validate the on-screen tasks as well as task flows.

- Paper prototypes used during stakeholder workshops and interviews. Co-create the design for main flows along with employees.

- Wireframes that are low-fidelity prototypes to capture and validate detailed functional and user experience requirements. Wireframes are used for stakeholder validation and usability testing with end-user representatives.

- Creating a UI specification document and visual design to define the specifications for various UI elements.

- Defining the overall test plan for the user experience track.

- Defining standards and guidelines for user interface elements.

UX Strategy Design

During this stage, you ask the strategic questions for the design. The strategic questions seek to answer the following:

- Road map for the next generation portal

- Existing challenges in employee adoption

- Challenges in engaging content

- Challenges in rollout and release management

- Challenges in self-service

As a result, you develop the UX road map, UX best practices, personalization strategy, localization strategy, information architecture, and employee-centric information architecture.

You leverage insights from user research, technology landscape, business priorities, and existing content to define the UX strategy.

- **Personalization strategy**: This is mainly driven by the employee needs, content scope, and communication goals. Personalization can be done broadly in two ways. Static personalization is mainly rules-driven. Based on user attributes (location, role, device, and such) and user preferences, you can personalize the user experience. In dynamic personalization, you segment the users dynamically based on their actions and behavior and personalize the experience. For instance, if the total number of employee blogs exceeds a specified limit, you can reward the blog author with redeemable bonus points.

- **Localization strategy**: For the localization strategy, you need to understand the content requirements for various geographies. You should also remove all duplicate and unnecessary content and check the design variations to accommodate content in various languages. In some scenarios, the regional content and messaging varies based on region-specific priorities and cultures.

Information Architecture and Visual Design

Information architecture (IA) is the process of organizing and labeling the information captured and designing the navigation to help users effectively perform their tasks and achieve their goals. The starts with conceptual sketches of the identified application/web site. These sketches will be duly validated with organization stakeholders to strengthen the understanding. IA addresses the usability issues that are critical while designing the user interface.

Basically, IA establishes the user's mental model in terms of task and information organization to establish the overall framework of the system.

- Information architecture is the culmination of defining the structure and model of the system.

- Techniques like card sorting are used to define the information architecture if required.

The main outcomes of information architecture are as follows:

- Site map that defines the overall site structure, page hierarchy, and such

- Navigation model that defines the navigation elements such as menus, breadcrumbs, and such

- Task flows that define the steps for completing a particular task

Navigation Model/Site Taxonomy

The navigation model/site taxonomy will provide a bird's-eye view of the proposed application structure and its constituents. This model is a simplified and high-level representation of a solution or idea of the application to be designed. This will also help in optimizing screen flows as per the user's tasks.

Wireframes

Subsequent to the navigation model, low-fidelity wireframes are created to illustrate the application design, content structure, and navigation. This iterative document will rely on information captured from usability analysis and on the data gathered from other tracks. The granularity and interactivity of wireframes may vary based on the needs or iterations guided by the requirements.

Wireframes are created to illustrate and evaluate the application design, content structure, and navigation for a finite number of given scenarios independent of the final presentation layer.

- Wireframing is a rapid mock-up prototyping technique used for iterative design.

- Wireframing is a quick and easy way of creating a screen mock-up, which consolidates the functional controls, user task menu, etc.

- Wireframing specifies the screen elements to the functional specification document.

Visual designs are the end-state look and feel of the application along with other factors.

Visual Design

The last step in this phase is to create visual design concepts for the identified wireframes. The visual design concepts cover branding and the end-state look and feel of the application, and this is largely influenced by the organization's corporate identity standards and user/stakeholder's personal preferences. Visual design includes five key sets of artifacts.

- Visual design concepts (for web and mobile interfaces)

- Style guide, content templates, and UI assets

- Corporate style guide/branding standards

- High-level information architecture

- High-level wireframes and page contents

Content Strategy and Management

Optionally you can also create the content strategy during the design phase. As part of the content strategy, content experts measure and repurpose the intranet's existing content using a set of heuristics and content evaluation techniques. The findings from the as-is evaluation are reported, and recommendations are made based on content standards and best practices and the collective experience to boost an organization's web presence and reach. The evaluation includes content, layout, navigation, user tasks, general site characteristics, and features over web pages, blog posts, multimedia, social media conversations, e-mails, newsletters, and RSS feeds.

Build, Test, and Measure Stage

During this stage you develop the experience assets as per the specifications and build the designs using the appropriate user interface technology.

Experience assets include HTML, stylesheets, page templates, navigation elements, site structure, and overall information architecture, as well as visual designs and visual assets such as style guides.

The main activities in this stage are the following:

- Development in compliance with W3C standards and other predefined standards

- Accessibility coding and testing

- Cross-browser compatibility coding and testing

- Usability assessment using heuristic analysis and eye tracking (to look at a user's scan paths, fixations, and areas of interest to find patterns of usage)

- Quality testing of experience assets to check for compliance, accessibility, and cross-browser compatibility

In subsequent sections, I will cover the concepts of design thinking in more detail.

Design Thinking

Design thinking is a user-centric approach to problem finding wherein you evaluate all the alternatives for a given problem to arrive at the most effective solution. Design thinking is effective for solving complex problems. Figure 3-5 shows the various steps of a design thinking exercise along with the core tenets of a design thinking exercise.

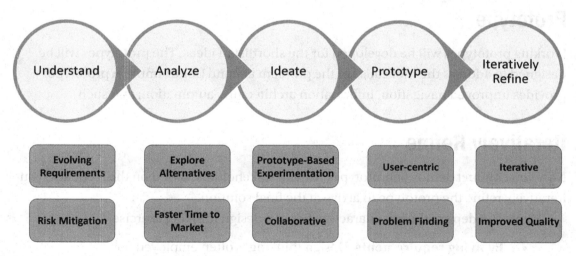

Figure 3-5. *Tenets of design thinking*

Understand

In the initial phases of design thinking, workshops are conducted with a selected set of employees from various groups (such as sales, marketing, support, and such). You want to conduct detailed workshops and interviews with specific user groups across teams and locations. The discussions will be interactive in nature, and they provide insights on the challenges faced by user groups. During the workshops you will understand the pain points and challenges with the current systems and processes.

Analyze

Once you understand the problems, you can try to identify the root cause of the problem. The problem root cause could be because of existing business processes, an absence of governance, and such.

Ideate

Based on your insights about the problem root cause, you can now discuss all the ideas that could potentially solve the problem. You can explore various alternatives to shortlist the promising solution options.

Prototype

Working prototypes will be developed for the shortlisted ideas. The prototypes will be designed to address the root cause of the problem at hand (for example, a prototype provides improved navigation, information architecture, automation, and such).

Iteratively Refine

Now you conduct demos of prototypes with all stakeholders. Based on the feedback, you iteratively refine the prototype to arrive at the final solution.

Figure 3-5 depicts the key characteristics of a design thinking exercise.

- **Evolving requirements**: Design thinking is often employed for problems with evolving or ambiguous requirements. Design thinking workshops are conducted to understand the problem better.

- **Explore alternatives**: During the ideation stage of the design thinking exercise, you explore various alternatives for a scenario.

- **Prototype-based experimentation**: Prototypes are exit points of a design thinking exercise. For a digital platform scenario, clickable prototypes visually communicate the navigation, design, and user experience to the stakeholders.

- **User-centric**: The design thinking exercise adopts a user-centric approach to problem-solving. The inputs from end users of the application are involved in activities such as user research, persona definition, and user journey mapping.

- **Iterative**: The prototypes are iteratively refined based on feedback from all involved users.

- **Risk mitigation**: The complex problems with evolving requirements have high-risk probability. Design thinking will be handy in such scenarios because the ideation stage, alternatives, and prototypes mitigate the risk.

- **Faster time to market**: Prototypes are converted into working models in a minimum viable product (MVP) and hence quicken the time to market.

- **Collaborative**: The design thinking exercise is a collaborative approach to problem-solving. The exercise involves stakeholders and end users in various stages such as the "understand" and "analyze" stages.

- **Problem finding**: During the initial stages of design thinking, you seek to find the right problems. Once you understand the right problems, you then analyze and ideate to find the appropriate solution.

- **Improved quality**: The iterative and collaborative nature of design thinking improves the overall quality of the deliverable.

UX Design Best Practices

The key user experience (UX) best practices are as follows:

- Understand the end user needs through data gathering sessions via techniques such as interviews, contextual interviews, and surveys.

- Interact with users early and often. Gather user feedback through the design process.

- Generate insights to map business goals and user needs.

- Review the revised flow and page design to identify potential usability problems.

- Create the design iteratively, from low fidelity to high fidelity.

- Test the design early and often.

- Base the visual design on brand guidelines and adhere to the visual design principles for a better end-user experience.

EXP Design Principles

The key principles of EXP design are as follows:

- **Minimalism**: The UX design should be simple and meaningful. The content should be clearly understandable in all channels.

- **Employee-centric**: The design should provide the features, information, and services based on employee persona. The information architecture and navigation model should reflect the employee's mental model.

- **Responsive**: The design should provide flexible layouts and images so that it adjusts to various devices and form factors seamlessly. Media queries, fluid layouts, and flexible images are the key components of responsive design, as depicted in Figure 3-6.

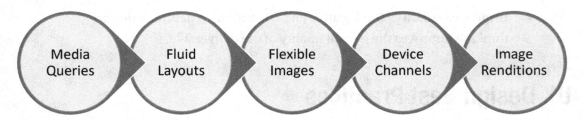

Figure 3-6. *Components of responsive design*

- **Mobile-first approach**: The design, navigation, and functionality should be primarily designed and tested for mobile devices.

- **Communicating visually**: The key ideas and information should be expressed mainly through visual elements such as graphics, icons, and visual aids so that it is easy for users to understand.

- **Personalized**: The information and functionality should be personalized based on user attributes (such as employee geography, employee department, employee skillset, employee job role, etc.) and based on employee preferences (such as opted communication preferences). The platform should know the user (based on persona) and use the insights (such as user interests, user activities) through personalization.

- **User-generated content (UGC)**: The design should accommodate user-generated content such as reviews, comments, ratings, likes, sharing, at-mentioning, and such.

- **Collaboration**: Collaborative features such as blogs, wikis, communities, and chat should be designed for an EXP to enhance information sharing. Less "formal" channels such as messengers and social features should be adopted in the EXP design.

- **Gamification**: The design should engage and incentivize employees for achieving organization goals (such as information sharing, contribution to knowledge base, etc.) through loyalty points, badges, user ranking, and such.

- **Intelligent**: The design should help the employees do their jobs faster through the usage of automated tools and services.

Accessibility

Accessibility includes inclusive methods and practices to remove barriers and make the Web accessible to everyone, including people with disabilities. Accessibility enhances the usability of the platform and is an important nonfunctional requirement. In this section, I will cover the crucial aspects of accessibility for an employee platform. Web Content Accessibility Guidelines (WCAG) is a set of accessibility guidelines, and it is widely used across the industry.

In the employee platform scenario, implementing accessibility standards and guidelines provides an inclusive environment for all employees. Conforming to accessibility guidelines also enhances the usability and hence the effectiveness of the platform. In fact, accessibility guidelines are part of legal and regulatory compliance in many countries.

Attributes of Web Accessibility

The key attributes of the web accessibility standards are as follows:

- **Perceivable**: Users should be able to perceive the web content through their senses. This includes using text alternatives for images, captioned multimedia content, text labels, color contrasts, and text descriptions for multimedia content.

- **Operable***:* Users should be able to easily operate the system. To adhere to this system, you should provide keyboard accessibility for main functionality and make the system easily navigable and provide enough time to use the functionality and content.

- **Understandable***:* Users should be able to easily understand the content. The web site information should be easily readable and understandable.

- **Compatible***:* The web site should be able to work on multiple user agents/browsers, devices, and form factors.

Figure 3-7 shows the detailed steps in implementing accessibility standards.

Accessibility Standards Definition	Implement Accessibility Guidelines	Validation
• Use WCAG guidelines to identify the relevant accessibility guidelines. • Prepare the accessibility document to mark relevant accessibility guidelines for pages, UI elements, actions, and other applicable elements.	• Create UI elements with the specified accessibility guidelines. • Build page-level and site-level accessibility guidelines. • Review the accessibility checklist for all the pages.	• Validate the accessibility features through accessibility testing tools such as Web Accessibility Toolbar and accessibility validator.

Figure 3-7. *Accessibility standards steps*

Sample EXP Designs

In this section, I'll discuss various designs for a next-generation EXP and call out the key functionality.

Generally, the home page of an EXP has a two-column or three-column layout wherein the functional widgets are tiled vertically. Figure 3-8 shows a sample EXP home page.

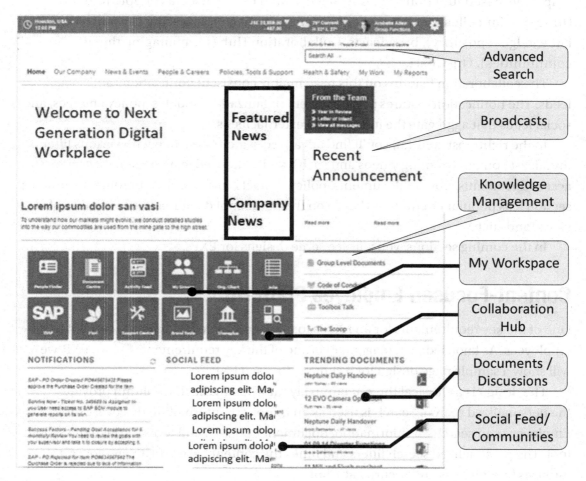

Figure 3-8. *Sample EXP layout*

The header section provides details of the logged-in user, a link to profile screen, and a settings icon where the user can change their preferences.

The EXP home page normally has a marquee image ("Welcome to the Next-Generation Digital Workplace" in Figure 3-8). The key highlights are displayed in image format or in accordion format (rotating images) can be displayed as a marquee image (sometimes as a scrolling accordion).

In Figure 3-8, you can see the personalized employee workspaces that provide employee-based functionality: Advanced search can be used as people finder (to search for colleagues), Knowledge Management (for accessing centralized knowledge repository), broadcasts, Collaboration Hub (for managing the user communities), Org Chart.

The collaboration features on this page mainly consist of notifications and social feeds. The notification features provide recent organization updates, policy changes, and social feeds that aggregate the internal and external feeds.

In the rightmost column, you'll find advanced search (to search with various filters), broadcast content (training videos and such), and a knowledge management section (to access documents, how-to documents, policy artifacts, and such). A trending documents section lists popular documents (based on the number of downloads, the number of views, and such).

In the coming sections, you will see some designs for EXPs.

Content-Focused Employee Platform

One of the key requirements for an EXP is to manage and deliver relevant content to the employees. As knowledge management is one of the key requirements for the EXP, we will show a sample page design for a content-focused EXP.

The design is a classical three-column layout wherein the first column provides the personalized search. Search is used as an important information discovery tool. Employees can search for information, documents, people, and tools through the search tool. The personalized search filters and ranks the content based on an employee's interests/preferences and security attributes.

An employee training calendar reminds the employee about upcoming trainings. The employee dashboard has a "how-to" section that provides personalized recommendations for how-to documents based on the employee's search history and preferences, as depicted in Figure 3-9.

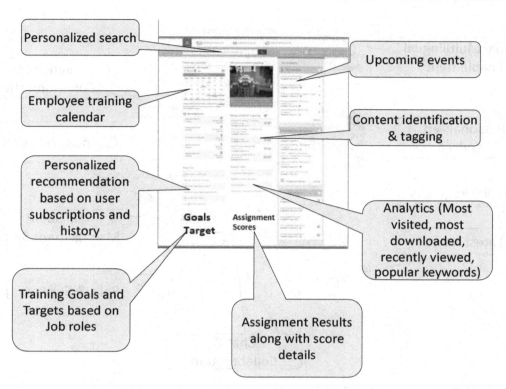

Figure 3-9. *Sample three-column layout of EXP*

In the middle column, the dashboard presents the newly added content. Employees can tag the content with meaningful words for quicker identification. We have a "Quick links" section that provides a list of the most viewed/downloaded articles and documents. Employees can bookmark the documents.

On the right side, employees can view the upcoming events and e-learning subscriptions (for learning on the go).

Employee Dashboard

In a typical employee dashboard, as depicted in Figure 3-10, you can see prominent features such as multilingual enablement (for a globally distributed intranet), personalized services, and leadership communication (that contains videos of senior leaders). The dashboard also features sections for service requests, latest news, and polls and surveys (for collecting feedback from employees).

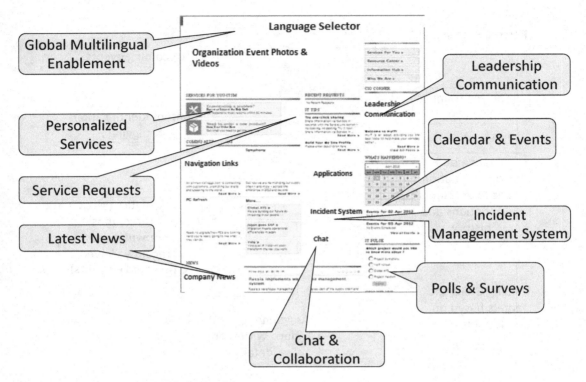

Figure 3-10. *Sample EXP dashboard*

The employee dashboard is omnichannel enabled, as depicted in Figure 3-11.

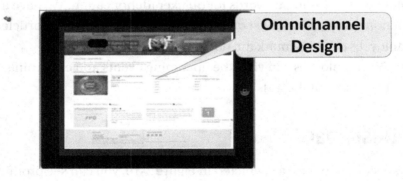

Figure 3-11. *Omnichannel view of EXP dashboard*

Figure 3-12 shows an employee profile dashboard. A typical employee dashboard mainly consists of a snapshot of employee activities that includes a personalized list of tasks, blogs, followers' list, and employee schedule.

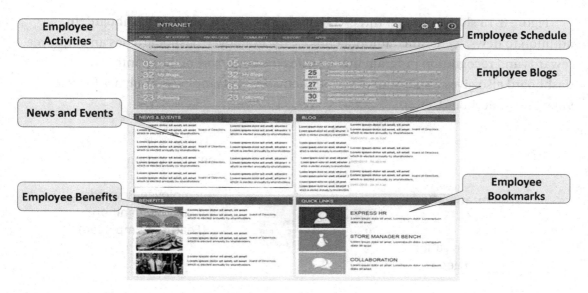

Figure 3-12. *Sample employee profile dashboard*

The employee dashboard page also consists of personalized details of the employee benefits, employee blogs, and employee bookmarks.

The design approach for an employee dashboard consists of the following:

- Combination of dashboard and organization-specific information

- Responsive design with a structured navigation and card layout to address all form factors

- Simplified data/information grouping (critical information such as user profile and work schedule on top and organizational information below)

- Contemporary look and feel with flat theme while remaining true to the brand identity

- Intranet applications that allow the employees to efficiently do their jobs

- Tools to collaboration tools with colleagues

- Personalized information delivery

Figure 3-13 shows another three-column layout of an employee dashboard. In addition to news, feeds, and announcements, the employee dashboard has an employee rewards and recognition program that features the employee of the month. The dashboard also gives a snapshot of various activities and employee analytics (article views, blogs authored, etc.).

Figure 3-13. *Three-column layout of employee dashboard*

Tiles/Cards-Based Design

Another popular EXP design is based on tiles. In a tiles-based design, various aspects of the same topic are grouped together. Content, videos, and clickable action buttons are part of a tile. Tiles are stacked vertically or horizontally.

In the design shown in Figure 3-14, you can see a "hamburger" mega navigation menu to improve the usability of the tiles-based design.

Figure 3-14. *Sample tile layout of EXP home page*

Figure 3-15 shows another view of a tile-based layout.

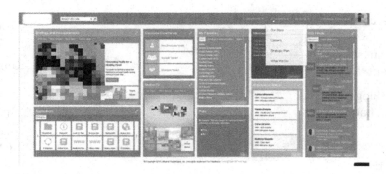

Figure 3-15. *Second sample of tile layout of EXP home page*

Employee Collaboration Platform

Figure 3-16 shows a typical collaboration dashboard of an EXP. The collaboration dashboard provides personalized information. The main element in the collaboration dashboard is a filtered search that enables an employee to search for relevant document and information. Employee request management allows employees to log incidents for seeking clarifications.

The collaboration dashboard provides links to core collaboration features such as blogs, wikis, communities, forums, and chat. These features enable employees to share information and effectively communicate and collaborate with colleagues.

The collaboration dashboard also features a training and learning plan for employees. A centralized knowledge management is provided as part of the collaboration dashboard through which employees can upload and download policy documents.

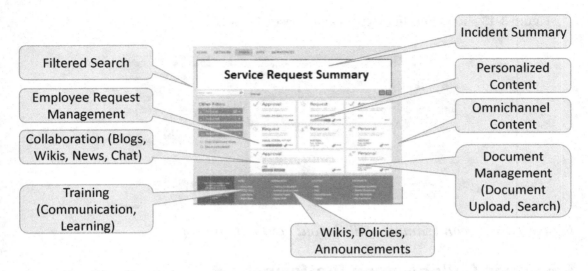

Figure 3-16. Sample employee collaboration dashboard

Employee Learning Platform

Self-learning and self-training are the key objectives of an EXP. Figure 3-17 shows a sample employee dashboard that focuses on learning and development. The employee dashboard is a three-column layout that has common employee features such as search, employee activities, news feeds, polls, and employee bookmarks.

Features such as gamification are designed to encourage and incentivize the employee learning. The gamification section features top learners and certification achievers to recognize and motivate other employees.

The dashboard also displays a training calendar and planned trainings to remind employees of upcoming trainings.

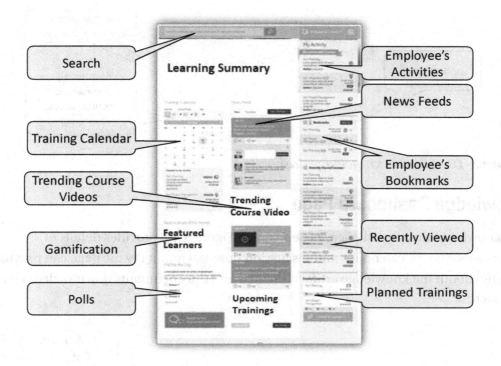

Figure 3-17. *EXP learning home page*

Knowledge Platform for an EXP

Because an EXP heavily relies on documents (such as how-to documents and process/policy documents), I will show some sample UX designs focusing on knowledge access.

In this section, I show three views of a knowledge repository.

Knowledge Home Page

Figure 3-18 shows the home page design for a knowledge access EXP. The knowledge artifacts are in various categories such as policy documents, how-to documents, help documents, on-boarding documents, and so on.

Figure 3-18. *Sample knowledge dashboard*

Knowledge Dashboard Page

The knowledge dashboard page, as depicted in Figure 3-19, provides details of documents, events, calendars, and discussion boards. Optionally the page can provide statistics about the knowledge artifacts created and the documents downloaded, viewed, and such.

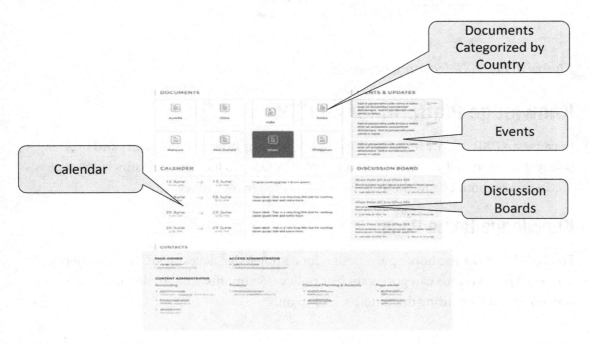

Figure 3-19. *Sample knowledge dashboard*

Knowledge Discovery Page

Search is the primary tool for knowledge discovery. Figure 3-20 shows a sample search page design. The search interface provides filter options such as document type, author, date range, and such. The search results also provide an option to sort the results based on parameters such as number of views, recency, number of comments, and such.

Figure 3-20. *Sample search page*

Validation

Usability testing is one of the key validation methods to assess EXP usability. It is a research technique that you can use to test UI design using paper mock-ups, interactive prototypes, or live applications with real users. This testing is called *formative testing* or *summative testing* depending on which stage of the design process it is done in.

- **Formative testing** is done during the initial stage of the design process to find and fix the usability problems as part of the iterative user-centered design process. The inputs and findings go back to iterate the design to make it more usable. There can be one or more formative tests before the design is finalized and goes into development.

- **Summative testing** is done when the UI design is in its final stage. This is part of the formal user acceptance testing milestone before the product is released to the target audience. The focus of this testing phase is on measuring the task completion time, success rates, and overall satisfaction.

Table 3-1 shows the main usability metrics.

Table 3-1. *Key Usability Metrics*

Category	Usability Metric	Example
Effectiveness	Task completion rate	What percent of users are able to complete the task of logging into their web e-mail system?
	Number of errors	How many errors did each user commit while completing a task?
	Number of assists	How many times was the user provided with a prompt/help to complete a task?
Efficiency	Time taken	How long does it take to search and find safety guidelines on the intranet?
	Task completion efficiency	What percent of users found the safety guidelines in a given unit of time?
Satisfaction	Subjective satisfaction index	Users rate questions like "I found the system unnecessarily complex" on a scale of one to five.

Sample Design Execution Plan

This section defines a sample plan for the design phase. Figure 3-21 shows a typical four-week plan for the discovery phase.

The discovery phase is sprint 0, where you mainly focus on understanding and elaborating the requirements. In the four-week exercise, you conduct interviews and focused workshops to get a deeper understanding of the requirements. The team conducts design thinking workshops, defines personas, and maps user journeys.

As part of the design thinking workshops, you create prototypes and iteratively refine the design. You also refine the information architecture (IA), interaction design, and UX guidelines.

The key deliverable of this phase are user stories, prototypes, wireframes, information architecture, and unique templates.

Project Stage		Discovery + Define			
Sprint 0 - Descovery	**Deliverable**	W1	W2	W3	W4
Discover requirements through Focus Group Workshops & Stakeholder Interviews. Define Problem Statement , Persona definition, User/Customer Journey Mapping User Groups from HR, Sales, Marketing, Production, Finance departments	Prioritized User Stories	✓			
Reasearch, Prototyping & Feasibility Analysis	Prototypes		✓		
Ideate Solution, Create Conceptual Sketches / Low Fidelity Wireframes	Conceptual Sketches or Low-Fidelity Wireframes		✓		
Define Strategy	Technical strategy			✓	
Firming up the ideation concepts & develop low fidelity prototypes	Low Fidelity Prototypes to validate with end users			✓	
Validate concept with end users/stakeholders and get feedback				✓	
Define & Finalize IA, SA, UX	IA, SA, UX				✓
Iterate design based on user feedback & Concept Signoff	Approx. 6-7 Unique Templates in the form of Low- Fidelity Wireframes				✓

Figure 3-21. *Sample four-week design plan*

Weekly Plan

Figure 3-22 shows a weekly plan for the entire EXP. This plan has five tracks (enterprise social, team collaboration, employee portal, document management, and mobile enablement) across four phases. I have mapped the main activities for each of the tracks in all phases.

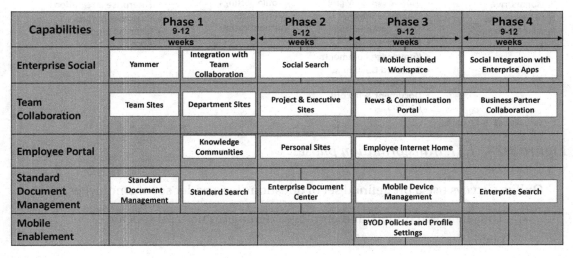

Figure 3-22. *Weekly EXP execution plan*

I have depicted another transformation for an EXP in Figure 3-23. During the first iteration, you target quick wins that consist of features such as collaboration, personal drive, and messaging. You leverage a product's built-in features for a quicker rollout of this phase. The initial platform and core integrations (such as security integration, database integration) will be enabled in the first iteration. Each iteration spans about 9 to 12 weeks.

During the expand phase, you include features such as conferences, communities, knowledge management, document management, and mobile enablement. These features will be built on top of the platform created in the first phase.

During the advance stage, complex features such as bring-your-own-device (BYOD) and multifactor authentication will be enabled. During the fully transform phase, you provide platform collaboration, complex integrations, business portals, and productivity improvement apps.

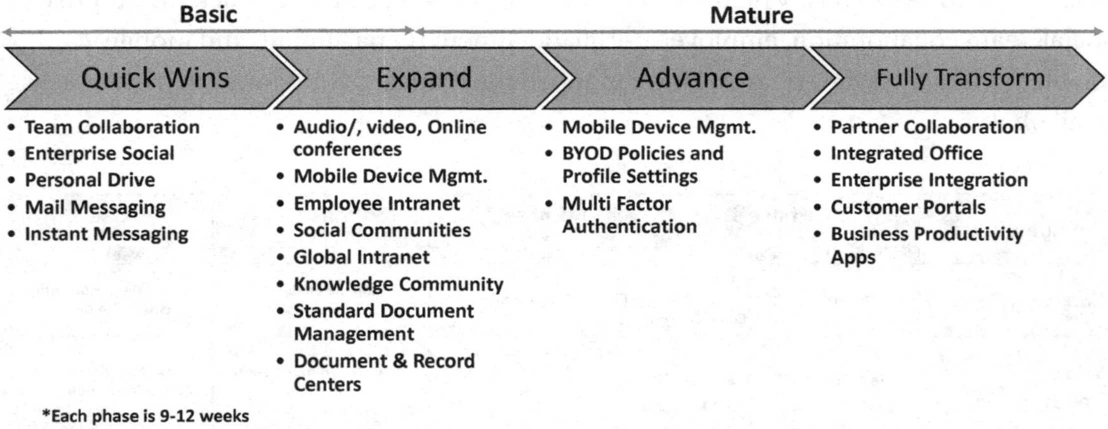

Basic		Mature	
Quick Wins	**Expand**	**Advance**	**Fully Transform**
• Team Collaboration • Enterprise Social • Personal Drive • Mail Messaging • Instant Messaging	• Audio/, video, Online conferences • Mobile Device Mgmt. • Employee Intranet • Social Communities • Global Intranet • Knowledge Community • Standard Document Management • Document & Record Centers	• Mobile Device Mgmt. • BYOD Policies and Profile Settings • Multi Factor Authentication	• Partner Collaboration • Integrated Office • Enterprise Integration • Customer Portals • Business Productivity Apps

*Each phase is 9-12 weeks

Figure 3-23. *EXP transformation phases*

Online surveys use a predefined set of questions for a wider set of employees.

- They help you understand employee demographics and specific needs.

- They provide broad trends in terms of employee needs and challenges.

- They enable the prioritization of functional requirements.

Summary

This chapter covered the following:

- The threefold advantages of experience design are business benefits, employee benefits, and operation benefits.

- An experience-based EXP architecture consists of layers such as the employee experience layer, orchestration layer, and system or record layer.

- The key benefits of the employee experience layer are quick information access, employee engagement, a consistent and standard user interface, omnichannel access, enhanced collaboration, and self-service tools.

- The high-level steps in experience design are the discovery stage, the design stage, and the build, test, and measure stage.

- During the discovery stage you finalize the UX scope, do stakeholder interviews, conduct a requirements workshop, define standards and UX goals, and do a content audit. The main deliverables from this stage are UX plan, competitive assessment, user personas, and such.

- During the design phase you design the information architecture, personalization, localization, user experience, interactive design, and others. The main deliverable are a UX strategy document, design comps, a style guide, the visual design, and wireframes.

- During the build, test, and measure stage, you develop a prototype, write the HTML, and do the usability testing. The main deliverables are production assets, page templates, and test reports.

- Design thinking is a user-centric approach to problem finding wherein you evaluate all the alternatives for a given problem to arrive at the most effective solution.

- The main stages of a design thinking exercise are to understand, analyze, ideate, prototype, and iteratively refine.

- The key EXP design principles are minimalism, employee centric, responsive, mobile-first approach, communicating visually, personalized, user-generated content, collaboration, gamification, and intelligent.

- The key attributes of accessibility are perceivable, operable, understandable, and compatible.

- Usability testing is a research technique that you use to test UI design using paper mock-ups, interactive prototypes, or live applications with real users.

CHAPTER 4

Digital Workplace Development

EXP development requires a thorough understanding of solution principles, development methods, best practices, and the software stack. In this chapter, I will discuss various aspects of digital workplace development. I will define the core requirements for EXPs along with the solution tenets. In addition, I will discuss the development aspects of core requirements including the user interface, integration model, search, and security. A robust infrastructure is a key success factor for the continued success of an EXP; hence, I will detail the infrastructure design and development principles.

Requirements and Solution Principles

This section covers the core requirements for EXP solutions, and then I will elaborate on the core solution modules in subsequent sections. Figure 4-1 shows the core requirements of an EXP.

© Shailesh Kumar Shivakumar 2020

S. K. Shivakumar, *Build a Next-Generation Digital Workplace*, https://doi.org/10.1007/978-1-4842-5512-4_4

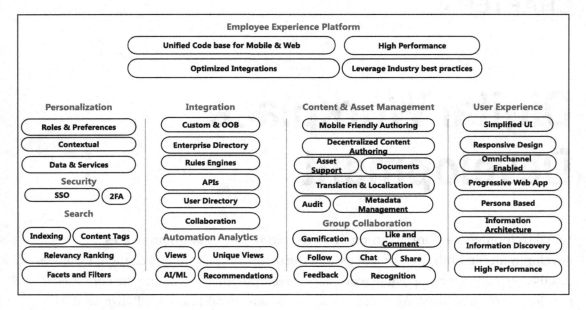

Figure 4-1. *EXP core requirements*

A modern digital workplace leverages industry best practices to develop a high-performance application with optimal integrations. I recommend having a unified code base for both mobile and web channels to provide a seamless omnichannel experience.

A forward-looking EXP should provide these features:

- **Personalization**: The EXP should provide user roles and preferences based on contextual and personalized data and features.

- **Security**: The EXP should support various security features such as authentication, authorization, single sign-on (SSO), and two-factor authentication (2FA).

- **Search**: The EXP should index information from various sources and should be able to index a wide variety of content types (such as web content, database tables, documents, etc.). EXP search should provide facets for filtering results and for ranking the top results.

- **Integration**: The EXP should provide integrations with various systems such as web services, user directories, rules engines, collaboration tools, and such.

- **Content and asset management**: Web content and assets (such as images and videos) are stored mainly in the content management system. EXP content and asset management should also provide features such as metadata management, mobile-friendly content authoring, and such.

- **Automation and analytics**: Adopting machine-led automation measures such as chatbots, smart recommendations, and cognitive search enhances the productivity.

- **Collaboration**: EXP collaboration enhances employee collaboration through features such as chat, reviews and ratings, gamification concepts, share, likes, and comments.

- **User experience**: A modern and forward-looking user experience includes features such as a simplified UI, responsive design, omnichannel enablement, persona-based information architecture, progressive web app design, and high performance.

Subsequent sections elaborate on the development of the core features such as the user interface, integration, search, security, and infrastructure.

Key Solution Design Principles

Solution design principles provide a best-practice approach that is proven to achieve a modular and extensible solution. Figure 4-2 shows the main solution design principles for an EXP.

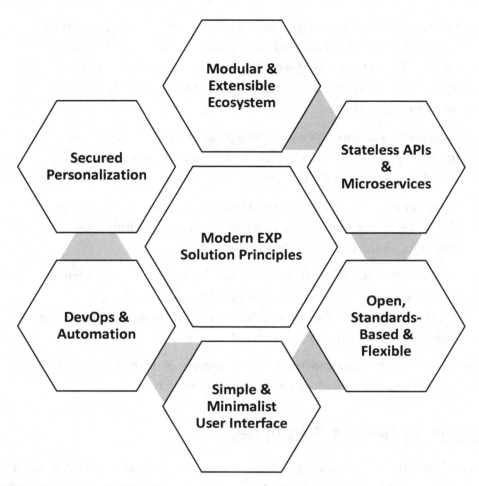

Figure 4-2. *Modern EXP solution principles*

- **Modular and extensible ecosystem:** An EXP should have a modular
design so that change/risk is localized to small units of functionality.
Modular design enables extreme flexibility to change, add, and
update new channels with minimal impact.

Components that are modular achieve high reusability and
scalability. The Singleton pattern can be used in implementing
the components. This solution follows the single responsibility
principle, which says to have self-contained modules with a single
source of truth. This also greatly reduces the coupling between
components of the application, enables a unidirectional flow of
data, and provides for easier maintainability.

- **Stateless APIs and microservices**: A microservices architecture ensures that the container becomes an independently deployable, testable unit. All services will be elastic/autoscaling-enabled, cloud-ready, and self-healing. They will have the ability to monitor/correct itself, will have a low cost of ownership, and will be able to be easily changed, deployed, and monitored.

- **Open, standards-based, and flexible**: The EXP platform should use open standards for presentation and integration so that it is easy to extend and enhance. HTML standards (such as HTML 2.0, XHTML), integration standards (such as REST), integration contracts (such as JSON, XML), accessibility standards (such as WCAG 2.0), encryption standards, and security standards facilitate future extensionality.

- **Simple and minimalist user interface**: A simple and minimalist design works across various devices and user agents. An uncluttered UI with an intuitive information architecture reduces a user's cognitive load and improves user satisfaction.

- **DevOps and automation**: DevOps-enabled releases provide a low time to market, from concept to rollout. Continuous integration and continuous deployment reduce the risk and increase the quality of the overall delivery.

- **Secured personalization**: The EXP should provide a personalized and secured view of data, content, functionality, and services. Personalization provides user preferences and interest-based information.

In addition to the previous items, the overall EXP development framework should also provide efficient governance (such as a change management process, a real-time monitoring process, a business continuity process, and such).

Migration of Legacy Platforms to EXP

When you are migrating the existing legacy platforms into the modern EXP, you should do the legacy portfolio analysis and identify the opportunities and priorities for the following:

- **Rehost and re-platform**: Change the hosting system and platform to the target platform. Cloud-native digital platforms are the preferred hosting platforms to provide on-demand scaling.

- **Refactor**: Consolidate the application, functionality, and data and reuse the components wherever possible. Standardize processes and decouple the user interface layer and the business layer.

- **Re-architect**: Refresh the technology, leveraging modern platform principles such as headless integration, stateless APIs, and modern UI frameworks.

- **Rewrite**: Redevelop the application with new technologies such as lightweight JavaScript frameworks and lightweight integration models.

- **Replace**: Decommission, do not move, and sunset the applications that are no longer needed.

Software Stack

Table 4-1 shows a sample software stack that can be used for building the EXP.

Note   I have listed a sample list of open source stack in Table 4-1. However, there are alternative commercial products and other open source technologies for each component.

Table 4-1. *Sample Software Stack for EXP Development*

Component	Technology Stack
Front-end UI framework	Angular 8, Angular Material, D3.js
API gateway	Apigee
UI layer	Angular, HTML5, CSS3, Bootstrap
Ingestion layer	StreamSets, Kafka Streams
Service layer and service contract	Java 9, Spring Boot, Istio Circuit breaker, Akka, Swagger
Testing	• Mockito (Java) • Jasmine, Karma framework (Angular) • Automation testing: Selenium and Appium • Performance testing: NeoLoad, Apache JMeter • Security penetration testing tool: Fortify
End-to-end testing	• Rest Assured (Java) • Protractor framework (Angular)
Caching layer	Apache Ignite in-memory cache, EhCache, Memcached
Database	• MySQL
Batch	Spring Batch
Security	• Authentication and authorization: a. Identity Access management using LDAPb. Authentications and authorizations: OAuth2, JWT, Kerberos, role-based access control, row-level security • LDAP software: OpenDJ 3.0 • Encryption: AES 256, HTTPS, SSL
Rule engine	Drools
Containers	Dockers and Kubernetes
Container application platform	OpenShift
Monitoring and logging	Elastic search, Logstash, Kibana, Graphana, and filebeats

(continued)

Table 4-1. (*continued*)

Component	Technology Stack
Reports	Jaspersoft
CI/CD	• Continuous Integration: Jenkins • Static code quality: SonarQube for Java, Codelyzer for Angular • Artifact repository: Nexus • Build tool: Maven, Gradle • Source control: Git, BitBucket • Performance tool: BlazeMeter • Automation deployment tool: Kubernetes • Ticket management: Jira

User Interface Engineering

In this section, I will cover the core solution tenets of UI engineering such as solution tenets, UX trends, the design process, and the reference architecture.

UI Core Solution Tenets

The core solution tenets of modern user interfaces are as follows:

- **Simple-user interface and lightweight**: Use a simple and intuitive user interface to enhance efficacy, which leads to user productivity and faster decisions. Leverage existing open source library components and responsive design to provide lightweight design.

- **Minimalist design**: Leverage best practices to design the minimalistic information systems to reduce cognitive load. Information design should be more visual to achieve a better user experience.

- **High performance**: Leverage a open source library framework and caching. The presentation platform should leverage other methods such as asynchronous loading, lazy loading, and pagination to provide optimal performance.

- **Omnichannel enabled**: The user interface should adopt a responsive design and adaptive design to provide a seamless omnichannel experience.

- **Decoupled design**: The front end is completely decoupled from the backend systems through the usage of the lightweight services layer.

- **SEO friendly**: UI frameworks serve prerendered versions of the HTML to bots/crawlers and leverage SEO best practices such as meaningful titles, keywords, page metadata, and friendly/ bookmarkable URLs to enhance the discovery of the web pages.

- **Continuous updates**: The UI updates are done continuously through continuous deployment.

- **High scalability**: Modern UI frameworks use CDNs and the cloud for on-demand scalability. The solution should autoscale along both the x- and y-axes (scaling out and scaling units of work independently).

- **Progressive web apps (PWAs)**: A PWA is designed for an omnichannel experience and leverages many native device features such as interactions, navigation, and so on.

- **Modular**: A modern UI has the ability to upgrade and reuse components through a decoupled architecture.

- **Secure**: A modern UI has token-based authentication and authorization to enable stateless and secure APIs.

- **Contextual and personalized**: A modern UI delivers the right information to the right user at the right time. Information is designed to show what is useful and relevant to match a user's needs and mental model.

- **Intuitive visual design**: A modern UI defines a user-centric visual hierarchy and information architecture.

- **Information architecture**: A modern UI defines a user-centric navigation model, site hierarchy, and menu.

- **High Usability**: Design the system to be easily usable and learnable.

Trends in UX

Understanding emerging trends helps to design the EXP with forward-looking features based on industry best practices. Figure 4-3 identifies the key trends in EXPs.

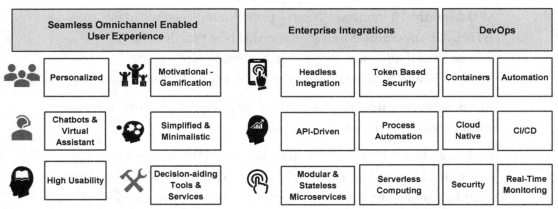

Figure 4-3. Key EXP trends

Figure 4-3 depicts the emerging trends in the EXP domain. Understanding these trends helps to design forward-looking and future-proof applications. The trends are as follows:

- **Seamless omnichannel-enabled user experience**: The key focus areas of a seamless omnichannel-enabled user experience are personalization (contextual and targeted delivery based on user preferences), gamification (adopting gaming concepts to digital world), chatbots/virtual assistants, simplified and minimalistic design, high usability, decision aiding tools, and services.

- **Enterprise integrations**: The main focus areas in integration are headless API-based integration (using lightweight APIs to integrate with a system of record), token-based security, serverless computing (such as AWS Lambda functions), process automation, modular and stateless microservices, and high performance.

- **DevOps**: The key focus areas in DevOps are containers (such as Kubernetes and Docker), automation (such as automation of release management), cloud native deployment, security, continuous integration and continuous delivery, and real-time monitoring of application and infrastructure.

Design Process

The design process consists of four distinct phases.

- **Discover**: The first step in the project lifecycle is discovery. In this phase, you predominantly conduct surveys, stakeholder interviews, and focus groups to understand the real pain points of the end users. This understanding is important to align the opportunities with the business needs and technical feasibility of solution. You also perform trend and competitive analysis to identify the service offerings of competitors and the latest design trends to be incorporated in the UX solution.

- **Define**: In the definition phase, you converge the information collected during the discovery phase to define user personas, new user journey maps, task flows, information architecture (IA), and interactions for responsive design implementation. You also create user scenarios to make informed design decisions during the next phase.

- **Design**: During design, all the information is analyzed, illustrated, and defined in the previous phases is used to realize the actual product. The team creates rapid low-fidelity and high-fidelity prototypes for quick feedback from stakeholders. It is an iterative process wherein the design is tested and improved to deliver an intuitive interface with the latest features and UX trends. After sign-off from the stakeholders on the wireframes and prototypes, the team of interaction and visual designers creates all the screen layouts for various devices, including web, tablet, and mobile.

- **Develop**: The final stage of the process is to create the web pages based on the UI specification sheet and style guide.

Reference Architecture

A reference architecture provides various solution components and technologies incorporating the solution design principles and the defined industry trends and standards. A reference architecture provides a blueprint for the solution.

A content-heavy EXP can be built with a JavaScript framework like Angular along with Drupal, as depicted in Figure 4-4.

- Progressive decoupling provides higher client side interactivity that provides rich user experience.

- Content Authors and site administrators can leverage features such as workflow, site preview of Drupal along with progressive decoupling.

- The user interface screens have static content sections driven by Drupal and JavaScript framework sections. UI developers can work on the JavaScript framework sections independent of the content authors.

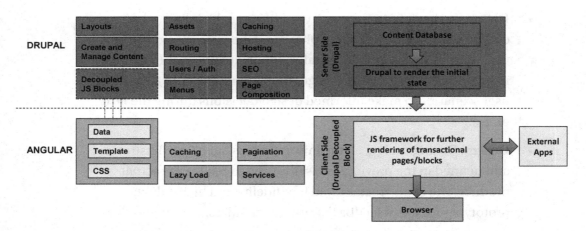

Figure 4-4. *Content-heavy EXP built with Angular and Drupal*

Figure 4-5 shows the detailed solution architecture when using Angular within Drupal.

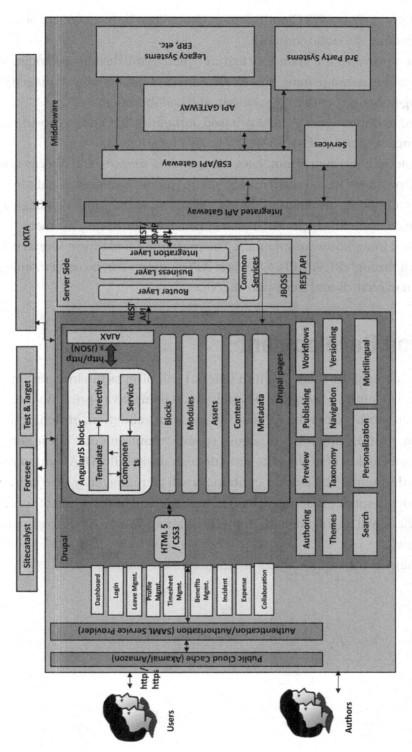

Figure 4-5. EXP solution architecture

Popular CDNs such as AWS CloudFront or Akamai can be leveraged to accelerate the web delivery (mainly the static content).

This solution provides the main EXP features such as the dashboard, login, leave management, profile management, timesheet management, benefits management, incident management, expense management, and collaboration.

Okta is used to implement OAuth 2.0–based authentication and to provide stateless APIs that leverage security tokens. SAML 2.0 is used for single sign-on.

AngularJS blocks consisting of templates, components, services, and directives will be hosted within Drupal. For web content management, you can leverage the built-in Drupal services such as authoring, preview, publishing, workflows, search, and multilingual features.

Server-side components include a business router/orchestrator, business components, and integration components. The presentation platform interacts with the backend system through REST APIs. ESBs and API gateways can be used to integrate with the system of records and third-party services.

Integration Development

As integration is one of the main solution tenets, I will discuss the integration details in this section. The entire services layer will be built using Java Spring Boot to process the API requests coming from the API layer to perform validation, enrichment, transformation, routing, and other business-specific requirements. These services will be hosted on Docker containers to provide high availability (HA) and to meet the scalability requirements. The Docker containers will be managed by the Kubernetes platform to provide service discovery, load balancing, and autoscaling of services. The microservices will aggregate data from the different source types to provide a 360-degree view.

Table 4-2 depicts the various layers in the integration module.

Table 4-2. *EXP Integration Layers*

Layer	Description
API layer	• APIs are set of routines, protocols, and tools required to expose business functionality to consumers. API components involve an API management platform that provides features to define, create, monitor, and measure the APIs and their usage runtime. The API management platform provides a gateway, portal, and analytics to provide complete functionality to manage and govern the API lifecycle. • The API gateway will apply security policies, traffic/quota management policies, and processes for the incoming API requests to the backend microservices.
Technical services	• These services are fundamental building blocks of the platform that cater to functionality such as notifications, rules, scheduler, and so on.
Integration services	• These services comprise adapters to the various backend systems. • These services will abstract the complexities and protocols required to integrate with various systems. • These services will be designed to accept/return entities from the canonical models defined during the modeling phase. • Some of these integration services will be built in order to enable a modular transition; some of them will be designed as wrappers over existing systems that are carried forward into the proposed architecture.
Business services	• These services are used to perform specific business tasks; they abstract the complexities and rules behind performing a specific business task.
Data services	• The services will perform the function to write into the messaging layer for temporary and permanent persistence.

Services Design

Asynchronous services are for calling external services and for transforming data to the schema defined by the business model. Services act as the common language enabler between external services and the UI. This will enable easier adaptability to change communication protocols and ensure a single format defined by models. Table 4-3 depicts key solution design considerations.

Table 4-3. *EXP Solution Considerations*

Goal	Considerations for the Design of the Solution
To implement a core part of the functionality as services and APIs for high resiliency, modularity, extensibility and scalability	• Microservice-based system with each service providing a unique functionality. • Modular, nonmonolithic system. • Clear distinct building blocks, with defined interfaces. • Microservices architecture to make sure that services are inherently stateless. • Microservice provides a clear separation of business logic and presentation, a higher degree of reuse, the ability to test/upgrade/replace distinct "units" of functionality, and the much needed ability to onboard more channels quickly. In an EXP, all services will be designed as microservices.
Cost-effective, scalable, and highly available runtime environment	• Services executed in Docker containers orchestrated using Kubernetes. Infrastructure will be containerized and managed across many hosts on Kubernetes. • The Kubernetes API is a set of loosely coupled primitives that operate under many different workloads. The Kubernetes API is used internally and externally by containers and extensions running on top of the system.
Minimal downtime of the services	• Service-level replication and scaling ensure a minimal set of services running seamlessly for the given functionality.
Elastic systems	• Responsive systems under varying load meeting the specified Transactions per second (TPS), leveraging the autoscaling feature.
Security concerns	• System to support authentication, authorization, security for data at rest, data in transit, API-level security, data governance, and security standards.

(*continued*)

Table 4-3. (*continued*)

Goal	Considerations for the Design of the Solution
Performance	• Achieved through highly scalable and concurrent model data processing in the microservices layer. • Integrated with highly scalable messaging system and data store, leveraging the distributed caching layer. • Faster computations and data transfers with data compressions.
Asynchronous and event-based system	• Nonblocking operations with reactive modelling. • Integrated with highly concurrent and scalable distributed messaging framework.
Consistency and standards in-grained across the streams (automation, DevOps, governance)	• Automation, DevOps principles, governance in-grained into the very fabric of the platform/process, environments tuned to delivery cycles, following "12 factor app design principles."
Consistent data model	• Single source of truth of data source replicated across the systems in distributed environment.
Non-functional requirements	• Horizontal scaling that ensures loose coupling through asynchronous, stateless, and idempotent APIs. • Performant, scalable, fault-tolerant, stable, cloud-agnostic infrastructure. • Resiliency despite partial failure and able to recover quickly to ensure zero loss of data.

Search Development

Search is an important tool in information discovery. EXP search is mainly used for people search, content search, and data search. In this section, I cover the prominent search development components.

Key Search Solution Components

Figure 4-6 depicts the key search solution components for EXP.

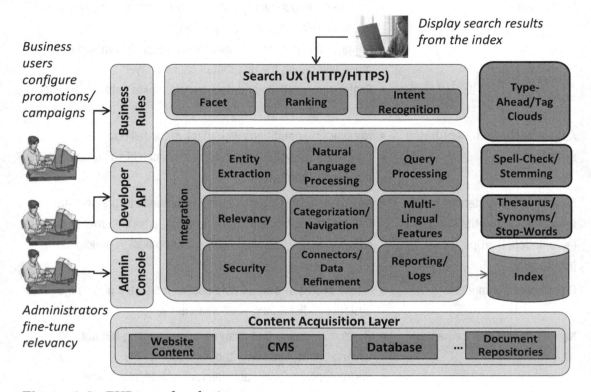

Figure 4-6. *EXP search solution components*

The key components of search solution components are as follows:

- **Content acquisition layer**: A search engine can ingest data from various content sources that can contain structured and unstructured content such as text, video, images, and such. The content in the content sources will be constantly growing, so the search engine has to keep refreshing the index from content sources on a periodic basis.

- **Search engine features**: The search engine should provide core features such as natural language processing, entity processing, intent recognition, query processing, indexing, and such. The search engine should also generate facets to filter the search results.

- **Search user engagement**: From a user experience standpoint, the search engine should implement features such as type-ahead, spelling corrections, synonym matching, facet-based navigation, and relevancy ranking of results.

- **Search design considerations**: The following are the main design considerations for the search engine:

  - **Data ingestion**: The search adapters should be able to connect and crawl a variety of content sources and a variety of content types.

  - **Relevancy ranking**: The search results should be ranked based on their relevancy to the identified intent. Business users should be able to artificially boost the relevancy to promote key products.

  - **Index strategy**: The search index strategy should be designed to index a variety of content and refresh the index at regular intervals to provide up-to-date results.

  - **Personalization**: The search engine should provide personalized search results based on user preferences and historical interactions.

  - **Security**: The search engine should ensure that search results comply with the information security guidelines.

Search Implementation

Figure 4-7 shows a sample search flow.

Note   I have used Apache Solr as an enterprise search engine for this sample solution.

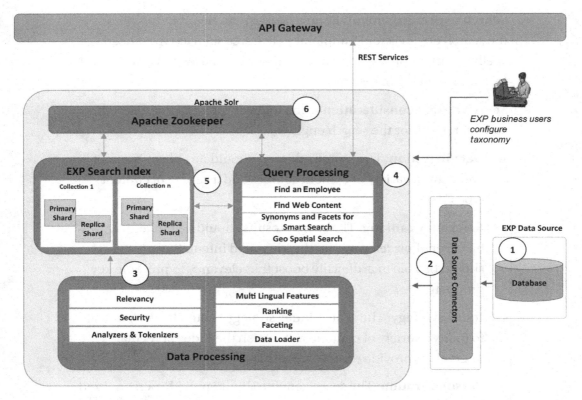

Figure 4-7. *EXP search flow*

The EXP search flow leverages the main solution components. Figure 4-7 explains the steps related to indexing, query processing, and data processing. The main features of the EXP search solution components are as follows:

- **Data sources**: The main data source for an EXP is the database. Additionally, you can also index content management systems and document management systems to index web content and documents.

- **Connectors**: The database adapter can be used to connect to the database and retrieve the content. Many CMS platforms provide secured web access to index the content and document repository.

- **Data processing**: The content ingested into a search engine will be processed based on the requirements such as metadata extraction for the classification of faceting, associating the data with ACLs, multilingual processing, and so on.

- **Query processing**: Search terms received from the front end, before retrieving results, undergo modifications such as spelling checks, stemming, lemmatization, and geospatial calculations to retrieve most relevant records.

- **Search index**: Data is categorized and grouped into logical units called an *index*. An index is divided into *shards*. There will be copies of shards called as *replicas*. Shards and replicas that belong to the same index are stored in different servers by providing horizontal scalability and high availability. One of replicas in each shard is automatically elected the leader. Additional collections can be added to support additional content in the future.

- **Apache zookeeper**: Apache Zookeeper is a component that contains information about all of the Solr servers. Zookeeper provides high availability by ensuring queries are not directed at Solr servers that have been taken out of rotation (either on purpose or when the server goes down).

Security Development

Security mainly consists of authentication, authorization, and SSO. Authentication is provided by products such as LDAP and Active Directory (AD). Authorization (also known as *fine-grained access*) can be implemented through policies, roles, and the permission model. You can define roles/user groups and associate the resource permissions (such as view, update, delete) for each of the roles. You can then associate roles to the users and user groups who inherit the resource permissions by virtue of the roles assigned to them.

SSO Development

EXP SSO leverages Security Assertion Markup Language (SAML) 2.0. SAML standard provides XML-based authentication and authorization information between Identity provider (that produces security assertions) and service provider (that consumes security assertions). SAML is one of the popular methods to implement SSO between IdP (identity provider) and SP (Service Provider).

The SAML 2.0 integration enables single sign-on by exchanging XML tokens with an external identity provider (IDP). The identity provider provides authentication service and creates an `entityId` token after successful authentication. The service provider, after receiving the `entityId` token matches the token information with user information (such as email address) to create a valid user session.

EXP can use two types of SSO with vendor applications.

- **IDP-initiated SSO**: In IDP-initiated SSO, the SSO process is initiated by the IDP and sends a SAML response to the SP.

- **SP-initiated SSO**: In SP-initiated SSO, the SP generates an authentication request that is sent to the IDP as the first step in the SSO process, and the IDP then responds with a SAML response.

Infrastructure Architecture

A robust infrastructure is required to provide a smoothly functioning EXP. The nonfunctional requirements such as scalability, performance, and availability are mainly dependent on the properly sized and tested infrastructure.

The following sections detail the server, storage, and network design aspects of an AWS Cloud infrastructure.

Key Cloud Design Considerations

Table 4-3 describes the key design considerations for an EXP cloud deployment.

Note   I have provided design considerations for AWS Cloud. As the core solution is cloud agnostic, any cloud platform can be leveraged for hosting/deploying the solution.

Table 4-4. *EXP Cloud Design Considerations*

Design Considerations	Design Considerations
Virtual private cloud (VPC)	• VPC-reserved isolated portion of the AWS region for hosting production and nonproduction environments. • Separate VPC for prod, nonprod, and management environments for better isolation and security with subnets. • VPC peering will be used for intercommunication. • Network ACLs and security groups to demark the web, application, and data tiers of the deployment within VPC.
Scalability and elasticity	• Leverage the AWS elasticity feature to rapidly scale up/down to cater for peak/troughs in the workload. • Autoscaling (dynamic/scheduled) addition of EC2 instances to scale up to meet the required throughput. Ramp down of instances will be planned outside business hours through scripts. • Scale-out architecture for web and app tier and scale-up architecture for database tier.

Performance and optimization	• Choose the correct "instance type" and "family" based on these workload characteristics:
	  • M4 instance types are considered for the web/app tier.
	  • M4 instance types for the EXP portal and the rest of the workloads.
	  • R3 instance types are considered for database workloads.
	• Provisioned IOPS and EBS-optimized instances for optimal I/O performance for EXP databases.
	• Database transaction logs and data files will be hosted in separate EBS volumes.
	• No peak workload sizing like a traditional system. No up-front provisioning. Establish processes for scale-up and scale-down to reduce the cost.
	• Shut down nonprod services and business hour services outside business hours through automated scripts.
	• Back up to S3 for better durability and define policies for moving "older" data to Glacier for archival purposes and longer retention.

(continued)

Table 4-4. (*continued*)

Design Considerations	Design Considerations
High availability	• Build system to cater to different types of failures; use EC2, EBS, and AZs to create a fault-tolerant architecture along with a comprehensive monitoring solution (SCOM, CloudWatch, SES, and SNS). • EC2 instances can be deployed across multiple availability zones to achieve infrastructure availability of 99.95 percent (a single solution to achieve high availability to manage the application as well as zone-level failures). • Active-active setup for web, active-active/passive for the app tier, and active/passive setup for SQL DBs through database log shipping/ AlwaysOn.
Security	• VPC for isolation and security for hosting the cloud platform. • Defense-in-depth security provided through the access control list at each subnet level and security groups at instance level. • Web Application Firewall (WAF) for protecting the Internet-facing portal. • SSL for secure communication between users and the applications hosted on the VPC (data in transit). • IAM framework for role-based access control for AWS resources. • Antivirus stakeholder and updated distribution server to stay up-to-date on the latest virus signatures. • Managed endpoint security (HIPS, vulnerability management) and patch management. • AD for user authentication and authorization for systems hosted in AWS.
Disaster recovery	• Multizone deployment for high availability and failover within a region for critical application and database components. • Periodic failover testing to secondary zone to ensure operational readiness in the event of a primary zone failure or disaster. • Back up data and AMIs stored in S3 and Glacier, which is replicated within a region. • Yearly and monthly backups are stored in Glacier.

(*continued*)

Table 4-4. (*continued*)

Design Considerations	Design Considerations
Deployment and management	• Faster and error-free provisioning of servers using golden AMIs (preconfigured and hardened OS images with the base configuration). • Cloud Formation templates for environment provisioning and management. • Integrate the CloudWatch alerts and SNS notifications with SCOM. • Use of predefined scripts for scaling instances to meet spikes in the workload. • SCOM will be configured to send alerts for event management. • EBS snapshots/database backup/restore for data refresh across environments. • SCCM for Windows patch management; AWS Linux repository will be used for patching Red Hat Linux servers.
Backup handling	These are the backup requirements for an AWS Cloud production environment: • Daily backup: retained for eight days • Weekly backup: retained for six weeks • Monthly backup: retained for three months • Yearly backup: retained for seven years (one copy of data is taken and kept for seven years at the end of every year)

Deployment Architecture

The deployment architecture of an EXP cloud environment is described as follows:

- The AWS cloud environment will host the production and nonproduction environments and the management components.

- The training, SIT, UAT, prototype, development, PT, and smoke PT environments will be hosted in the nonproduction VPC.

- The production, PT, and management tiers will be deployed across multiple availability zones.

- All shared services will be hosted in the management VPC including AD, DNS, NTP, NAT, Bastion, patch management server, proxy server, and vulnerability management server.

- The support team will log in to the Bastion servers and administrate the production and nonproduction environments.

- The independent SMTP solution based on AWS SES will be deployed on AWS Cloud.

High Availability Solution

Table 4-5 explains the high availability solution for the AWS solution components. The production infrastructure will be built with no single point of failure by distributing the components across two availability zones.

Table 4-5. *High Availability Configuration*

Application	HA and DR	Web/App Tier	Autoscaling	DB Tier	Load Balancing
Web Application Firewall (WAF)	Multi-AZ	Active-active	NA	NA	AWS ELB
Digital Experience Platform (EXP)	Multi-AZ	Active-active	For Web and App tier	NA	AWS ELB

Scalability

Scalability for EXP solution will be achieved by horizontal scalability and vertical scalability.

Horizontal Scalability

- Achieved by adding additional EC2 instances.

- Autoscaling can be enabled to automate the horizontal scalability by defining triggers to scale up/scale down using the CloudWatch metrics.

Vertical Scalability

- Achieved by saving the existing instance as an AMI and then relaunching it on a higher compute instance type. This is applicable for the DB tier. DB servers do not support autoscaling because of technology limitations. DB instance types can be changed to higher capacity after a reboot.

- DB instances will be sized to cater to the peak workload and thus will ensure the performance requirements of the EXP. Through proactive monitoring via SCOM and SQL performance counters, DB server resources will be analyzed, and appropriate configuration/instance changes will be proposed/implemented during the scheduled maintenance window.

Monitoring

Amazon CloudWatch can be used for monitoring. CloudWatch is an AWS service that monitors various health metrics associated with AWS resources. It can be leveraged to collect, analyze, and view system and application metrics. Amazon CloudWatch sets several predefined metrics, such as CPU utilization and disk I/O performance, that AWS measures. It supports publishing your own metrics directly to Amazon CloudWatch to allow statistical viewing in the AWS Management Console and to issue custom alarms.

Backup

AWS-native EBS snapshots will be leveraged as a backup solution. Each of the servers will cater to backing up instances in that particular AZ alone. Hence, the AZ1 backup server will back up all data such as the OS, data drives, web apps, and databases from all the instances present in AZ1. Similarly, a backup server in AZ2 would do the same. Environments other than production (called as *nonproduction* for document purposes) will have a single backup server in AZ1 to back up data from all instances distributed across both AZs.

Backup Strategy

The storage lifecycle policy is defined as follows:

- All full backups from all environments will be carried out on a weekly basis, during weekends at off-business hours.

- Incremental backups will be taken on all working days at the end of each business day.

- Incremental and full backups will be first stored in EBS for a week, after which they will be moved to S3.

- S3 will retain the data of full and incremental backups for three weeks.

- At the end of every three weeks, data will be further moved to Glacier for additional retention of three weeks. Hence, all production backups will be retained for six weeks.

- One copy of the full backup will be taken every month, which is retained in Glacier for three months (monthly backup).

- One copy of the full backup will be taken every year, which is retained in Glacier for years (yearly backup).

Table 4-6 shows the key points of a backup policy.

Table 4-6. Backup Policy

Environment	Backup Policy	Backup Storage and Retention		
		Primary (EBS)	Secondary (S3)	Archive (Glacier)
Production	• Database and file systems: Weekly full and daily incremental • DB transaction logs: Every two hours	Daily backup (one week) Weekly full back (two weeks)	Weekly full backup (3 weeks)	Weekly full backup (three weeks) Monthly backup (three months) Yearly backup (seven years)
Nonproduction	• Database and file systems: Weekly full and daily incremental • DB transaction logs: Every four to eight hours	Daily backup (one week) Weekly full (one week)	Weekly full backup (two weeks)	NA
EBS snapshot	• AMIs • OS images • Static file systems		Ondemand	

Database High Availability

The database platform will be built on relational database. The following section provides a high-level view of the database high availability solution.

AlwaysOn High Availability

This is a high availability and disaster recovery solution, which will enable the maximum availability of the critical user databases by using availability groups. The high availability for the database is provided by availability group. The availability group consists of set of primary databases and set of secondary databases for failover.

Disaster Recovery

Disaster recovery (DR) is necessary for business continuity and high availability. The following are the key points to implement disaster recovery in an AWS environment:

- Leveraging multiple availability zones provides coverage for most DR situations. Therefore, it is recommended that you leverage multiple AZs to build a high availability (HA) and DR solution in a region. In the context of AWS Cloud, an availability zone failure is considered a disaster. However, if an entire AWS region goes down, the AWS services will be active only in the region that is up and running, and the RTO is based on AWS service recoverability.

- It should be noted that data needs to be stored only in the AWS region due to data compliance issues. No backup/ data should be stored outside the AWS region.

- The servers will be placed in multiple availability zones with active-active/passive configuration. This enables a high level of availability and provide business continuity for the environment.

- The RPO for this approach is zero, i.e., zero data loss, and the RTO is less than eight hours.

To follow this multiple availability zone approach, the cost is minimal. See Table 4-7.

Table 4-7. *High Availability and Disaster Recovery Features*

Features	HA and DR Using Multiple Availability Zones
RPO/RTO	• RPO: Near zero data loss (depends on the replication strategy of various solution components and will be defined during the design phase). • RTO < eight hours.
Protection against	• Single availability zone failure or application-level failure.
High-level approach	• Run EC2 and application instances across zones in active-active or active-passive mode. • Use AWS Elastic Load Balancing to load balance the requests across multiple instances. • Databases will be replicated to secondary availability zone in active-passive mode. • Leverage DNS names for connecting the application to the database service. • Retain a copy of the latest backup in S3, which is replicated across the regions. • Failover/load balance services in the event of a failure of availability zone. • Recover/ restore services in secondary availability zone.

Summary

This chapter covered the following:

- A forward-looking EXP should provide features such as personalization, security, search, integration, content and asset management, automation and analytics, collaboration, and user experience.

- The key solution tenets are a modular and extensible ecosystem; stateless APIs and microservices; open, standards-based, flexible, simple, and minimalist user interface; DevOps and automation; and secured personalization.

- Key UX trends can be categorized into categories such as a seamless omnichannel-enabled user experience, enterprise integrations, and DevOps.

- Search mainly consists of the content acquisition layer, key search features, and search user engagement.

- Key cloud design considerations are virtual private cloud, scalability and elasticity, performance and optimization, and high availability.

- Security, disaster recovery, deployment, management, and backup handling are the key design considerations for setting up high available system.

CHAPTER 5

EXP Strategy

Crafting a next-generation digital workplace requires a deeper understanding of the trends in the employee experience space. By understanding the challenges for the modern digital workplace and analyzing the evolution of the employee experience, we can define the core transformation themes for a next-generation employee experience framework.

In this chapter, I define the employee experience framework and the main pillars that constitute the overall strategy for the employee experience.

Digital strategists can use this chapter as a reference for developing a strategy for their digital workplace.

I start the chapter by explaining various elements of the employee experience ecosystem such as the key focus areas, trends, and evolution. I then define the employee experience framework, transformation themes, solution design, and migration design.

Note *Employee experience* and *digital workplace* are used synonymously in this chapter.

Employee Experience Ecosystems

In this section, you'll learn about the trends in the employee experience space so you can understand the expectations of a modern employee platform. You'll also learn about the common challenges and key focus areas for building a modern digital workplace. I will then discuss the evolution stages of the digital workplace.

© Shailesh Kumar Shivakumar 2020
S. K. Shivakumar, *Build a Next-Generation Digital Workplace*, https://doi.org/10.1007/978-1-4842-5512-4_5

Trends in Employee Experience

A vast majority of today's workforce are millennials (born after 1980), and a good number of digital-native youngsters are entering the workforce. This population has been exposed to consumer-grade digital platforms (such as Facebook, Twitter, Instagram, WhatsApp, and such) for some time, and they expect a similar experience in intranet platforms.

Figure 5-1 gives the main technology trends in the digital workplace space.

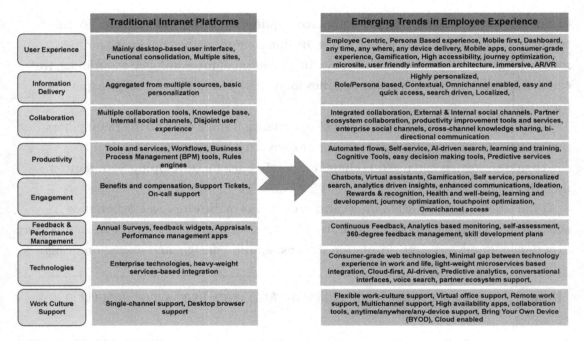

	Traditional Intranet Platforms	Emerging Trends in Employee Experience
User Experience	Mainly desktop-based user interface, Functional consolidation, Multiple sites,	Employee Centric, Persona Based experience, Mobile first, Dashboard, any time, any where, any device delivery, Mobile apps, consumer-grade experience, Gamification, High accessibility, journey optimization, microsite, user friendly information architecture, immersive, AR/VR
Information Delivery	Aggregated from multiple sources, basic personalization	Highly personalized, Role/Persona based, Contextual, Omnichannel enabled, easy and quick access, search driven, Localized,
Collaboration	Multiple collaboration tools, Knowledge base, Internal social channels, Disjoint user experience	Integrated collaboration, External & Internal social channels. Partner ecosystem collaboration, productivity improvement tools and services, enterprise social channels, cross-channel knowledge sharing, bi-directional communication
Productivity	Tools and services, Workflows, Business Process Management (BPM) tools, Rules engines	Automated flows, Self-service, AI-driven search, learning and training, Cognitive Tools, easy decision making tools, Predictive services
Engagement	Benefits and compensation, Support Tickets, On-call support	Chatbots, Virtual assistants, Gamification, Self service, personalized search, analytics driven insights, enhanced communications, Ideation, Rewards & recognition, Health and well-being, learning and development, journey optimization, touchpoint optimization, Omnichannel access
Feedback & Performance Management	Annual Surveys, feedback widgets, Appraisals, Performance management apps	Continuous Feedback, Analytics based monitoring, self-assessment, 360-degree feedback management, skill development plans
Technologies	Enterprise technologies, heavy-weight services-based integration	Consumer-grade web technologies, Minimal gap between technology experience in work and life, light-weight microservices based integration, Cloud-first, AI-driven, Predictive analytics, conversational interfaces, voice search, partner ecosystem support,
Work Culture Support	Single-channel support, Desktop browser support	Flexible work-culture support, Virtual office support, Remote work support, Multichannel support, High availability apps, collaboration tools, anytime/anywhere/any-device support, Bring Your Own Device (BYOD), Cloud enabled

Figure 5-1. *Key trends in employee experience platforms*

- **User experience**: Traditional intranet platforms were primarily designed for a desktop experience. Various functionalities are consolidated on the intranet landing page, and typically an employee has to navigate multiple web applications during the employee journey. The modern digital workplace platforms are designed with a mobile-first design and an employee-centric design. The employee experience involves aggregated dashboards and a persona-based design with an intuitive information architecture. Gamification and journey optimization concepts are commonly used to provide an engaging user experience.

- **Information delivery**: Intranet platforms provide aggregated information and basic personalization. Modern digital workplace platforms provide highly personalized and contextual information and role-based information access. Information discovery is enhanced through search and localized content delivery.

- **Collaboration**: Intranet platforms leverage multiple collaboration tools such as chat and conferencing tools and mainly focus on internal social channels. Because of the usage of multiple tools, there is a disjointed user experience. Modern digital workplace platforms provide built-in/integrated collaboration features, and they support both internal and external social channels. Digital workplaces also support partner ecosystems and enterprise social channels.

- **Productivity**: Traditional intranet platforms provide tools such as timesheet management and leave applications to enhance employee productivity. Business processes are implemented through business process management (BPM), rules engines, and workflows. Digital workplace platforms provide AI-driven automation and self-service features to improve productivity. Cognitive tools (such as cognitive search, smart recommendations), decision-making tools (such as calculators, scenario analysis tools), and predictive services are driving the productivity in modern digital workplace platforms.

- **Engagement**: Intranets provide basic engagement features such as benefits management, incident management, and on-call support. Modern digital workplaces engage employees through chatbots, virtual assistants, self-service features, personalization, idea hub, rewards and recognition, learning and development, employee journey optimization, touch point optimization, and omnichannel access.

- **Feedback and performance management**: Intranets have traditionally managed employee performance through management apps, annual surveys, and feedback widgets. Employee appraisals are done once in a year. Modern digital workplaces enable continuous feedback management throughout the year and provide 360-degree feedback management (obtaining feedback from peers, themselves, and supervisors) and flexible skill development and learning/training programs.

- **Technologies**: Intranet platforms primarily use enterprise technologies that involve heavy-weight services for integration. Digital workplace platforms leverage modern web technologies such as JavaScript frameworks and single-page applications (SPAs) to provide high responsiveness and interactiveness. Lightweight microservices are used for integration. Technologies such as AI, machine learning, cloud, predictive analytics, voice search, and conversational interfaces are used for higher employee engagement.

- **Work culture support**: The intranet applications support fixed work-time work culture in terms of availability. Intranet applications are mainly supported on single channels (like desktop browsers). Digital workplace platforms provide high availability to support a flexible work culture. The digital workplace provides remote login tools, virtual office tools, and collaboration tools to work from anywhere at any time on any device.

Key Focus Areas and Challenges for Modern Digital Workplaces

Drawing insights from emerging digital workplace trends, we can define the core focus areas for a next-generation digital workplace as follows. Organizations need to focus on these areas to build a modern digital workplace platform.

Challenges for Modern Employee Experiences

Table 5-1 lists the main challenges for building a modern employee experience.

Table 5-1. *Key Challenges and Remediation Steps for Employee Experience Platforms*

Challenges	Remediation Steps
Employee data distributed in multiple systems	Consolidate data to create a single source of truth and system of records. Consolidate disparate systems and services and provide an integrated view.
Homogenous experience for all employees	Persona-based design and journey mapping. Personalized information, services, and tools.
Challenges in employee tasks and activities	Digitize and automate employee workflows and tasks. Provide productivity enhancing and self-service tools.
Challenges in transforming insights into employee actions	Leverage analytics technologies to get insights into employee behavior.
Usage of legacy technologies for employee experience	Leverage modern and consumer-grade technologies for designing an employee experience.
Minimal use of personalization	Personalize the employee experience to deliver the relevant and contextual information.
Cultural issues/resistance to change	Create awareness campaigns and adopt gamification concepts/incentives to promote and encourage participation.

Key Focus Areas

The key focus areas for building an employee experience platform are as follows:

- **Seamless employee experience**: The end-user experience should match the consumer-grade experience and should provide a mobile-first user experience. The user experience across all sections and all channels of the platform and all linked systems should have a uniform and consistent experience. The navigation and information architecture should closely resemble the user/persona mental model.

- **Anytime, anywhere, any-device access**: The accessibility of modern digital workplace platforms should not be confined. Users should be able to access these platforms from anywhere on any device at any time.

- **Collaborative ecosystem**: Modern collaborative tools and social channels should enable employees to collaborate effectively, share information easily, and improve their productivity through tools. The platform should enable a centralized, collaborative platform for the enterprise.

- **Personalized, contextual, and quicker information access**: The EXP should provide personalized and contextual information, tools, and services based on employee roles, preferences, and transaction history. The platform should enable faster and easier access to relevant information.

- **Productivity**: Along with tools and services, many of the employee workflows and HR tasks are increasingly being automated. AI-driven tools such as smart search, cognitive tools, and decision-making tools are playing a major role in improving the employee productivity.

- **Engagement**: Traditional feedback tools and employee benefits have given way to chatbots and self-service tools. Employee chatbots play a variety of roles such as information delivery, query resolution, task automation, and such. People analytics are used to measure the effectiveness of tools and employee engagement levels.

- **Technology experience**: Employees expect the consumer-grade technologies and experiences that they use in their personal lives.

Evolution of Digital Workplaces

Employee expectations, changes in digital technologies, and business imperatives are driving the employee experience platform. Figure 5-2 identifies the evolution of the digital workplace.

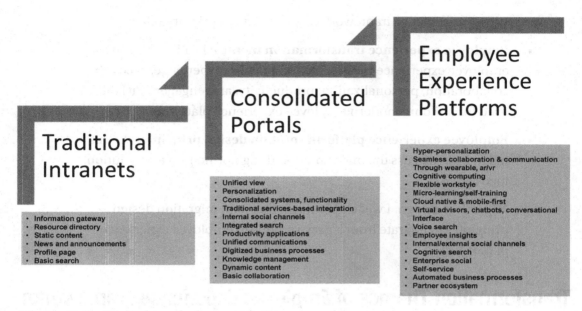

Figure 5-2. *Digital workplace evolution*

Traditional intranets were mainly used as information gateways to provide the organization with related news and other information. Intranets acted as online directories linking to various resources, pages, and departments. The content was mainly static web pages. Users could create profile pages. Intranets provided basic search features.

The next stage of evolution consisted of consolidated portals that aggregated information dynamically from various sources and provided personalized delivery. Portals mainly supported internal social channels and provided integrated search. Applications and communications were the main parts of the portals. The business processes were digitized and modeled using rules engine and workflows.

The next stage of the evolution is the employee experience platform discussed in this book. It provides a hyperpersonalized employee experience to support the flexible work culture of the employees. The main focus elements of the EXP are AI, analytics, and collaboration. Technologies such as cognitive computing, microlearning, self-service, cloud enablement, voice search, enterprise social, self-service, and partner ecosystem are supported. I discussed the key features of an EXP in Chapter 1.

Employee Experience Frameworks

An employee experience framework defines the main transformation themes for designing a next-generation digital workplace.

An employee experience framework consists of three primary pillars.

- **Employee experience transformation themes**: I will discuss the six employee experience transformation themes (experience, accessibility, collaboration, personalization, productivity, and engagement) that are used for building modern employee experience platforms.

- **Employee experience platform solution design principles**: In this pillar, I will discuss the main solution design principles and solution focus areas.

- **Migration design**: I will elaborate on the main migration design principles to migrate from legacy systems to employee experience platforms.

Transformation Themes of Employee Experience Frameworks

This section elaborates on the key focus areas for modern digital workplaces discussed earlier to define the core transformation themes.

- **Experience**: The EXP should provide a seamless, easy-to-use, omnichannel-enabled user experience. The information architecture and navigation model should be intuitive and easy to use.

- **Accessibility**: The EXP should be accessible from any device, anywhere, and anytime.

- **Collaboration**: The EXP should provide all the needed collaboration features, tools, and services to enable employees to effectively communicate, share information, and search.

- **Personalization**: The information and services should be personalized to make it more relevant and effective based on user personas.

- **Productivity**: The EXP should provide relevant tools and services to improve the productivity of the employees.

- **Engagement**: The EXP should provide features to actively engage employees.

Figure 5-3 shows the features and technologies for each of the transformation themes.

Transformation Themes

Experience	Accessibility	Collaboration	Personalization	Productivity	Engagement

Functional Features

Experience	Accessibility	Collaboration	Personalization	Productivity	Engagement
Mobile First	Anytime, Anywhere, Any-Device Access	Information sharing	Persona-based Design, Journey	Automation	Communications
UI Design	Localization	Document Collaboration	Contextual & Relevant Information Delivery	Task Management	Training & E-Learning
Usability	Regulation Compliance	Enterprise Social	Explicit/Implicit Personalization	Self-Service Enablement	Rewards & Recognition
Information Architecture	Error Handling	Team Collaboration	Targeted Content Delivery	Autonomy	Gamification
Dashboards/Integrated View	Quick Information Access	People Search	User Segmentation	Productivity Measurement	Insights
Branding & Communication	Assistive/Guiding methods	Conferencing	User Analytics	Effective Communication	Feedback, Polls & Surveys
Performance	Content Design	Mails	Preference Management	Work-life Balance	Inclusion

Technology Components

Experience	Accessibility	Collaboration	Personalization	Productivity	Engagement
Responsive Design	Search	Team Chat/Messenger	Personalization Rules	Travel, Project Management Tools	Ask Leader Tool
Single Page Applications (SPA)	Cross-browser Support	Blogs, Wiki, Forums, Calendar	Audience Targeting	Employee Feedback Tool	Live Event Streaming Tools
Search	Cloud-Ready	Content/Document /Asset Management	Microsites	Employee Training Tools	Idea Hub
Portals	Multi-Lingual Support	Groups/Community	Personalized Search	Performance Management Tool	Chat bots, Virtual Assistants
Mobile Apps	WCAG Checker	Media Streaming	Fine-grained Security	Incentive Management	Training & E-Learning Tools

Experience Definition

Experience	Accessibility	Collaboration	Personalization	Productivity	Engagement
Persona-based Experience	Process Automation	Digitized Flows	Mobile-First Approach	Consumer-grade Experience	Design Thinking

Horizontal Components

Experience	Accessibility	Collaboration	Personalization	Productivity	Engagement
Security	Integrations	Services	Reports	Workflow	Analytics
Governance	DevOps	Cloud/On-Premise Infrastructure	Project Management	Metrics & Monitoring	Reporting

Figure 5-3. EXP transformation themes and features

117

I will cover each of the transformation themes in detail.

Experience

The end-user experience creates the first impression for the user. The experience drives the user satisfaction, traffic, and retention. The following are the key features that are part of experience:

- **Mobile-first approach**: Modern digital platforms are primarily designed for mobile devices. Flexible layouts, responsive design concepts, and mobile apps are used for creating a mobile-first design. Testing the application on various mobile platforms, devices, and form factors with various loads are key to the overall success of a mobile-first approach.

- **User interface (UI) design**: The main elements of an effective UI design are consistency (the UI, layout, terminology, and navigation across pages and sites should match user expectations and follow web standards and industry standards), minimalism (present minimal functionality by eliminating the unnecessary features to reduce the cognitive load), engaging (through high interactivity, constant feedback, graceful error handling), and simplicity (through a simple and easy-to-use UI).

- **Usability**: The ease of using a system is a key success enabler for a digital platform. A system that is easy to use to achieve a goal or to complete a task acts as a force multiplier to the digital strategy. The main elements that enhance usability are visual cues, easier navigation, contextual hints and tips, easier learnability, high interactivity, and robust error detection and recovery. The UI designers can conduct alpha/beta testing (A/B testing) to proactively test the usability of the alternate designs.

- **Information architecture**: A user-centric information architecture that is based on the mental model of the user improves the information discovery. The site hierarchy, menu structure, breadcrumbs, search feature, expanded footer, and page metadata are all part of information architecture.

- **Dashboard/integrated view**: The EXP should provide an integrated view of activities for employees. The employee dashboard should provide aggregated information (application communications, company news, recent announcements, videos, broadcasts, feeds), personalized content (personalized search results, employee workplace, employee documents, employee activities, employee analytics, bookmarks), and relevant tools (calendar, search, collaboration tools, learning tools, service requests, knowledge base).

- **Branding and communication**: The UI design should use common branding and the consistent visual design elements across various pages and sites. Branding elements such as the logos, images, font styles, layouts, color scheme, and communication styles should be consistent across the organization.

- **Performance**: The performance of the pages on the Web and for mobile devices should be optimal. Employees should be able to complete the key tasks with minimal help in a minimal amount of time.

I already elaborated on various experience concepts in Chapter 3. The following are the innovations in user experience:

- **Augmented reality (AR)/virtual reality (VR) support**: AR/VR technologies can be used for employee training. AR/VR technologies provide immersive training simulations and can be used for the following purposes:

  - Product demos and walk-throughs

  - Compliance, regulatory, safety, and security trainings

  - On-the-job trainings

  - Task walk-throughs

  - Remote assistance

- **IoT support**: For designing an engaging employee experience, the IoT plays key roles.

  - High employee engagement

  - Employee analytics through connected devices

- Employee learning and training

- Productivity improvement through easily available tools

- High collaboration through easy conference room bookings and information sharing

- **Enhancing the employee experience with humanization**: Various aspects of the humanization of the employee experience include employee support (through support groups, personal counselling support, childcare support), inclusivity (support for diverse culture, workplace design for increasing accessibility), development (career development, cross-skilling, higher education support, and such), empathy, employee empowerment.

- **Integrating with existing tools and technologies**: The end-user experience should be seamlessly integrated with existing native tools and systems used by the employees.

- **Consumer-grade experience**: By providing a truly consumer-grade experience and matching the experience with that of popular consumer platforms, one can bridge the gap in employee experience.

Accessibility

Accessibility defines the degree to which the application is accessible to the end users. The key tenets of effective accessibility are seamless omnichannel availability (anytime, anywhere, and any device access), localization (support for various languages across geographies), regulatory compliance, error handling (consistent error handling and user-friendly error messages), text alternatives (for images, videos), proper labels and instructions, assistance methods (through visual cues, hints), quick information access, and user-friendly content design.

We use technology component such as WCAG compliance checker, search feature, and cross-browser support to implement accessibility.

We detailed the accessibility in Chapter 3.

Collaboration

Collaboration features such as content collaboration, team collaboration, and information sharing are quintessential features of an employee experience platform. The platform should also provide features such as document collaboration (such as co-authoring of document), people search (search based on skill sets, job roles, names, departments, and such), conferencing (audio and video conference), enterprise social (external/internal blogs), and a centralized knowledge base (for document sharing).

To create a robust collaboration platform, you need technical components such as content management, document management, media streaming, chat, forums, blogs, wiki and communities, messenger, calendar, and such.

The following are innovations in collaboration:

- **Story sharing platforms**: The employee platforms should provide a collaborative tool through which employees can share their experiences and feedback through a story sharing platform.

- **Enterprise social**: Organizations provide social features such as blogs, wikis, and forums for employees to express their opinions and share their thoughts. Leaders can communicate their viewpoints through leader blogs and forums.

- **External and internal social channels**: The platform should provide integration with external social channels so that employees can collaborate with their professional connections effectively.

I already elaborated on collaboration concepts in Chapter 4.

Personalization

Because an organization consists of various kinds of employees, you need to define the employee personas and provide engaging and personalized experiences for each persona. A persona is based on user research and represents a group of employees with common usage patterns, motivations, attributes, and goals. Persona-based design is used to refine the user experience and user journeys. I already discussed some aspects of persona-based design in Chapter 3.

The platform should support implicit personalization (personalization based on a user's implicit actions) and explicit personalization (personalization based on a user's explicit preferences, interests, and options) and user preference management. The platform provides contextual and relevant content, tools, and services based on employee attributes (such as job role, interests, preferences, and such).

The platform should provide user segmentation, which segments the users based on their dynamic attributes such as geography, language, demographic attributes and such. User segmentation helps to provide targeted content based on their segments. Analytics can be used to monitor employee actions (such as page views, downloads, search keywords, etc.) and use the insights to further personalize the behavior.

Technical components include personalization rules (configuring user profile attributes for visibility rules and information display rules), audience targeting (sending contextual information based on user segments), personalized search, and fine-grained search.

The following are innovations in personalization:

- **Location-based services**: The employee platforms should provide collaborative tools through which employees can share their experiences and feedback through the story sharing platform.

- **Hyperpersonalization**: The information and services are personalized to provide one-to-one messaging based on geolocation, device type, transaction history, time, and other attributes.

- **Predictive analytics**: Analytics tools are used to mine the employee's historical data and provide actionable insights and recommendations to influence future actions.

- **AI-based personalization**: Machine learning and AI tools are increasingly used to personalize experience.

- **Facial recognition, voice commands**: Augmented reality (AR) tools are used to personalize the experience using facial recognition and other means.

Productivity

An employee experience platform should empower the employees to do the tasks faster with minimal effort. One of the key drivers of an EXP is to improve the productivity of the employees.

Productivity quantifies the improvement in task completion times for employees. Bringing conditional automation for the key workflows and tasks (such as employee applications, content reviews, and such) improves the task completion timelines. An EXP should also provide tools and services related to task management (such as task tracking, SLA management tool, skill-based task assignment tool), self-service (through tools such as search, knowledge base, training, e-learning, skill improvement), productivity measurement (through analytics and reporting tools, feedback tools, goal management tools), effective communication (personalized communication, alerts/ notification), work-life balance (through remote working tools, telecommuting tools), perks/incentives (such as paid time off, instant appreciation tools, wellness program, employee development applications), and collaboration tools.

The following are the innovations in productivity:

- **Continuous feedback**: An organization needs to plan for regular and continuous feedback to employees. Often 360-degree feedback covering all hierarchy levels is also effective in the overall development of the employees.

- **Autonomy**: An organization can assign the task based on an employee's skill set and enable employees by providing all the necessary support and greater autonomy. Highly engaged employees can perform better with little micromanagement by taking complete ownership of the task.

Engagement

Employee engagement is one of the key pillars of an employee experience framework. Active employee engagement motivates employees, connects them with the organization, aligns them with business goals, and increases the retention rate, thereby reducing the overall attrition. Engaged employees also contribute to the increased revenue and business goals of the organization and drive the organization's growth.

The main features and technology components of employee engagement are as follows:

- **Communications**: The EXP should provide communications tools that enable direct communication between employees and the management team to enable direction and transparent communication. The leadership team can articulate and broadcast the organization's vision, goals, and strategy directly to employees. Tools such as "Ask the leader" can be used by employees to ask any questions of the leadership team, and "leader blogs" can be used by the leadership team to provide their point of view and establish an open and transparent dialogue with employees. The live streaming tools can stream events such as leadership townhalls to employees across all geographies. The EXP should also provide tools such as news, communities, discussion forums, mails, and videos for executive communications. Employees and leaders can share their opinions, photos, and videos of important organization events.

- **Microlearning and training**: Organizations should provide smaller learning units for specialized skills to enable self-paced learning for the employees. The platform should provide flexible training tools, e-learning tools, and other competency development tools. Employees can leverage these tools for competency development and widening their skill set. The e-learning tools should provide the flexibility to learn from anywhere on any device at any pace.

- **Idea hub**: Fostering employee innovation actively engages employees, and hence organizations can design an "idea hub" to provide an ideation platform for employees.

- **Employee contribution**: The platform needs to encourage and reward employee participation and contribution to various initiatives such as knowledge management, blogs, and such.

- **Gamification**: The platform should use the concepts of a game such as scores, points, badges, levels and instant recognition to improve the employee participation and provide incentives to foster contribution.

- **Insights**: You should be able to measure the impact of various engagement tools. You can achieve this through analytics and monitoring tools. For instance, you can track the number of unique views for a broadcasted video and the number of replies for a leader blog to gauge the effectiveness of communication.

- **Feedback management**: A 360-degree feedback includes obtaining the feedback from managers, peers, and reporters to provide a holistic view of strengths and areas of improvement for an employee. The feedback management tool provides opportunity for others to rate an employee on various predefined parameters, and they can provide feedback on an employee's strengths and areas of improvement.

- **Rewards and recognition**: The online rewards and recognition tool can be used to provide timely and instant recognition for high-performing employees. Timely recognition improves employee engagement.

- **Inclusivity**: Using persona-based design encourages inclusivity for all employee groups. The EXP should cater to both knowledge workers and nonknowledge workers.

- **Surveys**: Polls and surveys can be used as tools to get feedback from employees about organization policies, employee experience, and such.

- **Analytics reports**: Employee engagement levels can be measured by tracking and monitoring employee contribution and participation. Analytical tools can be used to measure the impact of communications and the reach of engagement methods. Such reports can be further utilized to improve the engagement effectiveness.

- **Sharing**: Employees should be provided with tools to share the information, expertise, best practices, knowledge, resources, documents, and experience with the wider community.

Modern organizations constantly innovate to find new and impactful methods for employee engagement. I have listed a few such methods here:

- **Interact with leader**: Selected employees can be rewarded by providing opportunities to interact with the senior leaders. This engagement not only provides an opportunity to understand the day-to-day tasks of a leader but also improves their connection with the organization.

- **Crowd-sourced ideas**: Organizations can launch campaigns to crowd-source product ideas, productivity improvement ideas, revenue generation ideas, automation ideas, solution to main challenges, and so on, to the employee community. Such campaigns and challenges provide win-win opportunities for both employees and organizations.

- **Storytelling tools**: Organizations can provide opportunities to employees to share their stories. A story sharing platform empowers employees to share their experiences and voice their opinions and ideas to a wider community.

- **Internal support groups**: Employees can reach out to internal support groups and communities to resolve their queries through peer-to-peer support. Organizations can also provide professional counselling services to the employees. Employees can also create "communities of practice" to share expertise and best practices.

- **Seasonal campaigns**: Organizations can launch awareness campaigns, seasonal campaigns, health-related campaigns, quality campaigns, and safety campaigns to create awareness and train employees.

- **Employee health, fitness, and well-being initiatives**: Organizations invest in employee health through fitness trainings, health checkups, medical insurance, and such. The EXP can provide digital enablers for these initiatives through campaigns, mobile apps, gamified leaderboards, and such.

- **Maintaining the immediacy of social media**: Providing tools for social media feeds, sharing on social media, posting on social media, and finding social media connections at workplace all keep employees engaged and help them expand their networks and collaborate more effectively.

- **Conversational interfaces**: Conversational interfaces such as chatbots leverage natural language capabilities and use data from enterprise systems to provide contextual and relevant responses. Chatbots can be used for a variety of purposes such as recruitment and employee onboarding, task management, employee servicing, self-service, incident management, collaboration, training and development, and such.

- **Voice bots and virtual assistants**: Voice-recognizing bots equipped with natural language processing and virtual assistants are used to actively engage employees and resolve their queries.

Figure 5-4 shows various modules of transformation themes.

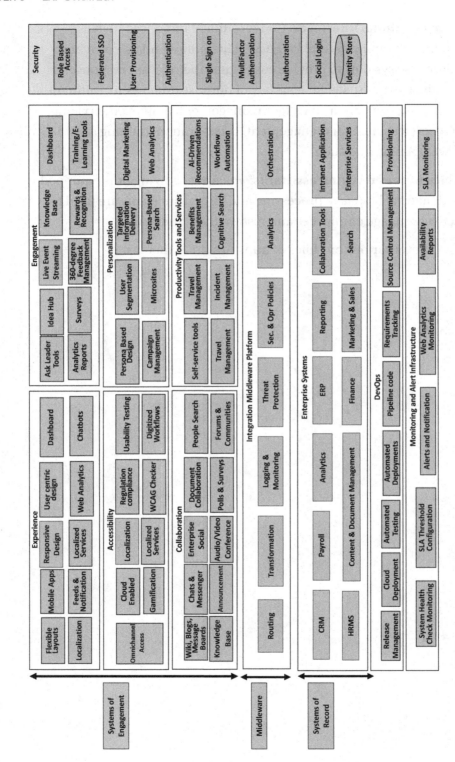

Figure 5-4. EXP transformation themes

Employee Experience Platform Solution Design

Crafting a robust employee experience platform requires a detailed analysis of the requirements. In this section, I will discuss the holistic requirements, solution design principles, and key focus areas of a solution.

Holistic View of EXP Requirements

The initial step while designing any employee experience platform is to understand the main requirements. An integrated view of the requirements helps to design a robust employee experience platform aligned with long-term strategic needs.

Figure 5-5 provides the holistic view of EXP requirements.

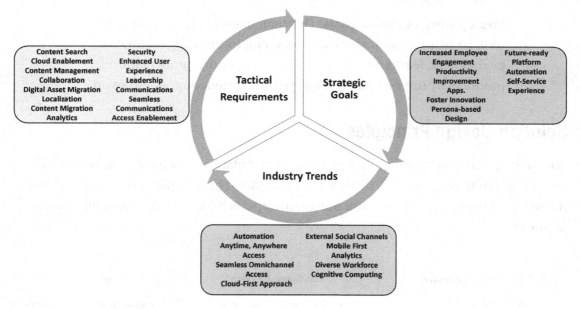

Figure 5-5. *Holistic view of EXP requirements*

A holistic view of requirements consists of three dimensions.

- **Tactical requirements**: The key short-term intranet requirements such as content management, security, search, user experience, localization, integrations, digital asset migration, and other requirements will be part of this category. Normally the tactical requirements consist of short-term goals such as search, improved UX, content requirement, cloud enablement, collaboration, migration, security, and so on.

- **Industry trends**: This category includes emerging trends in the employee experience space such as automation, external partner integrations, cloud-first approach, mobile-first approach, cognitive computing, predictive analytics, and so on.

- **Strategic organization goals**: This includes an organization's long-term strategic goals such as increased employee engagement, access enablement, leader/persona-based design, future-proof platform, productivity improvement, self-service experience apps, and so on.

Solution Design Principles

For crafting next-generation employee engagement platform solutions, I have defined the core solution principles, as depicted in Figure 5-6. The six solution principles define the overall design, architecture, and execution approach for the employee engagement platform.

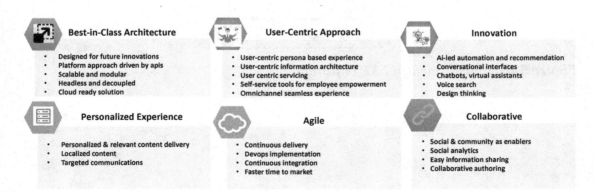

Figure 5-6. *EXP solution design principles*

- **Personalized experience**: The user experience will be designed to cater to various devices and personas in a seamless way. The proposed platform has the ability to support implicit and explicit personalization. Implicit personalization involves leveraging a user's attributes (such as location) to personalize content, and explicit personalization leverages a user's explicit preferences to personalize the experience. The platform should support localization and targeted communications.

- **Collaborative**: The solution is designed to maximize the platform's built-in collaborative features to enable employee collaboration and productivity improvement through information sharing and search. Collaborative features such as blogs, wikis, and articles will be prioritized for initial iterations. External social platforms will be integrated to bring in relevant conversations.

- **Best-in-class architecture**: This category includes forward-looking, proven, and best-in-class architecture principles for designing the platform. The solution is well-aligned with the emerging architecture and industry trends. The salient features of the recommended solution architecture are as follows:

  - **Platform principle**: The solution should be based on platform principles, providing a framework and reusable building blocks for continuous development and integration.

  - **Scalable and modular**: The solution modules and integration modules will be designed to be extensible and scalable. The API-driven and stateless integration provides higher scalability.

  - **Headless integration**: The systems of record (SORs) such as CMS, DAM, workflow, and such will be integrated in headless mode through APIs so that systems of engagement will be completely decoupled from the system of record.

  - **Decoupled**: Systems of engagement (SOE) and systems of record will be fully decoupled so that you have flexibility to change the back-end systems.

- **Cloud-ready**: All the layers and solution components are made cloud-ready.

- **Open standards**: It uses open standards at all layers so it is easy to integrate and extend.

- **User-centric approach**: You need to take a consulting-led approach to identify personas and the unique requirements for each persona. Information delivery and tools will be personalized for each persona. The site structure, navigation model, and information architecture will be designed to cater to all personas. The self-service tools and application services will be developed to empower employees and improve their productivity. The following are the key attributes of a user-centric approach:

  - **Persona-based design**: Users with common goals, expectations, and needs are grouped into a "persona."

  - **User profiles**: The user's profile management functionality provides features such as account management, preference management, application management (opt-out/opt-in), and such.

  - **Integrated enterprise search**: Search is used as a primary information discovery tool across the entire platform.

  - **Engaging and inspirational content**: You need to provide engaging content that depicts the organization's cultures and values and that conforms to brand identity.

  - **Dynamic home pages**: The home page content is dynamically delivered based on users' preferences, users' transaction history, and users' persona.

  - Quick and easy access to important information

  - Quickly complete a task by providing relevant tools and optimized processes

  - Conversation tools such as chat bots and messengers

  - Reflect company's culture through uniform brand identity

- ***Agile***: The agile methodology will be adopted for the solution delivery. The execution methodology consists of sprints to deliver a minimum viable product (MVP) to market more quickly. Continuous integration, continuous deployment and continuous testing will be used to archive higher quality.

- ***Innovation***: Implement machine learning methods to provide smart recommendations. To enhance information discovery integrate chatbots, virtual assistants and voice search into the employee platform. Adopt design thinking approach to problem solving.

Solution Key Focus Areas

Based on this understanding of the common challenges and industry trends, I have identified a set of solution themes to address the common challenges, as shown in Figure 5-7.

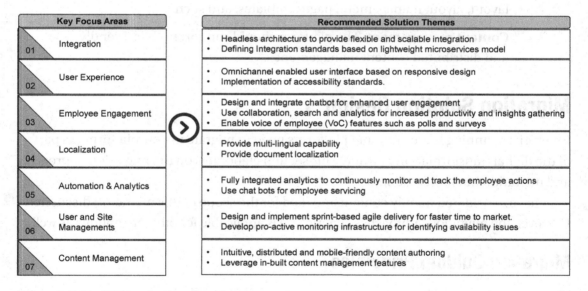

Figure 5-7. *EXP solution key focus areas*

- **Integration**: For efficient integration with systems, use a headless integration model with back-end systems. The usage of a light-weight microservices-based integration also improves high scalability and performance.

133

- **User experience**: A seamless omnichannel experience can be enabled by implementing a responsive design, for mobile apps, and meeting accessibility standards.

- **Employee engagement**: Various tools such as chat bots, collaboration, surveys, search, and voice of employee (VOE) can be used for improved employee engagement.

- **Localization**: The platform should enable localization by leveraging the multilingual capability of the products and integrating the content workflows with translation services.

- **Automation and analytics**: The platform should provide automation features such as workflow automation, chatbots, and such. The platform should also use analytics to provide insights into employee behavior.

- **Site management**: The platform should provide flexible site management capabilities such as preferences management, flexible layout, layout management, page templates, and such.

- **Content management**: The platform should support mobile-friendly and distributed content management.

Migration Solution Design

Enterprises running legacy intranet platforms need to migrate to new platforms as part of the digital transformation journey. This section elaborates on the migration approach and migration implementation.

I have considered mainly content and data for the scope of this migration discussion. However, the migration approach is generic and is applicable for other migrations as well.

Migration Guiding Principles

The key migration guiding principles are as follows:

- Seamless experience for site owners with minimum or no business disruption

- Maximum automation using tool-based migration and scripted validations

- Support for repetitive and iterative migration through scripts

- Support for incremental, batch, and complete migration options

- Standardization and best-practices implementation for better maintainability and for ease of future upgrades

- Utilization of existing software/hardware resources

- Efficient deployment approach to optimize the resources with minimum efforts

- Automated verification of migration

Migration Approach

Figure 5-8 shows the overall migration approach.

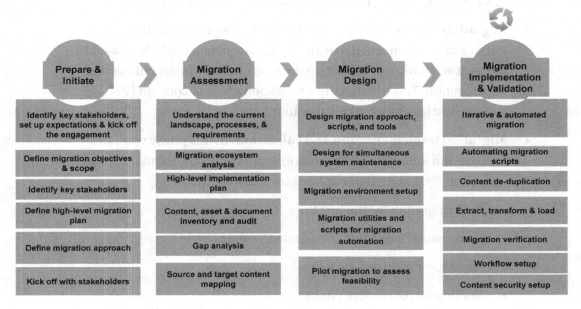

Figure 5-8. *EXP migration approach*

The main stages of migration approach are as follows: prepare and initiate, migration assessment, migration design, and migration implementation and validation.

- **Prepare and initiate**: In this stage you identify the main migration objectives and scope. You fine-tune the overall migration approach for the organization and define the overall migration plan. You define the high-level migration plan covering the migration phases, define the migration scope items, and kick off the migration after getting buy-in from stakeholders.

- **Migration assessment**: During the assessment phase, you understand the current tools and migration ecosystem. You also take an inventory of the content and documents. This includes compiling the overall volume of content and documents and identifying various document types, content types, metadata structure, and such. You also identify any existing gaps with the organization content during this stage.

- **Migration design**: During migration design, you develop the migration scripts needed to extract, transform, and load (discussed in the next section). You will set up the migration environment needed for migration. You will execute a migration proof of concept (PoC) to validate the feasibility of the migration.

- **Migration implementation and validation**: In this phase you execute and automate the migration scripts and validate the migration. The execution methods includes the following:

  - Bulk migration for the first time

  - Incremental migration to migrate the changes

  The validation includes the following:

  - Verification of content count

  - Verification of content integrity

Migration Framework and ETL

In this section I cover the overall migration framework and the detailed steps of extract, transform, and load.

Migration Framework

Figure 5-9 shows the various components of a migration framework.

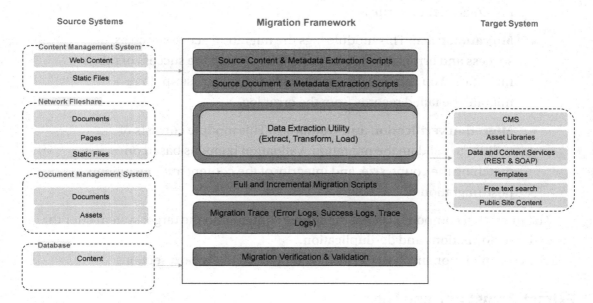

Figure 5-9. *EXP migration framework*

The source system components consist of web content and static files and pages in the content management system, document management system (DMS), network file share, and database.

The core migration framework components are as follows:

- **Source content and metadata extraction scripts**: These are the scripts to extract the web content and metadata from source system. You leverage the APIs and services exposed by the source system to extract the content. If the source system supports a bulk export utility to export the data dump, you will leverage it.

- **Source document extraction scripts**: Generally the documents from the document management system (DMS) and network file share are extracted through a bulk export feature to a compatible system or to an intermediate file system (from which the documents are loaded back to the target system).

- **Full and incremental migration scripts**: The migration framework should support scripts that can do one-time full migration or incremental migration (that can only migrate the changes since the previous migration run).

- **Migration trace**: This module logs the migration actions such as success and errors that can be used for analyzing the success of the migration. You can also design a "migration repair" script to re-migrate the failed records from the error log.

- **Migration verification and validation**: This module consists of utilities to validate the migration. Validation happens based on matching the count, size, and integrity of the content and documents post-migration.

The migration components load the source content into the target system after the needed transformations and de-duplication.

The core migration involves ETL, which is detailed in the next section.

Extract, Transform, and Load

Figure 5-10 shows the key ETL processes.

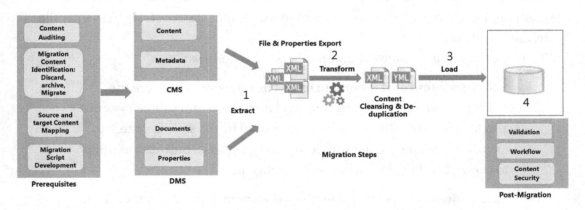

Figure 5-10. *Sample ETL flow*

The migration normally involves ETL, which is a three-step process.

- **Extract**: Extract content files and properties from the source CMS and DMS. You can use the content/document extraction APIs and services supported by the source system. Alternatively, you can leverage any bulk export tools. Along with content and documents, the relevant metadata (such as author, size, permissions, workflow status, and such) is also exported. If both the source and target repositories are compatible (by supporting standards such as JCR, WebDAV, XML, JSON, HTML, XHTML, and such), then you can directly load the source content into the target system. If the target system is not compatible with the source system, you export the source system content into a standard format (such as XML or JSON or CSV) and use the transform step to convert this data into a format compatible with the target system.

- **Transform**: The transformation step converts the data from the source system into a format compatible with the target system. Transformation is needed to bridge the incompatibility gap between the source system and the target system. During this step you also process the content and document by removing duplicates and cleansing the content.

- **Load**: During the load step, you leverage the APIs and services to load the transformed content and documents into the target system. After content validation, you will publish the content and documents on the target system.

Summary

This chapter covered the following:

- In this chapter I discussed key focus areas, trends and evolution, the experience framework, transformation themes, solution design, and migration design for next-generation employee experience platforms.

- The key trends in the EXP space are related to user experience, information delivery, collaboration, productivity, engagement, feedback and performance management, technologies, and work culture support.

- The key focus areas for building employee experience platforms are seamless employee experience; anytime/anywhere/any-device access; a collaborative ecosystem; personalized, contextual, and quicker information access; productivity; engagement; and technology experience.

- The digital workplace evolution is from the traditional intranet to a consolidated portal and finally to an employee experience platform.

- An employee experience framework consists of employee experience transformation themes, employee experience platform solution design principles, and migration design.

- The key employee experience transformation themes are experience, accessibility, collaboration, personalization, productivity, and engagement.

- The experience theme consists of a mobile-first approach, UI design, usability, information architecture, dashboard/integrated view, branding and communication, and performance.

- The accessibility theme consists of omnichannel availability (anytime, anywhere, and any-device access), localization (support for various languages across geographies), regulatory compliance, error handling (consistent error handling and user-friendly error messages), text alternatives (for images, videos), proper labels and instructions, assistance methods (through visual cues, hints), quick information access, and user-friendly content design.

- The collaboration theme consists of document collaboration (such as co-authoring of document), people search (search based on skill sets, job roles, names, departments, and such), conferencing (audio and video conference), enterprise social (external/internal blogs), and centralized knowledge base (for document sharing).

- The personalization theme consists of implicit personalization (personalization based on a user's implicit actions) and explicit personalization (personalization based on a user's explicit preferences, interests and options), user segmentation, and user preference management.

- The productivity theme consists of key workflows and tasks (such as employee applications, content reviews, and such), task management (such as task tracking, SLA management tool, skill-based task assignment tool), self-service (through tools such as search, knowledge base, training, e-learning, skill improvement), productivity measurement (through analytics and reporting tools, feedback tools, goal management tools), effective communication (personalized communication, alerts/notification), work-life balance (through remote working tools, tele-commuting tools), perks/incentives (such as paid time-offs, instant appreciation tools, wellness program, employee development applications), and collaboration tools.

- The engagement theme consists of communications, microlearning and training, idea hub, employee contribution, gamification, insights, feedback management, rewards and recognition, Inclusivity, surveys, analytics reports, and sharing.

- An employee experience platform solution design consists of a holistic view of EXP requirements, solution design principles, and solution key focus areas.

- Migration solution design consists of migration guiding principles, a migration approach, and the migration framework.

CHAPTER 6

Digital Workplace Testing

EXP testing is needed to validate the EXP's functionality, thereby improving the overall quality of the platform. End-to-end testing involves executing various test scenarios such as functional validation, data validation, nonfunctional validation, and such.

In this chapter, I discuss various aspects of testing. I will elaborate on security and performance testing in detail, as these testing functions are critical for the EXP scenario.

EXP Validation Scenarios

A thorough validation of an EXP needs end-to-end testing of various functional and nonfunction scenarios. Table 6-1 lists the main test categories and various test types that are needed for a typical EXP solution.

Table 6-1. *EXP Validation Categories*

Test Category	Test Type
Functional	• System integration testing • User acceptance/end-to-end testing • Regression function (built with artifacts from the previous types) • Automation (if applicable)
Nonfunctional	• Load testing • Endurance testing • Scalability/stress testing • Availability testing
Security testing	• Web application penetration testing • Source code review • Web services security testing
Compatibility testing	• Mobility testing • Cross-browser testing

© Shailesh Kumar Shivakumar 2020
S. K. Shivakumar, *Build a Next-Generation Digital Workplace*, https://doi.org/10.1007/978-1-4842-5512-4_6

EXP Validation Lifecycle

The EXP validation lifecycle consists of the following stages:

- **Test strategy and planning**: During this phase, you formulate the overall test strategy and define the test plan.

- **Test design and review**: Based on the test requirements, you create the test scenarios and test cases and test scripts.

- **Test execution**: During this stage, you execute the test scripts and validate the scenarios.

- **Test reporting**: You collect the metrics and document the learnings and artifacts in the knowledge repository.

Table 6-2 details the testing activities and deliverables at each level.

Table 6-2. *Testing Activities and Deliverables*

Test Stage	Activities	Deliverables/Exit Criteria
Test strategy and planning	• Define test strategy covering various testing services (functional and nonfunctional). • Formulate the test approach along with entry and exit criteria for each phase. • Generate sample set of devices and prioritize and categorize devices for testing. • Draft test plan for the requirements.	• Finalized test strategy. • Finalized test plan.

(continued)

Table 6-2. (*continued*)

Test Stage	Activities	Deliverables/Exit Criteria
Test design and review	• Develop test scenarios and test cases. • Design performance workload model and scripts. • Design device-specific scenarios and test cases. • Design security testing scripts. • Prepare the user acceptance test (UAT) test cases. • Define test data setup requirements. • Prepare test traceability with requirements. • Conduct test reviews.	• Test environment setup. • Ready to execute test scenarios and test cases (with prioritization). • Test data setup. • Requirement traceability matrix.
Test execution	• Perform test readiness review. • Execute test cases. • Conduct functional/nonfunctional testing. • Defect management process. • Test summary reporting. • Regression testing.	• Test readiness review. • Test execution results. • Daily status reports and weekly status reports.
Test reporting	• Gather test metrics for the executed test cases. • Update test repository, maintain knowledge artifacts.	• Defect reports. • Code coverage reports. • Code quality reports. • Metrics report where all metrics meet the Expected KPIs. • Security test summary report. • Achieved test repository/testing artifacts.

End-to-End Testing Approach

The EXP validation lifecycle has various stages aligned with the project lifecycle. Figure 6-1 depicts the end-to-end testing stages.

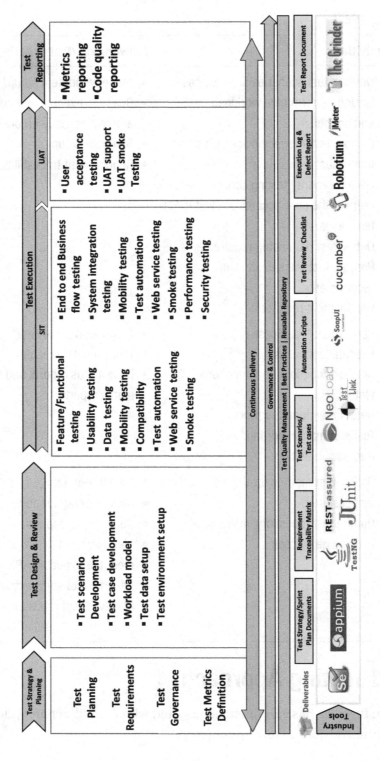

Figure 6-1. End-to-end holistic testing approach

In each of the test phases, you will use various testing tools to conduct unit testing, functional testing, web testing, test automation, test management, and so on.

Testing Tools

As mentioned, at each stage of the project, you will use various tools to fulfil the stage-specific goals. Table 6-3 lists a sample set of open source tools that can be used during the different phases of the project.

Table 6-3. *Testing Tools*

	Tools
Development	JUnit, PQM, Eclipse, SVN, JIRA
Continuous integration	Sonar, Jenkins, Hudson
Functional and web testing	Selenium, TestNG, Appium, Rest-assured, Robotium, Cucumber, SOAPUI
Performance and load testing	Jmeter, NeoLoad, Grinder, BlazeMeter
Application support	JIRA
Security testing	Burp Suite Free, ZAP, Firefox add-ons, SWAAT, Find Bugs, Soap UI Free

I will discuss the details of various types of testing in the subsequent sections.

Functional Testing

Functional testing involves testing each EXP functionality and feature. Functionality testing usually validates all the business use cases, business rules, or use stories (in agile projects).

In functional testing, you will have well-defined expected results, exception flows, and test data.

- Login and logout features (including the exception scenarios such as incorrect password, password reset, inactivity session timeout, and such)

- EXP dashboard features (such as news, announcements, policies, incidents, and such)

- EXP admin functionality (such as role assignment, account management, and such)

- EXP workflows (such as approval workflow, content workflows, etc.)

- EXP collaboration (such as blogs, wikis, communities, etc.)

Localization Testing

Localization testing is carried out to validate whether the system is ready to be configured for different languages and how the system behavior after configuring it for different languages.

In localization testing, you will test the following details:

- Personalized information and different configuration settings

- Linguistic accuracy

- Locale-specific items such as date/time formats, currency, sorting, alignment, text, page layout, and graphics

- Accuracy of content translation capabilities

- User interface labels, titles, and contextual help content

- Content of the system under test as per the requirements

- UI design along with specific color schema, language, and images

- Geo-specific legal and disclaimer content

- Locale-specific error messages, telephone numbers, weights, tutorials, release notes, contextual help, and such

Localization testing will mainly be carried out manually along with functional testing.

Usability Testing

Usability testing is conducted to validate the robust user experience and to ensure an enriched feeling to the user. The usability testing will focus on the following:

- **Ease of information discovery**: You test how easy it is for different personas to find the relevant and contextual information, as well as the availability of personalization, search, and site hierarchy.

- **Ease of accessibility**: You test the compatibility of the user interface on multiple devices, form factors, and browsers. Accessibility testing also validates the conformance of the user interface to accessibility standards.

- **Ease of learning and understand**: How easy is it for the new user to learn and understand the new system? Here you look at the contextual help, chat bots, FAQs, and documentation.

- **Ease of using the system**: How easy is it to use the new system? Here you look for consistency in the user interface, navigation, and error handling methods of the system.

- **Information architecture**: You validate the usability of the information architecture (site navigation, context menus, and such).

- **End-user testing**: Here you validate the user experience of the business flows for different personas to understand how the user thinks, how the user uses the application, and the ease of application navigation. Discover which parts of the EXP are failing and how to improve the overall user experience.

    - Usability evaluation will be done to identify issues related to emotion design, navigation, presentation, consistency, and overall user experience to give the end user a better experience. A/B testing is the most popular testing to identify the usability issues.

Compatibility Testing

Compatibility testing is carried out to validate the behavior of the system across all supported browsers and devices. Compatibility testing is conducted across various end-user systems such as the following:

- **Browsers**: Popular desktop and mobile browsers.

- **Operating systems**: Popular desktop and mobile operating systems.

- **Mobile devices**: Various mobile devices with multiple form factors, resolutions.

- **Backward compatibility**: Wherever required, you also conduct compatibility testing by validating the system on older versions of the software.

Integration Testing

Integration tests involve the validation of major software components (EXP portal, API services, EXP database), data flow (from EXP portal to downstream), cross-application flows (to and from ancillary and source systems), and eventually the correctness of test data from a business transaction's perspective. The integration approach also involves identifying key production-like integration scenarios designed around the integration touch points for the EXP system with ancillary systems and other source systems. As a part of integration testing, the focus is to test chains of transactions that flow together along with end-to-end business process validation between various modules.

The following are the key considerations of the integration testing:

- Error handling scenarios such as application error handling, system error handling, and network error handling.

- Performance of the integration methods during normal loads and peak loads.

- Validation of integration contracts (such as handling optional and mandatory elements and validation rules).

- Iterative integration testing and continuous integration testing are recommended to identify issues during the early phases of the project. Big-bang integration testing (testing all the integrated system components at once), top-down integration testing (testing the top-level components before moving to low-level components), bottom-up integration testing (testing low-level components before testing high-level components), and hybrid integration testing (combination of the top-down and bottom-up approaches) are other forms of integration testing.

Data Testing

Data testing ensures you have valid data in the database and that the data flows across all layers. Data testing validates the entire data flow journey from source systems and ancillary systems to the EXP database. The following are the key considerations of data testing:

- **Data migration validation**: Validate the completeness and correctness of data post-migration from legacy systems to the new platform.

- **Data flow testing**: Validate the data that flows from the UI layer to the services layers to the database layer.

- **Data security testing**: Validate the security of data at rest and of data in transit. Based on information security categories (top secret, confidential, public), you validate if the data is encrypted at rest and while in transit.

Security Testing (Vulnerability Assessment and Penetration Testing)

Security testing is one of the crucial components of the digital workplace as the system handles a lot of sensitive information. Security testing validates the handling of sensitive data, security standards, system vulnerability, and adoption of secure coding practices.

The overall security testing is a phased approach for identifying vulnerabilities and ensuring the identified vulnerabilities undergo timely remediation. See Figure 6-2.

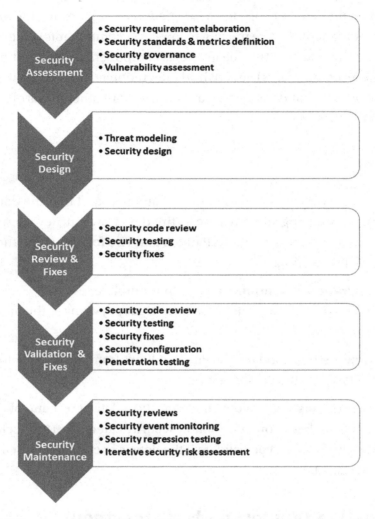

Figure 6-2. *Phased approach for security testing*

By implementing this methodology, all security system weakness will be identified and mitigated before bringing the systems into production. Use cases are derived from the OWASP Top 10 Testing Framework. This will also involve dynamic code reviews and static code analysis.

As part of the security maintenance process, you need to carry out the following activities:

- Vulnerability assessments are conducted once in a year for all the key assets, and a detailed testing is performed for the new system prior to release.

- An annual penetration testing will be performed for systems that are delivering business-critical services and any changes/additions of critical assets supporting the business services.

Web Application Security Testing

Figure 6-3 shows the common testing approaches and testing tools for web application security testing.

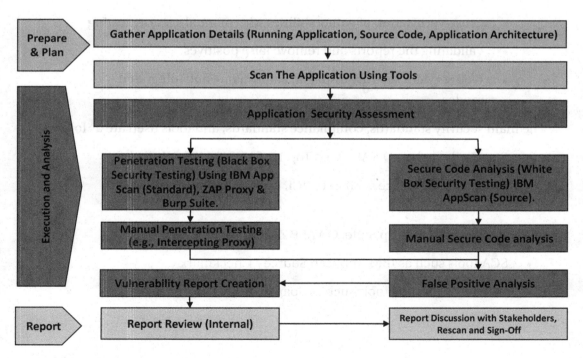

Figure 6-3. *Web application security testing*

- **Secure code analysis (SCA)/static application security testing:** The security code review identifies potential security vulnerabilities at the code level. This testing scans the source code and identifies potential security issues. This testing can be done through the following methods:

  - Automated testing using static analysis tools such as IBM AppScan

  - Manual vulnerability analysis

  - Validating the reports and removing false positives

- **Penetration testing/dynamic application security testing:** Manual and tool-based penetration testing is black-box testing to identify the security vulnerabilities of the web application. An EXP application will be analyzed for a comprehensive set of well-known vulnerabilities, which will also cover the OWASP Top 10 (`www.owasp.org/`). The main methods adopted are as follows:

  - Automated security scanning

  - Cross-verification of vulnerabilities with manual security testing

  - Validating the reports and remove false positives

  - Web services security testing in stand-alone and integrated modes

The main security standards, compliance standards, and tools used are as follows:

- Standards such as OWASP Web Top 10, SANS Top 25, NIST

- Industry compliance such as to PCI, HIPAA (application-level compliance check)

- Proxies such as Burp Suite, OWASP ZAP

- SCA tools such as IBM AppScan Source / Checkmarx

- Webservice testing tools such as SoapUI, RestClient, Resteasy

- Automated security scanners such as IBM AppScan Standard

- Open Source Security Testing Methodology Manual (OSSTMM)

- CREST Penetration Testing Guide

Table 6-4 provides brief details of the common security vulnerabilities discovered in source code analysis (SCA) and penetration testing. I also give the remediation measures to address each of the vulnerabilities.

Table 6-4. *Security Vulnerabilities and Fixes*

Vulnerability Name	Security Test Category	Brief Details	Recommended Fixes
Information management vulnerability: plain-text password in configuration file	Source code assessment	Password is stored in human-readable plain-text format, which is vulnerable to authorization attacks.	Secure the password through encryption and obfuscation and manage it in a central place.
Injection vulnerability	Source code assessment	Injection attacks such as SQL injection attacks and LDAP injection attacks through usage of reserved and dynamic query parameters. Attacker can manipulate the data.	Input validation. Request filters. Query validation. Encode special/reserved characters. Use Prepared JDBC statements.

Insufficient data validation vulnerability	Source code assessment	Input values such as form field values, request parameters, and HTML query parameters are not validated. Attackers use unvalidated parameters to target the application's security mechanisms such as authentication and authorization or business logic, and as the primary vector for exercising many other kinds of error, including buffer overflows. If the unvalidated parameters are stored in log files, used in dynamically generated database queries or shell commands, and/or stored in database tables, attackers may also target the server operating system, a database, back-end processing systems, or even log viewing tools.	Input validation is necessary to ensure the integrity of the dynamic data of the application. Validation is useful to protect against cross-site scripting, SQL and command injection, and corrupt application data fields. Even if there are no directly vulnerable uses of a piece of data inside one application, data that is being passed to other applications should be validated to ensure that those applications are not given bad data. Validation, especially for size and metacharacters that might cause string expansion, is even more important when dealing with fixed-size, overflowable buffers. You should validate input from untrusted sources before using it. The untrusted data sources can be HTTP requests or other network traffic, file systems, databases, and any external systems that provide data to the application. In the case of HTTP requests, validate all parts of the request, including headers, form fields, cookies, and URL components that transfer information from the browser to the server-side application.

(continued)

Table 6-4. (*continued*)

Vulnerability Name	Security Test Category	Brief Details	Recommended Fixes
			The primary recommendation is to validate each input value against a detailed specification of the expectation for that value. This specification should detail characteristics such as the character set allowed, length, whether to allow null, minimum value, maximum value, enumerated values, or a specific regular expression. For example, make sure all e-mail fields have the same format. Also, limit name fields and other text fields to an appropriate character set, no special characters, and with expected minimum and maximum sizes. An input pattern violation can be evidence of an attack and should be logged and responded to appropriately. There are several possible approaches to input validation in an application. The recommendation is to implement the features in a single component that is invoked in a central location. If this is not possible, then enforce a strong policy for the use of a common set of input validation functions.

Poor cryptography vulnerability	Source code assessment	The application uses an insecure source of randomness, potentially enabling an attacker to improve the odds of predicting the next secret generated by the generator. This form of attack is used in sequence number prediction, cryptographic attacks, and session spoofing.	The application should use a cryptographic strength random number generator, such as the java. security. SecureRandom class. There are commercial and open source libraries available that have strong random number generator classes. You should choose a tested and widely used implementation. As with all cryptographic mechanisms, the source code should be available for analysis.
Cross-site scripting vulnerability	Source code assessment	Content being passed into the InnerHTML() or OuterHTML() method should be checked for tainted data. Since this data is further used to insert text, HyperText Markup Language (HTML), and/or script inside of a page, steps should be taken toward validating this data. Content inputted to the InnerHTML() or OuterHTML() methods should not be trusted without further validation. Using such content without validation can lead to a variety of cross-site scriting and HTML injection attacks.	It is recommended that all InnerHTML() or OuterHTML() methods be replaced with InnerText() or OuterText() methods. These methods simply write the data as plain text to the browser without rendering HTML or script. If the InnerHTML() or OuterHTML() methods are necessary, further validation on the input is recommended. Validation of such content when it is exposed to the user should be performed in the same manner as server-side input validation. Input validation should not be solely performed by client-side JavaScript components exposed to the user. Validation implemented in this manner can be bypassed by means of manipulating the browser and/or the submitted request. Use server-side validation or a combination of client-side and server-side validation.

(continued)

Table 6-4. (*continued*)

Vulnerability Name	Security Test Category	Brief Details	Recommended Fixes
Insecure communications vulnerability	Source code assessment	The application does not use a secure channel, such as SSL, to exchange sensitive information. Therefore, it is possible for an attacker with access to the network traffic to sniff packets from the connection and uncover the data.	All sensitive data across all layers should be transmitted over an SSL connection.
Improper error handling	Source code assessment	In a web application, if unvalidated user input is included in the stack trace, an attacker can introduce malicious scripts into the stack trace and launch a cross-site scripting attack against the viewers of the stack trace. If the stack trace is returned to a user, a reflected cross-site scripting attack will be launched in the user's browser. If the stack trace is redirected to a log file and later viewed by application administrators using a scripting-enabled log viewer, a stored cross-site scripting attack can also be launched against the application administrators.	Production applications should never use methods that generate internal details like stack traces unless that information is being directly committed into a log that is not viewable by the end user. The log messages should be encoded to prevent XSS attack.

If the application APIs provide a detailed error message when an exception is thrown and this error message is returned to a user, it might reveal application internal information to attackers. Error messages should not provide attackers with any implementation details when an illegal action is detected by the application or an exception is thrown. This includes indicating exactly what is allowed or exactly what was illegal about the user's input. Such detailed information can help an attacker craft new attacks that will pass through the validation filters.

Stored cross-site scripting	Penetration testing	Malicious scripts can be added to application pages. The scripts once added can be either stored in the database or executed each time a user opens that page or the user can be tricked into clicking a link, which will execute a script in their browser.	User inputs should be validated and filtered using a blacklist or whitelist approach (whitelist is always preferable). Input/output encoding can be done to avoid cross-site scripting.

(continued)

Table 6-4. (*continued*)

Vulnerability Name	Security Test Category	Brief Details	Recommended Fixes
Restrict to URL access	Penetration testing	The security framework should include security filters that check the authorization and access rules before allowing the access to the URLs.	Use POST method to send sensitive data and also display an error message if someone tries to manipulate a URL.
After SSO logout, user can retrieve the visited pages	Penetration testing	After successfully logout, still users can see the past visited pages by click the back button through cached pages.	Restrict the users to visit the cache pages after logout.
Header in the test response contains following unwanted options: PUT, TRACE, OPTIONS, HEAD	Penetration testing	The Allow header in the test response contains following unwanted options: PUT, DELETE, TRACE, OPTIONS, PATCH, HEAD.	GET and POST need to be enabled; disallow HTTP methods that are unneeded.
Information disclosure in HTTP headers	Penetration testing	This information can help an attacker gain a greater understanding of the systems in use and potentially develop further attacks targeted at the specific version of server.	Critical information about system components (e.g., server name, version, installed program versions, etc.) of a web application and database servers should be obscured and not revealed via HTTP responses or error messages.

Information leakage: error handling	Penetration testing	Server details, OS details, programming language details may be leaked in the error logs.	A proper and centralized error handling method is necessary to avoid the information leakage. Sensitive information such as server/OS version, user credentials, personal data and such.
Missing secure attribute in encrypted session (SSL)	Penetration testing	Cookies that are not set with "secure" attribute can be exploited for impersonation or identity theft.	Set the "secure" attribute for the cookie so that it is always sent in an encrypted session.
Missing HttpOnly flag in session cookie	Penetration testing	If the "HTTPOnly" attribute is not set for the cookie, untrusted scripts can steal the information in the cookie.	Set the HttpOnly attribute for the cookie.
Missing HTTP Strict-Transport-Security header	Penetration testing	HTTP Strict Transport Security (HSTS) method restricts the client communication only via secured protocols such as HTTPS. The web server can instruct the user agents, browsers via Strict-Transport-Security response header.	Include the Strict-Transport-Security header in the response body.
Missing CSRF token	Penetration testing	Cross-site request forgery (CSRF) attack exploits an authenticated user to execute state changing actions such as funds transfer, email update and such.	A CSRF token should be passed in each POST request.

Performance Validation

Performance testing validates the overall performance of the system.

Server-Side Performance Testing

Server-side performance testing will verify that the application can handle the expected amount of load while adhering to defined standards of responsiveness, reliability, and scalability.

There are a few key steps that should be followed to design a robust performance testing solution.

- **Objectives and SLA definition:** Based on the work package, the objective and SLA definition will change.

- **Workload modeling:** Depending upon the work package, a separate workload modeling exercise might be carried out to simulate a realistic scenario. You can categorize the work package as live or as under production. Depending upon the state of the application, you can choose different approaches to derive a realistic workload. Depending upon the workload, key test types can also be identified. Script creation of web-based workflows of the APIs and web UI can be done using NeoLoad.

- **Test execution:** This phase involves generating load against the application as per the defined objectives. You can use a commercial tool such as NeoLoad if the Transactions per second (TPS) requirement is high. The tests would include different types of tests.

    Sample stress testing:

    - Combined stress test with ancillary APIs, end-user APIs, end-user UI scripts, for 22,500 concurrent users to generate 1.5 times the normal load

The peak user loads are assumed to be used for all the tests, and the user loads can be revisited based on the scope of work that is defined. During the test execution, you can gather performance statistics of different servers at regular intervals.

- **Analysis and tuning recommendations**: The QA team utilizes the performance statistics captured in the previous phase to understand application behavior. Depending upon the application and its current resource utilization, the QA team will provide tuning recommendations.

- **Performance tuning specific tests**: After the analysis phase, if the application is not performing to the expected level, you need to execute one performance tuning specific test and enable performance logging on the server and applications. The details from the monitoring tools will help you to perform in-depth analysis of the application to pinpoint performance problems and provide tuning recommendations accordingly.

Key Metrics to Be Captured for Performance Testing

During the execution of the load and stress testing, the following metrics will be collected. The server infrastructure metrics will be captured using the performance testing framework and the native cloud monitoring tools for CPU, memory, disk, I/O, network, and processes. The following server and user performance metrics are collected from the load testing tool:

- Response times for critical transactions

- Hits per second

- Transactions per second

- Failed transactions throughput

Troubleshooting Performance issues

To troubleshoot the performance issues of the existing EXP, use the following approach:

- Identify the key pages and transactions for each of the EXP application pages using the 80-20 approach.

  - The pages and transactions that are used most often and the ones that are mostly used by users (such as home page and search page)

  - The pages and transactions that are business critical and that have high impact on business revenue

- For each of the identified pages and transactions, analyze the following:

  - Analyze the end-to-end performance across all layers.

  - Analyze the performance manually and by leveraging the tool.

  - Identify web components, server-side components, services components, and infrastructure components affecting the performance.

- Based on the performance analysis, recommend short-term tactical interventions and long-term strategic interventions.

- Identify the list of design and architecture changes that can impact the long-term performance of the end-to-end application.

- Proactively define other frameworks such as an early warning system and monitoring system that impacts the overall performance.

- Proactively call out any process gaps or process interventions that impact the overall performance.

Performance Design Recommendations

Adopt the performance-driven development strategy as a crucial development guideline. The following are some of the performance-by-design principles:

- **Simple and lightweight**: Frequently accessed pages such as home page and landing pages much be designed to be simple and lightweight. This involves the following:

- Include only key functionalities to keep it lightweight.

- Use compressed and optimized marquee images.

- Make all pages accessible through search.

- Provide expanded footer links for main pages.

- **Lean architecture**: Design a lean UI using a JavaScript framework with a microservices-based services layer.

- **Fine-tune the key functionalities for performance**.

- Evaluate the included third-party scripts from performance and security dimensions.

- **Layerwise caching**: Apply caching at various layers such as web server layer, application server layer, services layer to get optimum performance.

  - The user agent/browser layer can cache the assets such as JS/CSS and images. You can set the appropriate cache headers for this.

  - The service layer can cache the application objects, lookup values, and service responses for frequently used service invocations.

  - The database layer can cache the query results for frequently used queries.

- **Performance guidelines**: Come up with organization-level performance guidelines involving images, JS/CSS coding, and other aspects. Some of them could include the following:

  - Use optimal format of images (such as PNG)

  - Use CSS sprites.

  - Do JS code validation with JSLint.

  - Load the content and images only on-demand.

  - Minimize iframes and page redirects.

Table 6-5 provides the common UI performance optimization guidelines.

Table 6-5. *UI Performance Optimization*

UI Performance Optimization	Performance Gains	Tools and Techniques
Merge JavaScripts and Stylesheets.	• Merging avoids mulitple resource requests	• YUI
Minify the JavaScript and stylesheet files.	• Minification reduces the overall page size.	• JSMin • YUI
Place the JavaScripts at the bottom of the page and stylesheets at the top of the page.	• Optimal placement of JavaScripts and Stylesheet files enhances the perceived page load time.	
Assets optimization • Use CSS sprites. • Use lossless compression or PNG files.	• Reduces number of resource requests and reduces page size.	• Smushit Image Compressor • Trimage
Caching • Leverage browser caching by setting a long expiration for static assets. • Leverage web server caching.	• Improves page load time by loading the data from the nearest cache.	• Add expires header in the web server config file
Compression • Enable gzip compression for HTTP traffic.	• Enhances the page load times on various devices.	• Content-encoding header

Test Automation Framework

In this section, I discuss the methods for automating the EXP testing.

UI Testing Automation

The UI automation scripts will be created by recording the test steps. The same automated scripts will be reused to conduct compatibility testing across OSs/devices and browser versions and to validate different environments with different sets of test data.

The following are the benefits of UI automation:

- Higher automation coverage to reduce release cycle time

- Higher automation coverage across various platforms and OS/browser

- Helps maintain defect removal efficiency (> 98 percent)

- Enables predictability in release dates due to standardization of QA processes

- Reduces testing cycle time

- Helps in easy maintenance and implementation of automation

- Improves test coverage across multiple rollouts and devices

API Automation

API interfaces will automate all the RESTful service messages. The microservices will be tested through the API calls, and entire API/web services testing will be automated using the REST-assured library with the TestNG automation framework.

- For each API or web service, you need to analyze the following:

  - API functionality, business rules, boundary conditions, test scope, input paramter validations.

  - Use test methods such as equivalence classes, parameter validation to validate the APIs

  - Iteratively test the APIs and compare the actual with expected results.

169

- Web/microservices testing will involve the following:

  - Validate the operations of the microservices.

  - Determining the JSON request format that the tester needs to send

  - Determining the response JSON format

  - Using a tool to send requests and validate the response

  - Validated the API with the web service test automation tool REST-assured

Key Metrics

Table 6-6 provides the metrics that can be used to track the testing's effectiveness.

Table 6-6. *Key Testing Metrics*

Metric	Formula
Test schedule variance	(Actual calendar days – Planned calendar days) / Planned calendar days
Defect detection efficiency (DDE)	(# valid defect by) / (# valid defect by + # valid SIT defect in UAT, # valid SIT defect in production during warranty) * 100
Test coverage	(Total test cases executed in release) / (Total test cases for all requirements)
Test execution productivity	(Actual # of test cases executed per day / Target number of test cases to be executed) * 100
Defect rejection ratio	(# of defect fixes rejected / Number of defects fixed) * 100
Automation test coverage	Number of test cases automated / Total number of test cases that can be automated

Summary

This chapter covered the following:

- The main categories of testing are functional, nonfunctional, security testing, and compatibility testing.

- The EXP validation lifecycle consists of test strategy and planning, test design and review, test execution, and test reporting.

- Functional testing involves testing each EXP functionality.

- Localization testing is carried out to check whether the system is ready to be configured for different locales and how the system behaves after configuring it for different locales.

- Usability testing is conducted to validate the robust user experience and to ensure an enriched feeling to the user.

- Compatibility testing is carried out to validate the behavior of the system across all supported browsers and devices.

- The integration tests involve validating the major software components (EXP portal, API services, EXP database), data flows (from EXP portal to downstream), and cross-application flows (to and from ancillary and source systems), as well as eventually validating the correctness of test data from a business transaction's perspective.

- Data testing ensures you have valid data in the database and the data flows across all layers.

- Security testing validates the handling of sensitive data, security standards, system vulnerability, and adoption of secure coding practices.

- The UI automation scripts will be created by recording the test steps.

CHAPTER 7

Digital Workplace Case Study

In this chapter, I discuss in detail an end-to-end EXP case study. In the case study, I cover various concepts such as the employee journey map, user experience design, functional design, and platform development. We will understand all the steps and processes involved in the EXP development process. The chapter depicts an elaborate digital workplace development detailing end-to-end steps for design, employee journey mapping and such.

Case Study Background

In this case study, I discuss the ground up development of an employee experience platform. The employee platform will cater to a digital-savvy workforce by leveraging modern digital technologies.

As part of the existing technology ecosystem, there are multiple legacy platforms such as HRMS systems, CRM systems, and content management systems (CMS). The integration of an intranet with these legacy platforms was done using heavy-weight XML-based web services, which impacted the overall system performance.

The main features of the new employee platform are as follows:

- The platform should provide seamless collaboration tools and features.

- The platform should provide seamless personalization features.

- The HR processes should be simplified with automated workflows.

- The user experience should work seamlessly on all major desktop browsers and mobile platforms.

© Shailesh Kumar Shivakumar 2020
S. K. Shivakumar, *Build a Next-Generation Digital Workplace*, https://doi.org/10.1007/978-1-4842-5512-4_7

- The platform should be scalable for 100,000 users and will respond within one second.

- The platform should enable agile delivery for a faster time to market.

Employee Platform Design Principles

To build the forward-looking employee platform to satisfy the requirements, we must lay out the design principles as depicted in Figure 7-1.

- Collaboration involves enabling employee-to-employee connections through tools such as messengers and chat. Other collaboration features such as groups, forums, enterprise social, and communities enable collaboration among groups of employees. Remote login and audio/video conferencing will allow employees to telecommute. Employees can use people search for finding and connecting to people based on their skill sets. The EXP should provide collaborative ideation wherein employees can contribute to the corporate "idea hub." The EXP will provide a feature called "Ask the leader" wherein employees can ask questions to the senior leadership team.

- Employee engagement leverages personalization (providing personalized content and tools) and gamification (adopting gaming concepts to encourage employees) to actively engage employees on the employee platform. Productivity improvement and decision-making tools help employees to complete the tasks quickly. Virtual assistants and chatbots should provide conversational interfaces to help employees discover information quickly and to provide clarifications. Rewards and recognition and benefits management will act as motivators for employees.

- Process redesign impacts the overall employee satisfaction levels through quicker process completion times. Process redesign includes various process optimization features such as auto-approvals, fewer process steps, process simplification, one-click employee onboarding, and such.

- Automation is another key solution tenet that optimizes the overall operational cost and improves employee productivity. Many of the employee activities such as ticket management, employee onboarding, employee learning, and development will be automated through bots and tools.

- Experience redesign involves providing a seamless omnichannel experience through responsive design. The redesign exercise also involves interactive design, an intuitive information architecture (navigation model, site hierarchy), persona-based design, and employee journey mapping to provide a superior user experience to the employees.

- Productivity improvement is one of the primary goals of the EXP. We should enable employees with productivity improvement tools that provide faster/contextual information. The EXP should also provide decision-making tools such as timesheet planners, career goal planners, tax planners, and such. Self-service features enabled by cognitive search will play a major role in improving the overall productivity. Providing business self-service, wherein the business stakeholders can configure/control the system without involving IT, optimizes the overall process execution time.

Collaboration	Employee Engagement	Process Redesign	Automation	Experience Redesign	Productivity
• Messenger • Forums, groups, communities • Enterprise social • Audio/video conference • People search • Ideation • Question & answers feature	• Personalization • Gamification • Virtual assistants • Chatbots • Rewards and recognition • Benefits management	• One-click onboarding • Auto-approvals • Reduced process steps • SLA-based approvals • Process simplification	• Conversational Bots • Process automation • Employee ticket management • Employee onboarding • Employee learning & development	• Seamless omnichannel experience • Interactive and responsive UI • Lean portal model • Light-weight services • Intuitive information architecture • Persona based • Employee journey mapping	• Faster, contextual information • Decision-making tools • Business friendly controls and configuration • Effective search • Self-service

Figure 7-1. *Employee platform design principles*

Table 7-1 outlines various transformation categories, mapping the current scenarios and challenges to the future architecture of the case study.

Table 7-1. *Employee Platform Transformation Categories*

Transformation Category	Current Scenario	Future Architecture
User experience	Varied UI, inconsistent experience, duplicate functionality	User-centric UI, consistent and uniform experience, intuitive information architecture
Employee processes	Complex, multistep processes and manual processes	Automated steps, optimized workflows, simplified processes
Solution architecture	Multiple tools and technologies, nonscalable solution	Scalable architecture, stateless, microservices based, modular, reusable, open source, cloud-based scalability
Analytics	Minimal usage of analytics	Analytics-driven insights, analytics-based personalization and recommendations
Time to market	Slow (release time of three to six months)	Fast, agile (four- to six-week sprints)
Total cost of ownership	High	Low

Design Deep Dive

In this section, we will look at the various elements of EXP design as related to the case study. The section elaborates on the main solution tenets such as experience redesign (including persona design and employee journey mapping), process redesign (including process automation and process optimization), and automation (bot-based automation and process automation).

Persona Definition

As you know, a *persona* represents a group of people and defines various characteristics of the group. All users belonging to one persona have similar goals, information needs, and journey maps. We can define user personas based on similar needs, goals, and challenges. Personas create a better understanding of the application's target user population and their core needs. We also define the common platform usage patterns for each of the personas.

Personas help us to understand the user's challenges, mental model, and usage of the UI. We can then develop the user-centric user interface, information architecture, key features, automation tools, and optimized processes based on personas.

Figure 7-2 shows a sample persona definition for Alex, a project manager.

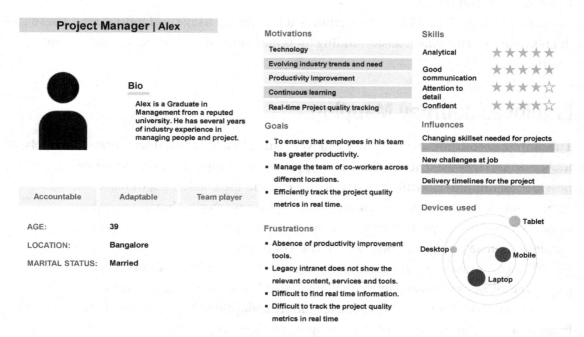

Figure 7-2. *Sample project manager persona*

A persona definition represents the distinct user groups in the target user platform. In this example, Alex represents a project manager persona. We have filled in his details along with the persona's motivations, goals, skills, influences, and frustrations/challenges.

In the example, one of the key goals of the project manager persona is to improve the productivity of the team members. An EXP can help achieve this goal by providing various productivity tools such as collaborative tools, project management tools, and such. For the team management goal, the EXP can provide features such as performance management and team management. The EXP can provide an integrated project management tool that tracks the project status, quality metrics, risks, milestone planning, and such.

A persona definition also identifies the main challenges and frustrations for the persona. The key challenges for the project manager persona are the absence of productivity tools, absence of personalized tools, challenges with real-time information discovery, and lack of real-time project tracking. Based on these insights, we can design these features into the EXP.

Persona analysis provides other details such as device usage and influencers. These details help us to provide decision-aiding tools and target device-specific content and testing.

Employee Journey Mapping

The employee journey involves the employee paths, touch points, interactions, channels, tools, and services used across the entire application. Mapping the employee journey provides an unique opportunity for us to understand the challenges, transformation opportunities, and self-service opportunities of the case study. Hence, we can use employee journey maps to improve the overall employee engagement, improve employee satisfaction, and optimize the costs of the EXP.

Without employee journey mapping, organizations don't know how to actively engage employees across various touch points and channels. Organizations also need to enable low-touch services to increase platform adoption. Organizations have a fragmented and limited view of all employee interactions.

A comprehensive employee journey map provides insights about the most popular tools/services and the underlying business processes and opportunities to improve the KPIs. We can also improve productivity, improve employee satisfaction, and reduce and improve release cycles through optimal journey analysis.

Figure 7-3 depicts the high-level steps in an employee journey mapping for the case study.

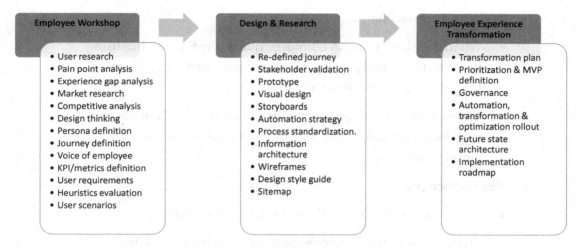

Figure 7-3. *Employee journey mapping process*

Employee Workshop

The first step in the employee journey mapping is an employee workshop wherein you conduct user research, pain point analysis, persona definition, as-is journey mapping, and KPI/metrics definition. We will look at all these activities in detail in this section.

User Research

As part of user research, you determine the user details (name, designation), goals/aims, responsibilities, needs/wants, day-to-day tasks and scenarios, and main challenges for the sample set of users.

Sample user research for the case study is as follows:

- **Name**: John

- **Role**: Support Executive (SE)

- **Needs and goals**:

    - Resolve customer queries quickly

    - Access relevant information quickly

    - Understand customer details in real time

    - Understand the products and services of the organization

    - Ability to access all the customer service systems such as search, knowledge base, CRM, and reports

- **Tasks and scenarios:**

  - When the SE receives an employee query, the SE searches using the search tool and gets the relevant documents and content from the centralized knowledge base.

  - The SE should be able to get all the public details of employees such as the employee role, recent tickets, software used by employee, and such.

- **Key challenges:**

  - The SE is not able to find the right information quickly.

  - There is no centralized knowledge base storing the product documents, how-to documents, best practices, and troubleshooting tips.

The following are the best practices in an employee journey mapping:

- You need to involve cross-functional teams to understand the underlying business functions, technology, and operations.

- You should iteratively refine the employee journey to ensure that the employee journey is up-to-date at all the times.

- You should define the key performance indicators (KPIs) and track them regularly to assess the effectiveness of the employee journeys.

Journey Definition

An as-is employee journey map defines how the persona uses the product or platform for a specific scenario. Each persona has specific goals and expectations during a journey map while traversing various stages of the journey. We can explore various engagement opportunities and understand challenges during the journey map.

In a journey map, we depict other elements such as the journey sequence (a series of steps to complete the scenario), interaction (persons/tools/services with whom the persona interacts to complete the scenario), cultural aspects (such as aesthetics, influencers), touch points (such as devices, services), and artifacts (documents used).

Figure 7-4 shows a sample employee journey map for the "blog authoring" scenario of the case study.

Journey Phases	Research for blog feature	Employee logs a ticket	Author the blog	Mail blog admin for review	Share the blog post	Blog reports
Stakeholders and Touch Points	Employee wants to author a blog about a product.	Employee needs to get permission for blog	Employee uses authoring tool for authoring blog	Employees mail blog administrator for review and approval	Employee wants to share the blog with friends & colleagues	Employee gets the regular report of blog usage.
	How does the employee find blog feature? Where is blog available?	How does employee log the ticket? Is there any knowledge base or chatbot available?	How friendly is blog authoring tool? Are there online tutorials for blog authoring?	How employee interacts with blog admins?	What tools can an employee use for sharing the blog post?	Is there a blog or site that can help me with pet care. Can I get personalized regime for my dog?
Empathy map: Seeing Feeling Thinking	:)	:-|	What are the pain points and causes? :-|	:-:	:-(	:-(
Artefacts			What artefacts is the user using?			
Opportunities	• Can we provide blog in the home page? • Can we provide search feature to get recent blog posts? • Can we provide feeds for blog posts?	• Can we automatically provide blog permission to all employees? • Can we provide knowledge base about blogs? • Can we provide chatbot feature to help employee? • Can we provide self-service option to request blog permission?	• Can we provide rich text editors? • Can we provide mobile friendly and distributed blog authoring? • Can we provide language translation • Can we provide meaningful tags and metadata for efficient information discovery?	• Can we automate the review and publishing flow? • Cab we automate the review process and workflow? • Can we provide SLA-based alerts and notification to the process owner?	• Can we provide external sharing and mailing option? • Can we provide social media sharing option? • Can we provide other options such as liking, commenting, rating and reviews? • Can we automatically share the published blog in latest blog section?	• Can we provide sentiment analysis? • Can we provide regular alerts for blog views, rating and comments?

Figure 7-4. Employee blog journey map

181

Employees normally blog to detail products and services, express their opinions, share information, provide updates on new policies, and such. As depicted in Figure 7-4, an employee has to navigate six journey phases for end-to-end blog publishing. For each of the phases, we have depicted touch points, empathy maps, artifacts, and opportunities.

As depicted in Figure 7-4, there are many manual steps in the entire journey such as logging incidents for blog permission and mailing the blog admin for review and approval.

As the first journey step, an employee does some research for a blog feature. The main employee touch points in this stage are the home page, search box and collaboration page featuring blogs. In the current scenario, the blog feature is present at two levels below the top-level pages. As an improvement opportunity, we can feature the most popular features like a blog on the home page or landing pages. Once the employee identifies the blog feature, the employee requests permission to author the blog by logging an incident. We can eliminate this manual step and make this transaction truly frictionless by automating the blog permission request by providing a self-service portal for providing blog permission. We could also provide a chat bot to automate blog access. Once the employee gets blog access, the employee starts the blog authoring. The current platform provides a legacy and traditional blog authoring feature. We can provide intuitive mobile-friendly content authoring tools equipped with rich-text editors, tags/metadata, and content translation capability. Once the blog is authored, the employee e-mails the blog admin to review and approve the blog. We can automate this manual step by automating the blog review and publishing flow. For an employee to share the blog, the employee currently manually e-mails the blog link to friends and colleagues. We can provide social sharing tools and tools for liking, commenting, reviewing, social sharing, and rating options. As the last step, the employee gets analytics reports about the blog. We can provide a sentiment analysis tool and regular alerts about blog viewing metrics.

Figure 7-5 shows another example of an employee journey for the case study. The diagram identifies various touch points and journey steps involved in the employee learning journey.

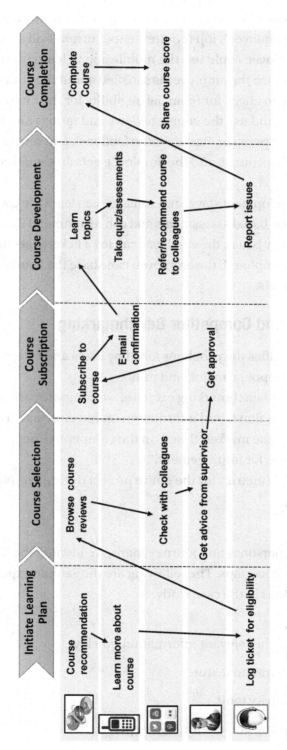

Figure 7-5. Employee learning touch points

The journey is initiated with the "course recommendation" from the EXP to the employee based on the employee's job requirements, current skill sets, career goals, and aspirations. The employee could use the mobile app to learn more about the recommended courses. Once the employee is satisfied about the course relevance, the employee can log a ticket to check for financial eligibility for the interested courses. As a next step, the employee could use the course reviews and ratings and get feedback from colleagues and from the supervisor. Based on the feedback and recommendation, the employee subscribes to the course, and the employee gets an e-mail confirmation about the course subscription.

During the course development stage, the employee can learn the course and complete web assessments or mobile-based assessments and can recommend the course to friends/colleagues. In the case of any issues, the employee can log a ticket to get the issues resolved.

When the course is completed, the employee can share the course score on internal and external social channels.

Heuristic Evaluation and Competitor Benchmarking

Heuristic evaluation identifies the problems faced by users and categorizes them into categories such as showstoppers, major, and minor.

During the competitor benchmarking exercise, we compare various parameters such as user experience, process flows, and information architecture against the competitors and popular platforms on the market. Based on the competitive benchmarking, we can identify the gaps and scope for improvement.

We also define the KPI/metrics for the entire project during this phase.

Pain Point Analysis

Based on the analysis of personas and journey maps, we identify the improvement opportunities and experience gaps. The following are the sample experience gaps we have identified for personas in the case study:

New Joinee:

- Not able to find the relevant information quickly

- Minimal collaboration features

- Lack of productivity tools

- Minimal e-training and e-learning support

Project Manager

- Not able to find the real-time project details

- Lack of automation and productivity improvement tools

- Lack of remote access features

Design and Research

In this phase, we iteratively redefine the user journey to ensure that the touch points are optimized for all the personas. We validate the redefined user journey with all the concerned stakeholders (a select set of employees and business stakeholders). Using the redefined user journey as a reference and based on the insights from employee workshop, we define the new user experience and visual design. After the review and approval of the visual design and modified user experience, we create the style guide, wireframes, prototype, information architecture (site hierarchy, navigation model, menus), and storyboards. We define the design style guide (UI element specifications) and site map (that maps the site hierarchy) as part of the design and research track.

During the same phase, we also define the automation strategy for future phases and standardize the business processes.

Employee Experience Transformation

Based on the business priorities of the case study, we define the rollout plan for various features and functionality. We define a minimum viable product (MVP) for each of the iterations and bundle the MVPs into sprints for the delivery. Based on the priorities and the business impact, the implementation road map identifies various milestones, and the future architecture will be defined to address the experience gaps and to implement the long-term vision. Automation, transformation, and optimization features will be rolled out based on the defined strategy and priorities.

Automation Opportunities in the EXP

In the employee engagement space, there are multiple automation opportunities. I have elaborated on the main automation opportunities in the following section.

Bot-Based Automation

Bots can be used in multiple ways for active employee engagement and for improving the overall productivity of the employees. The following is a list of the main scenarios where bots can be used in the case study:

- Chat bots can be deployed as conversational interfaces to help employees find information quickly. Chat bots can also be used to perform other activities such logging tickets, applying for leaves, filling in timesheets, and such.

- Bots can automate tasks such as document verification and event-based follow-ups.

- Some of the learning and development activities and competency management tasks such as recommending relevant courses, tracking the employee learning progress, creating learning assessments, filling in progress reports, and personalized learning can be automated using bots.

- Bots can be used for automating talent recruitment activities (such as résumé screening and offer management), employee on-boarding, first-level service request handling, and automatic ticket triaging.

- Bots can be used for employee engagement activities such as voice search, rewards management, and benefits management.

- Bots can manage and automate operations and maintenance activities such as time and attendance management, reporting, expense management, and such.

- Bots can aid decision-making activities through decision-making tools, content recommendation tools, and benefits calculators.

- Bots can be used to respond to employee queries using Natural Language Processing (NLP) in a centralized knowledge base.

Process Optimization and Automation

Based on the insights gathered from the employee journey mapping, we can identify the automation opportunities for the case study. These are some of the process automation opportunities for the case study:

- Approval workflows such as leave approvals and basic system access approval can be automated.

- The process for sending event reminders, notification, and SLA violation alerts can be automated.

Solution Design of the Case Study's EXP

Figure 7-6 shows the solution architecture of the sample EXP. The architecture identifies the key layers as the presentation platform, integration middleware platform, enterprise systems, DevOps, security, and monitoring and alert infrastructure.

The presentation platform primarily addresses the presentation concerns such as rendering and personalizing the user experience. To provide a seamless omnichannel experience, the presentation platform has various modules such as a responsive UI (that provides a flexible UI design across various channels and devices), site management (designing page templates, site hierarchy, site metadata, and such), dashboard/unified experience (integrated view of employee information and activities), personalization (user role/preferences-based information and tools), service request/incident management, user account management (managing user profile and user preferences), information architecture (menus, site map, site structure, page metadata), search engine optimization (to improve search results ranking with meaningful keywords and metadata), mobile apps, polls and surveys (to get the employee feedback), workflows, collaboration, alerts and notification, search (to improve information discovery), and web analytics (to track the employee web page actions).

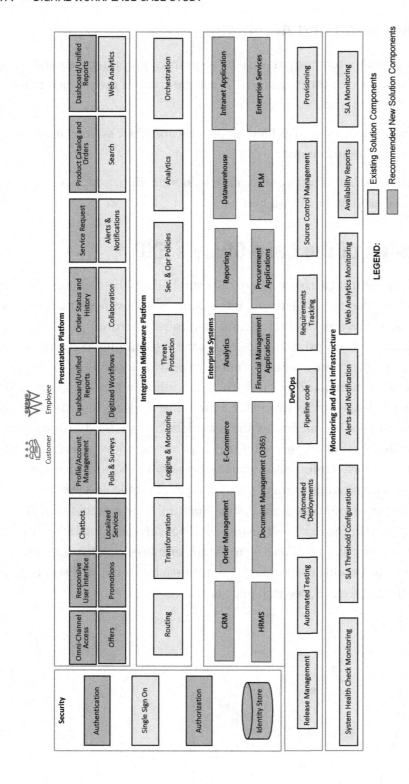

Figure 7-6. EXP solution architecture

The integration middleware layer is mainly responsible for handling integration concerns centrally. As the integration middleware manages the integrations, the main modules in this layer are routing (map and route the request and responses to appropriate end points), transformation (protocol and data transformation needed for source and target systems), logging and monitoring (errors, response codes, timestamps, source/destination details), threat protection (API/service-level security, token-based authorization), service governance (service monitoring, standards enforcements, service performance management and such), analytics, and orchestration (sequential invocation of services for a business process).

Enterprise systems are also known as systems of record/sources of truth and are mainly used by organizations to centrally store the master data. This layer includes systems such as CRMs (to store campaign data and user profile information), ERPs (for storing employee master data), e-commerce systems (for managing orders), analytics, reporting systems, relational database systems, enterprise web applications, human resource management systems (for storing user information), document management systems (for storing documents), content management systems (for storing web content), financial applications, procurement systems, product lifecycle management systems, and enterprise services.

DevOps enhances and automates the release management processes. We can create a DevOps pipeline using a continuous integration tool to automate the code review, testing, build, deployment, alerts/reporting, provisioning, and such activities.

The security layer is mainly responsible for handling security concerns such as authentication, authorization, encryption, single sign-on, user provisioning, and identity store management.

The monitoring and alert infrastructure regularly monitors the system hardware through heartbeat monitoring (for checking the system/service availability), SLA monitoring (checking the CPU, memory thresholds, and alerts in case of threshold violation), real-time user monitoring (through global monitoring bots), web analytics monitoring (to monitor the site usage patterns, user traffic), and synthetic monitoring.

Solution Tenets

Figure 7-7 shows the key solution tenets for an employee experience platform for the case study.

Technology Modernization	Application Modernization	Migrations	Consolidation	Experience Redesign
• Open source technology stack • Platform principle • Technology standardization • Leveraging artificial Intelligence and Machine learning technologies for automation	• Cloud enablement • Decoupled, microservice based • Retire, refactor, redesign • Scalable & extensible	• Data migration • Functionality migration	• De-duplication of data /functionality/content • Single source of truth/system of record creation	• Seamless omnichannel experience • Interactive and responsive UI • Lean Portal model • Light-weight services

Figure 7-7. *Key solution tenets of EXP*

Technology modernization primarily involves exploring and leveraging open source technology and open standards in the modern enterprise. Other solution tenets are standardizing the technology (by creating a uniform technology stack), adopting platform principles (by creating modular, scalable, and extensible modules), and leveraging artificial intelligence and machine learning technologies for automation.

Application modernization involves adopting futuristic principles for the existing applications. This includes service enablement of existing applications through a multi-speed IT approach (wherein the digital systems of engagement change faster than legacy systems of record), cloud enablement of the applications by moving existing applications to cloud or by using the software-as-a-service (SaaS) model, and creating a decoupled architecture by using a headless architecture and modular components. Evaluate existing applications to identify applications that can be retired (decommissioned), refactored (reusing partial application), and redesigned (rewriting the application) to make the application scalable and extensible.

Migration involves migrating the data, functionality, content, documents, and user data into target systems or a cloud platform as part of application modernization.

Consolidation involves creating centralized repositories for data, content, documents, and enterprise data to create a system of record. During the consolidation process, we de-duplicate the data. Functional consolidation involves identifying duplicate functions and creating reusable and module functions across the enterprise ecosystem.

Experience redesign involves creating user-centric, omnichannel user interfaces by making them interactive and responsive. Modern user experiences are based on lean principles (light-weight and simplified UI) using light-weight services.

Maturity Model of an EXP

A *maturity model* provides various maturity levels of enterprise processes and technology ecosystems. Enterprises can use the maturity model to assess their current maturity levels, and it helps enterprises to define a road map for the future. Figure 7-8 shows an EXP maturity model.

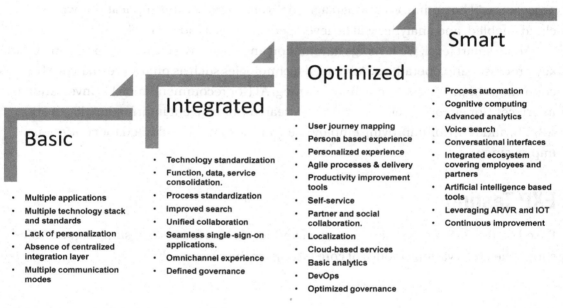

Figure 7-8. *EXP maturity model*

The basic level is the first level wherein the organization has multiple applications providing a disconnected experience. Often organizations have multiple technology standards, and the organization data will be distributed across various repositories. The user experience lacks key features such as personalization, collaboration, and integrated view.

The next level in the maturity model is the integrated level, wherein the data, functionality, and services will be consolidated, leading to a centralized system of records. Organizations define technology and integration standards and process standards. The user experience provides integrated dashboards that use single sign-on and provide an omnichannel experience. Standard operating procedures (SOPs) will be defined as part of system governance for handling business-critical systems and applications.

At the optimized level, organizations aim to provide a user-centric user experience with efficient information discovery. Organizations use persona-based design, employee journey mapping, localization and personalized delivery, self-service tools, and productivity tools to enhance the performance of the employees. Existing governance processes will be optimized through agile delivery. Services and applications will be cloud enabled, and analytics will be leveraged to understand user behavior.

At the smart level, we leverage automation and cognitive computing to automate the key processes and operations. Advanced technologies such as predictive analytics (for continuous improvement), machine learning/AI (for recommendation), conversational interfaces (for enabling self-service), voice search (for efficient information discovery), AR/VR, and IOT (for improving employee experience) will be adopted for continuous improvement.

EXP Testing

Based on the EXP requirements, we can conduct various modes of testing. Figure 7-9 shows the given various modes of core testing for the cases study.

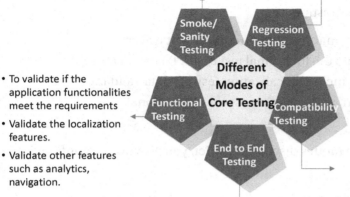

- Basic health check on each build to make sure the main functionalities are working fine to proceed with further stages of testing.

- Validate the current iteration functionality for web portal
- Validate the previous iteration to make sure functionality is not broken
- Regression suite of critical business flows created and validated against the same

- To validate if the application functionalities meet the requirements
- Validate the localization features.
- Validate other features such as analytics, navigation.

- Validate the application functionalities across in-scope browsers for all the critical business flows to ensure that identical user experience is provided irrespective of the browser used to access the application
- Browsers testing for Chrome, Firefox, IE, Safari for the latest & minus 1 versions
- For mobile testing, considering Android phone (Android Browser), iOS phone(Safari), Android tablet (Opera Mini), iPAD (Safari)
- Validate both portrait and landscape of the application as part of mobile testing

- **Validate end-to-end features**

Smoke/ Sanity Testing **Regression Testing** **Different Modes of Core Testing** **Functional Testing** **Compatibility Testing** **End to End Testing**

Figure 7-9. *EXP testing categories*

- **Smoke/sanity testing**: You usually do the smoke testing when the validation team gets a new release. The validation team quickly validates the core functionality (such as page loading, main integrations, page navigation, key button clicks, etc.). Smoke testing provides a quick validation of the overall sanity of the release after which the validation team proceeds with further testing.

- **Regression testing**: During regression testing, you validate all the previously working functionality (pages, flows, integrations, and such) to identify any broken issues. Regression issues ensure a stable release and backward compatibility of the new releases.

- **Compatibility testing**: You test the EXP against all the supported browsers and mobile devices during the compatibility testing. This ensures that all the features of the EXP work consistently and as expected on the supported browsers and devices.

- **End-to-end testing**: As part of end-to-end testing, you test all the moving parts of the EXP such as the presentation layer, API layer, and services layer. You also test the key transactions and processes from end to end as part of this testing.

- **Functional testing**: You mainly use the requirement use cases and user stories to create the functional test cases. Based on the requirements, you also include localization testing, data validation, business rule validation, and analytics as part of functional validation.

In addition to the core testing modes discussed earlier, you also do the nonfunction validation as follows:

- **Performance testing**: You test the performance SLAs (load times, response times, transaction completion times) of all EXP pages.

- **Availability testing**: You test the overall availability of the EXP application over a period of time.

- **Load/stress testing**: You subject the EXP to above-average loads and monitor the system behavior to understand the application's breakpoint.

- **Endurance testing**: You test the application with average loads for an extended time duration to check for any memory leaks or any performance degradation.

Key Success Metrics of an EXP

Metrics are needed to measure the performance of the EXP and use it for continuous improvement. Hence, you need to define the critical success factors and success metrics based on the business goals during the initial stages.

Table 7-2 shows the main success metrics and EXP best practices for achieving the success metrics for the case study.

Table 7-2. *Success Metrics and EXP Best Practices*

Success Metrics	Brief Details	EXP Best Practices
Easy information access and reduced cognitive load	Employees should be able to find the relevant information quickly.	Personalization, cognitive search, targeted content delivery, chatbots/virtual assistants
Improved self-service	Self-service tools and applications are made available to employees.	Search, centralized knowledge base, chatbots, virtual assistants, collaborative tools, automation
Improved personalized information delivery	Provide personalized information and tools.	Personalization, role-based access, permission model
Improved automation	Automate structured tasks.	Employee process automation, automated publishing
Productivity improvement	Employees should be given tools to complete their tasks faster.	Time sheet management tools, mobile apps for core functions
Easier collaboration	Employees should be able to effectively collaborate with their colleagues.	Forums, people search, communities, groups, calendar, event management, enterprise social, partner collaboration
Decision-making tools	Employees should have easier access to decision-making tools.	Effective search, smart recommendations, benefits calculators

Sample Transformation of Legacy Platform to EXP

Figure 7-10 depicts a sample transformation journey of the legacy EXP for the case study organization.

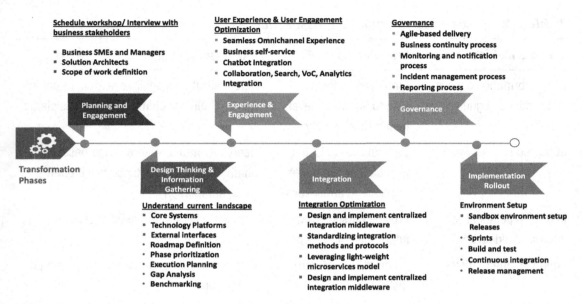

Figure 7-10. *Sample transformation phases*

The transformation journey for the case study consists of the following transformation phases:

- **Planning and engagement**: You interview the stakeholders and employees to understand the scope and key goals of transformation.

- **Design thinking and information gathering**: As part of this phase, you do as-is analysis, benchmarking, and pain-point analysis. Once you understand the key requirements, you identify and prioritize the phases and do the execution planning.

- **Experience and engagement**: As part of this phase, you define the experience and engagement elements such as UI design, self-service, chat bot, collaboration, and such.

- **Integration**: In this phase you identify the main integration ecosystem (such as centralized integration middleware) and design the integration methods (such as microservices and APIs).

196

- **Governance**: You define the main governance processes such as agile delivery, business continuity process (leveraging disaster recovery process), monitoring and notification process (including the system monitoring, real user monitoring), incident management process, and reporting process.

- **Implementation rollout**: Once you set up the environment, you roll out the sprint-based releases as per the planned rollout.

Summary

This chapter covered the following:

- The key design principles of an EXP for the case study are collaboration, employee engagement, process redesign, automation, experience redesign, and productivity improvement.

- The high-level steps in the employee journey mapping for the case study include employee workshops, design and research, and experience transformation.

- As part of user research for the case study, you get details such as user details (name, designation), goals/aims, responsibilities, needs/wants, day-to-day tasks and scenarios, and main challenges for the sample set of users.

- The key solution tenets for an employee experience platform for the case study are technology modernization, application modernization, migration, consolidation, and experience redesign.

- The maturity model of an EXP for the case study consists of the basic, integrated, optimized, and smart levels.

- The key EXP success metrics for the case study are easy information access and reduced cognitive load.

  - Improved self-service

  - Improved personalized information delivery

- Improved automation
- Productivity improvement
- Easier collaboration
- Decision-making tools

CHAPTER 8

Digital Transformation to Next-Generation Workplaces

I have discussed the main features and solution tenets of a next-generation digital workplace. I have also discussed the key challenges related to user experience, productivity, and integration with legacy intranet platforms. Many organizations embark upon the digital transformation journey to provide superior employee experiences in order to improve employee productivity and improve overall employee satisfaction. Reimagining and redesigning legacy intranet platforms is often done through a digital transformation exercise.

The digital transformation of legacy Intranet platforms is a multidimensional exercise involving various aspects such as technology modernization, process digitization, data and content migration, user experience redesign, and such.

In this chapter, I discuss the main digital transformation framework and scenarios for transforming legacy intranet systems into modern digital workplace platforms.

Legacy Modernization Overview

Organizations embark on a legacy modernization journey to scale the existing platform and develop a future-ready platform. Legacy modernization provides a competitive advantage to the organization by providing on-demand scalability, simplified processes, quicker turnaround time, reduced risk, a modular architecture, a standardized technology stack, improved quality, a 360-degree view of employees, and cost optimization. During legacy modernization, organizations can also implement productivity levers such as automation, a self-service model, gamification, agile delivery, and such. As part of legacy modernization, organizations can deliver the platform and services from the cloud.

© Shailesh Kumar Shivakumar 2020

S. K. Shivakumar, *Build a Next-Generation Digital Workplace*, https://doi.org/10.1007/978-1-4842-5512-4_8

The following are some of the key challenges in the legacy modernization journey of intranet platforms:

- The legacy intranet platforms that consist of multiple tools and technologies (no common platform) pose challenges in the modernization journey. Defining a standard technology stack and migrating legacy technologies are time-consuming tasks and carry a high risk.

- Without a proper migration approach (including appropriate migration tool, migration plan, target platform selection, and validation through pilot migration), legacy modernization carries a high risk of failure.

- Complex legacy applications, closed/monolithic architectures, and nonscalable application architectures pose challenges in modernization.

- Legacy platforms that have point-to-point/direct integration need a high degree of redesign effort during migration. Minimal readiness for services-based integration also requires a high migration effort.

- Legacy systems usually have distributed data across various systems, and there is no single source of truth or system of record for data. Additionally, factors such as data redundancy, data duplication, and data integrity issues impact data migration.

- A lack of well-defined governance processes for content authoring/publishing flows and platform maintenance processes increases the maintenance effort.

- An absence of a metadata strategy (minimal usage of tags/metadata) impacts information discovery and search quality.

- Other key challenges include a resistance to change, culture issues, lack of proper governance and a change management process, lack of proper documentation of business rules, and an inability to get real-time insights.

Goals of Legacy Modernization

Organizations embark on a legacy modernization journey to achieve the following goals:

- Use modern digital technologies to provide an immersive experience to employees.

- Scale and improve performance, modularity, and reusability of existing systems.

- Enable multi-speed IT (where systems of engagement change faster than systems of record) and provide sustainable and flexible architecture.

- Roll out features such as interactivity, personalization, real-time insights, targeted content, self-service, automation, productivity improvements, advanced analytics, and such.

- Increase operational efficiency using automation.

- Provide flexibility and extensibility to onboard future innovations.

- Reduce turnaround times and time to market.

- Optimize and maximize legacy technology investments to be ready for the future.

- Stay competitive, relevant, and be future-ready against digital disruptors.

- Monetize existing services and data using digital as a core enabler to drive revenue.

- Identify transformation opportunities and quick wins.

The next section defines a legacy modernization framework to transform a traditional intranet platform to a next-generation digital workplace.

Legacy Modernization Framework

In this section, I define the legacy modernization framework to modernize a legacy intranet platform. The framework acts as a reference for legacy transformation and covers various aspects of the modernization journey. As legacy modernization is a complex transformation process, I cover various aspects of legacy modernization through three dimensions.

- **Legacy modernization process**: I define the main steps in the modernization process. In this section, I cover the main process stages and the activities in each of the process stages.

- **Digital transformation blueprint**: I define the transformation principles, operations transformation, infrastructure transformation, and security transformation in this dimension.

- **Transformation deep-dive**: I provide details of the transformation related to experience transformation, process transformation, operations transformation, and data transformation.

Legacy Modernization Process

The legacy modernization process defines the core transformation stages and the activities in each stage. The key steps to modernizing legacy Intranet platforms are depicted in Figure 8-1.

- **Digital strategy definition**: In this stage, you define the overall vision for the digital program. You lay out the key business goals, success metrics and KPIs, and main drivers for the transformation. You define the digital transformation blueprint (discussed in the next section) that shows up in various elements of the transformation. Based on the business drivers, you also define the transformation goals and strategy for automation, productivity improvement, and self-service.

- **Maturity assessment and benchmarking**: You assess the current ecosystem, processes, and tools/technologies in this stage. Through stakeholder interviews and focused group discussions you understand the challenges, gaps, and pain points of the current system. You also assess the scope for automation (such as process automation, operations automation, and such), productivity improvement (through decision-aiding tools, enhanced workflows, and such), and self-service (such as business self-service, auto-approval forms). You also benchmark the key areas (such as user experience, information architecture, performance) against industry-leading platforms. At the end of this stage, you arrive at an overall assessment scorecard that can be used in the later stages for defining the transformation approach.

- **Modernization**: In this stage you define the future state of the architecture and detail the approach for experience transformation, process transformation, data transformation, and operations transformation (detailed in later sections). You also identify the product and solution components needed for the transformation. You detail the migration plan and do a pilot migration to validate the migration approach.

- **Rollout**: During this stage, you identify the business impact of each of the transformation items identified using the prioritization matrix. The priorities are used for defining the overall release plan. Once the releases, milestones, and iterations are identified, the execution team builds, validates, and releases in iterations. Continuous integration (CI) and continuous deployment (CD) principles will be adopted for the releases. CI enables a smarter, cheaper, faster, nimbler, and better service rollout. Based on the feedback from end users, you continuously improve the metrics in subsequent iterations.

	Cloud Migration Analysis	Cloud Migration Design	Cloud Migration	Cloud Operations & Maintenance
Activities	• Cloud readiness assessment • Business drivers • Cloud platform selection • Regulatory compliance analysis • Target cloud platform selection • Application & data consolidation analysis • Infrastructure consolidation analysis • Roadmap definition	• Cloud fitment analysis • Application migration design • Services design • Data/Content migration design • Security migration design • Infrastructure migration design • DevOps design • Migration approach • Backup & DR	• Cloud environment setup • Cloud data center design • Application re-design/rewrite • Code refactoring • Data migration • Application migration • Infrastructure migration • Security migration • Integration migration • Migration scripts	• Cloud governance • SLA monitoring and reporting • Optimization & automation
Best Practices	• Creation of single source of truth • Consolidate applications and services	• Remain, retire, rewrite, refactor, re-architect, migrate • Release management automation	• Proper cloud sizing • Serverless functions • Container based micro services • Automation • Backup and DR setup • Migration verification	• CloudOps • CI/CD setup • SLA based alerts and monitoring • Performance monitoring • Availability monitoring • Metering • Fine-tune cloud environment for cost optimization

Figure 8-1. *Legacy intranet modernization steps*

Digital Transformation Blueprint

A *transformation blueprint* provides the reference point for the entire transformation process by defining the core transformation principles and key transformation elements. A transformational blueprint is developed during the digital strategy definition stage.

Figure 8-2 depicts a sample digital transformation blueprint with various transformation elements. The blueprint defines the transformation principles and three transformation elements (operations, infrastructure, and security). Based on the business goals and program vision, the transformation elements need to be identified.

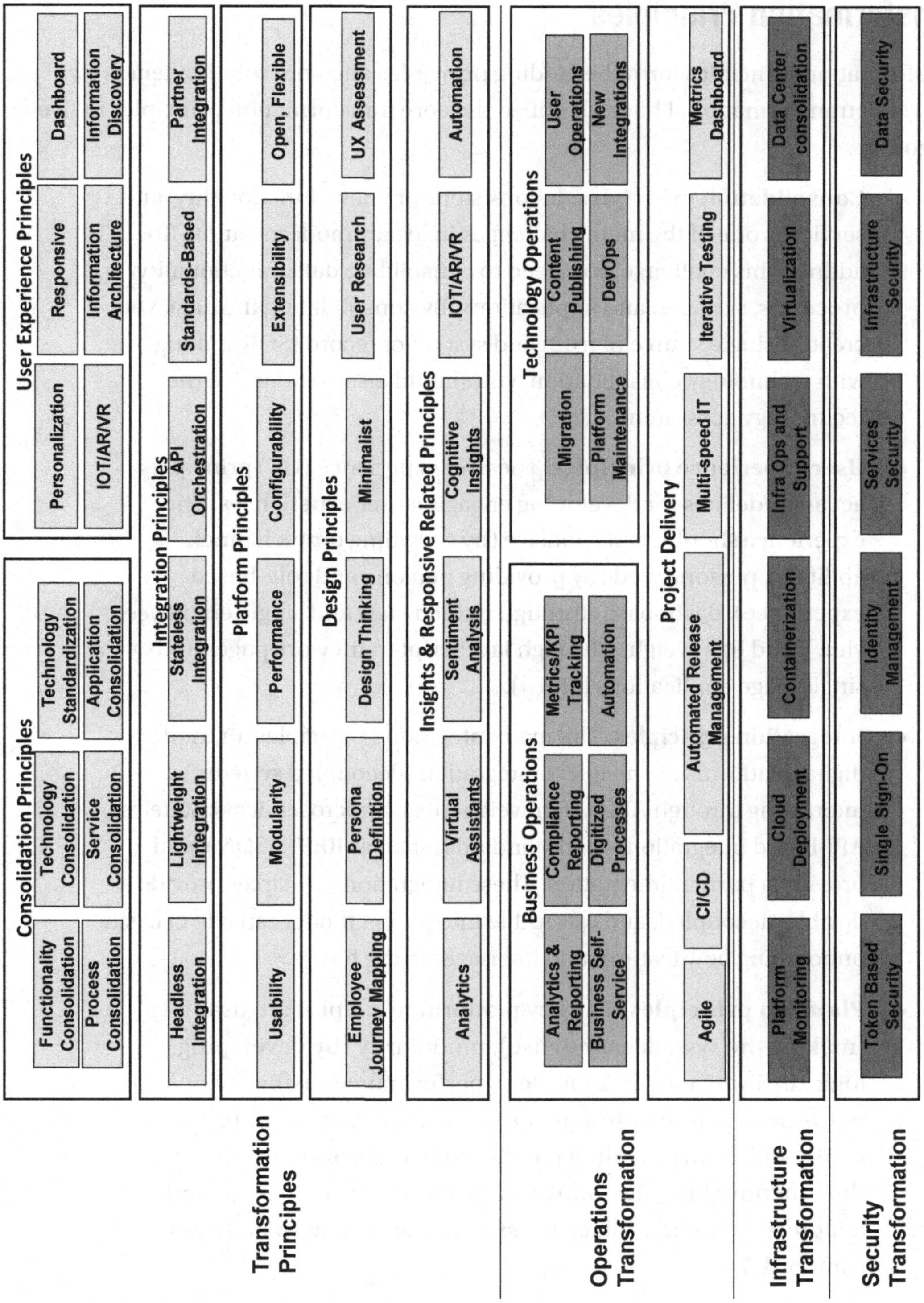

Figure 8-2. Sample digital transformation blueprint

Transformation Principles

Transformation principles form the guiding principles and core solution tenets for the overall transformation. I have identified the core transformation principles in five categories.

- **Consolidation principles**: Inconsistency in data, functionality, and service is one of the main challenges in legacy modernization. To address this challenge, you need to consolidate data, functionality, processes, services, and applications. By consolidating the data, you create a single source of truth and system of record (SOR). Along with technology consolidation, you should also standardize the technology ecosystem.

- **User experience principles**: The user experience (UX) principles act as guidelines for developing engaging user experiences. The experience should be responsive (by providing omnichannel abilities), personalized (by providing persona and role-based experience), dashboard (through unified view and single employee view), and lightweight (through JavaScript framework pages and single-page applications [SPAs]).

- **Integration principles**: The main integration principles for modern digital platforms are headless integration (decoupled systems interacting through APIs), lightweight (using microservices), stateless, API-based integration, open standards (such as REST, JSON), and providing partner integration. These integration principles provide a flexible, decoupled, and extensible integration model capable of easily onboarding new features and interfaces in the future.

- **Platform principles**: The key platform principles are usability (making the system easy to use), modularity (by developing logically independent modules), performance (using performance-based design and iterative performance testing), configurability (providing configurable controls to extend/modify the functionality), flexibility/extensibility (through pluggable adapters and marketplace ecosystem), and open (using open standards).

- **Design principles**: The main UX design principles are employee journey mapping (mapping employee's journey steps), persona definition (identifying user groups that share common characteristics), simple and minimalist design (providing minimal features on key pages), user research, and UX assessment. I have detailed journey mapping, persona definition, and user research in Chapter 2 and Chapter 3.

Operations Transformation

Operations is one of the key focus areas for businesses. A digital program vision and business goals help to identify the transformation elements. The following are the main operational elements:

- **Business operations**: Providing prescriptive analytics and preventive analytics on a regular basis helps organizations to minimize the maintenance costs. A modern digital platform should also provide compliance reporting on a regular basis to help organizations comply with legal regulations and business compliance needs. Business self-service features (such as web-based configurations, self-service portals) minimize IT involvement, thereby reducing the cost and turnaround times. During the assessment phase, you can identify automation and digitization opportunities for business processes. The monitoring and reporting feature should regularly monitor the platform based on defined metrics/KPIs and should provide reports to business stakeholders.

- **Technology operations**: Regular technical operations include platform maintenance (such as patching, upgrading, system configuration, and such), content publishing operations (such as translation, publishing to various formats, and such), user operations (such as user provisioning, access controls, and such), migration (data migration, content migration, user migration), DevOps (for deployment and release management), and new integrations (such as third-party integrations). The platform should provide easy-to-use configuration controls to automate and support the technology operations.

- **Project delivery**: To support quick turnaround times and faster time to market, the project delivery framework should incorporate the agile methodology (using shorter sprints for releases), minimum viable product (MVP) iterations, continuous integration and continuous deployment (regular and iterative integration, testing and deployment) for automated releases, and multispeed IT (a process that enables quicker change management between systems of record and modern digital platforms). As part of delivery, you should also provide a dashboard view of code quality, delivery SLAs, build status, and such.

Infrastructure Transformation

Transformation of infrastructure is needed to support enterprise agility, responsiveness, flexibility, and cost optimization. The primary elements of infrastructure transformation are monitoring the setup (to monitor the availability and performance of systems in real time), cloud deployment (leveraging cloud platforms for infrastructure, services, and platform needs), containerization (deploying application and services in containers for increased scalability and failover), InfraOps and support, virtualization (virtualizing OS and hardware), and data center consolidation. I discuss an automated maintenance and machine-led operations model in Chapter 11.

Security Transformation

A complex enterprise ecosystem needs robust security. The key security-related transformation elements are token-based security (through the exchange of access tokens with microservices), single sign-on (SSO) with all enterprise systems, robust identity management (authentication and authorization), services and application security (through application firewalls), infrastructure security (through access controls, server hardening, and such), and data security (through fine-grained data access controls). I will discuss the EXP security details in Chapter 10.

Transformation Deep Dive

You learned about the core transformation principles and key transformation elements in the transformation blueprint. In this section, I will elaborate on the most essential transformation elements such as experience transformation, process transformation, operations transformation, and data transformation, as depicted in Figure 8-3. For each of the transformations, I define the key components and the transformation methods used.

	Key Components	Transformation Tools/Methods
Experience Transformation Providing interactive, responsive, and engaging user experience	• Mobile-first experience • Employee engagement • User first approach • Analytics based insights • Personalized experience • Integrated omnichannel • Data visualizations • Information discovery • Collaboration • Information architecture • Productivity improvement	• Persona-based design • User journey mapping • Minimalistic user interface • SEO & web analytics • Conversational service • Cognitive search • Virtual assistants • Responsive design • Voice search • Immersive AR/VR self-service • Chatbots • Design thinking • Targeting & segmentation • Dashboard/Single employee view
Business Process Transformation Digitizing and optimizing processes	• Optimized business processes • Process transformation • Analytics driven actions • Gamification • Real time insights • Legal & regulatory compliance	• Process digitization • Process automation • Process standardization • Predictive analytics • Process gap analysis • Retire, redesign, refactor legacy processes • API-based integration • Performance based design • Lean processes • Robotic process automation (RPA)
Operations Transformation Digitizing and automating operations	• Cloud migration • DevOps implementation • Technology standardization • Agile release management • Productivity improvement tools • Autonomous computing	• User/Content/Infrastructure migration • Agile delivery • Cloud-first approach • DevOps pipeline implementation • IoT enablement • Self managing • Self optimizing • Continuous availability • Fault tolerant & fail fast • Self monitoring & self configuring • Self healing • Cloud fitment analysis • Maintenance automation • Multi-tenancy model
Data Transformation Data migration, cleansing, and data de-duplication	• Data assessment • Data flow assessment • Data migration • Data consolidation	• Automated migration • Migration validation • Retire, reuse, modify/cleanse data • Data de-duplication • Data sanitization • Centralized system or record

Figure 8-3. Key components and tools for transformation

We will look at each of the four transformation elements in the coming sections.

Experience Transformation

Transforming a user experience is a vital part of all transformation journeys. Experience transformation aims to provide an interactive, responsive, and engaging user experience to the user.

The key components of the experience transformation are as follows:

- **Mobile-first experience**: Design and test the user experience primarily on mobile devices. Provide mobile apps for the core platform features (such as dashboards, chat bots, and such). Effective usage of iconography provides a consistent experience across all channels.

- **Employee engagement**: You can actively engage employees through chat bots, virtual assistants, voice search, immersive AR/VR, and conversational services. Active engagement is one of the key levers for improving employee satisfaction and productivity. Conversational interfaces (such as chat bot, voice search) can be used for various engagement activities such as employee onboarding, personalized learning, employee assistance, incident management, scheduling meetings, personalized recommendations, and such.

- **User-first approach**: The design, information architecture, and navigation should be user-centric. You can achieve this by persona-based design and user journey mapping.

- **Analytics-based insights**: You can leverage analytics tools such as web analytics, search analytics, and social analytics to gain insights into an employee's goals, needs, and satisfaction. The insights can be used to fine-tune the functionality and user experience.

- **Personalized user experience**: The platform should provide personalized (based on role, user segments, user profile attributes) content, services, tools, and information. User segmentation and targeted information delivery can be used to personalize the user experience.

- **Integrated omnichannel experience**: The platform should provide seamless and integrated omnichannel experience through responsive design and mobile apps. Dashboards and single views can be used to provide an integrated user experience.

- **Data visualizations**: UI elements such as charts, graphs, and process flow steps visually convey the information quickly to the end users.

- **Information discovery**: Through the usage of enterprise search, metadata, and taxonomy, you can provide quicker and relevant information. Cognitive search can be used to provide intent-based search results.

- **Collaboration**: Tools such as chats/messengers, forums, groups, virtual conferences, shared calendar, and communities can be used for collaboration among employees to improve productivity and information sharing.

- **Information architecture**: Minimalistic design and persona-based design can be used to develop intuitive information architecture (with elements such as site hierarchy, navigation flow, menus, breadcrumb, and such).

- **Productivity improvement**: Decision-aided tools, automated workflows, intuitive information architecture, and analytics all play vital roles in improving productivity.

Business Process Transformation

Transforming existing business processes to make it more efficient is an important aspect of digital transformation. The key elements of business process transformation are as follows:

- **Optimized business processes**: Business processes can be optimized through process digitization and process automation. Existing business processes will be analyzed, and you can identify ways to automate the process steps to improve the overall process completion time. Performance-based design and robotic process automation (RPA) can be leveraged to optimize the processes.

- **Process transformation**: Transforming manual processes into digital processes, simplifying the process steps, and automating the process steps are part of the process transformation. For instance, multipage registration process can be transformed into a one-click registration by eliminating unnecessary form fields. You can evaluate existing business processes to understand and categorize the business processes into retire, redesign, or refactor.

- **Analytics-driven action**: Leveraging predictive analytics, organizations can make proactive and informed decisions. For instance, an employee churn prediction model can predict the likeliness of an employee quitting the organization so that the organization can take proactive measures.

- **Gamification**: Leveraging the gaming concepts such as points, levels, badges, and ranks can be used to create incentives for employees to keep them engaged and motivated. For instance, the platform can provide badges based on the level of employee contribution to the knowledge base, and employees with the highest level of badges can be rewarded with shopping points.

- **Real-time insights**: Data processing and analytics can be leveraged to get real-time insights. For instance, the site exit reasons and the performance degradation reasons can be obtained through real-time insights.

- **Legal and regulatory compliance**: The business processes should be redesigned to comply with the applicable legal and regulatory rules.

Operations Transformation

In this category I include business and technical operations that are ongoing to maintain the platform. Operations transformation optimizes the maintenance cost and improves the release time. The following are the main components of operations transformation:

- **Cloud migration**: Migrating from on-premise infrastructure to the cloud provides greater control over the cost and service quality (scalability, performance, availability, and such). As this is a crucial transformation topic, I have elaborated on this in the next section. We need to assess the cloud readiness of the existing ecosystem and deploy the solution components to the cloud. As part of cloud migration, we need to migrate data, content, services, and infrastructure to the cloud platform.

- **DevOps implementation**: Designing an optimal DevOps pipeline to automate the build and release management activities reduces the overall release time. DevOps automates various release management activities such as build, testing, deployment, reporting, notification, and such.

- **Technology standardization**: Standardizing the technology stack makes it easy to extend and integrate with external interfaces. A platform built on standard components also reduces the overall maintenance effort and license costs.

- **Agile release management**: For the project delivery, you need to adopt agile delivery based on four- to six-week sprints. This helps in iterative development and faster time to market.

- **Productivity improvement tools**: Tools and services such as business self-service, administration user interfaces, automated scripts for patching, and upgrades all reduce the overall operation costs.

- **Autonomous computing**: The platform should support autonomous computing to optimize maintenance costs. The key attributes of autonomous computing are continuous availability (continuous and maximum availability of business-critical services), containerization (using features such as containers and rolling updates), fault tolerance and fail fast (using components such as circuit breaker), self-monitoring and self-healing (through methods such as auto restarts), and self-optimizing and self-managing (through smart resource management).

Data Transformation

Data transformation is needed to support system consolidation and to get real-time data-based insights. The following are the core components of data transformation:

- **Data assessment**: Perform a data assessment to identify the issues with data such as data duplication, data redundancy, and date integrity issues. Classify the data into retire (don't migrate), reuse (migrate), or modify (cleanse/modify before migration) that helps in data migration. Data assessment also maps source data to target data, document data-related business rules, deals with data ingestion systems, and identify data dependencies.

- **Data flow assessment**: Analyze the data flow across various systems to identify the opportunities for optimization. For instance, a batch data load can be converted into on-demand or event-based data load to improve the data freshness.

- **Data consolidation**: Consolidate various data sources into a centralized repository to create a single source of truth/system of record.

- **Data migration**: Once the data assessment is done, perform data de-duplication and data sanitization, and develop automated migration scripts for data migration. Migration scripts can use the data mapping information to convert/transform the source data to the target format wherever needed. Conduct migration validation to ensure the completeness and integrity of data migration.

Cloud Migration

The cloud is the preferred hosting and delivery platform for organizations. Cloud platforms offer opportunities for cost optimizations, on-demand scalability, and high availability with reduced infrastructure costs. Cloud-based technologies bring speed and agility to organizations and optimize the infrastructure cost. The key business drivers for cloud migration are cost optimization, quicker time to market, application scalability, and continuous availability.

Key Success Factors for Cloud Migration

These are the key success factors for cloud migration:

- **Assessment**: Perform a cloud assessment for the employee application to analyze the cloud fit for legacy applications. The applications that cannot be migrated as-is need to be identified for architecture redesign.

- **Virtualization**: For the organizations with virtualized environments (OS, network, and such), cloud migration will be the logical next step.

- **Technology standardization**: The technology ecosystem across various enterprise applications (such as security providers, integration technologies, database, and such) should be standardized to enable easier cloud migration.

- **Data and service consolidation**: The data, content, and assets should be consolidated into a centralized "system of records" to avoid data integrity issues.

- **Containerization**: Deploying microservices in cloud-based containers optimizes the development and testing cycles. Containers also provide on-demand and elastic scalability to handle high loads.

- **Monitoring and notification setup**: Set up robust monitoring for server health checks (such as CPU utilization, memory utilization, disk utilization, and such), real-time alerts for SLAs (such as performance SLA, availability SLA), and error reporting (real-time reports on HTTP response codes such as 404, 500, 502, and such from error logs).

- **Legal and regulatory compliance**: As part of cloud migration, you need to ensure that you are in compliance with all applicable legal and regulatory requirements. Regulatory compliance includes topics such as data localization requirements, GDPR requirements, accessibility requirements, data retention policies, and data anonymization policies. Based on the application domain, you also need to test for compliance with industry-specific standards (such a PCI standard compliance for financial industry, HIPAA standard compliance for insurance industry, GDPR standards, and such). Additionally, business requirements dictate other requirements such as disaster recovery requirements, reporting requirements, and so on.

- **DevOps setup**: Deployment and release management activities such as code build, testing, code reviews, cloud deployment, and others should be automated as part of the DevOps setup.

Steps for Cloud Migration

Figure 8-4 shows the main steps for cloud migration.

Digital Strategy Definition	Maturity Assessment & Benchmarking	Modernization	Rollout
• Vision for the digital program • Defining success KPIs and metrics. • Digital transformation blueprint • Automation strategy • Productivity improvement strategy • Self service strategy • Program governance	• Stakeholder interviews • Focus group discussions • Automation scope assessment • Productivity improvement assessment • Self-service assessment • Application portfolio assessment • Competitive benchmarking • Assessment scorecard • Gap assessment	• Future state architecture definition • Solution component mapping • Approach for experience transformation, process transformation, data and operations transformation • Migration approach definition • Pilot migration	• Prioritize tracks based on cost and impact • Prioritization matrix • Build, testing and release • Iterative releases • Continuous integration (CI) & continuous deployment (CD) • Continuous improvement

Figure 8-4. *Cloud migration steps*

Cloud Migration Analysis

The activities for cloud migration analysis are as follows:

- **Cloud readiness assessment**: You need to assess the readiness of the existing technology ecosystem and perform an application audit for cloud deployment. As part of this, you need to assess the cloud compatibility of enterprise application technologies, integration technologies, and systems of records (such as the database, ERP, and CRM). You can use the assessment to define the cloud migration path (retire, rewrite, migrate) during the design stage.

- **Regulatory compliance analysis**: You need to analyze all the applicable regulatory and compliance requirements for the applications selected for cloud migration. I discussed the categories of regulatory compliance in the previous section.

- **Target cloud platform selection**: Based on the business requirements (security, integration, performance, scalability, availability, and such), you need to select the target cloud platform; choose public cloud, private cloud, or hybrid cloud. The following are the common rules of thumb for selecting a public cloud, private cloud, or hybrid cloud:

  a. **Public cloud**: You can choose this option if the application is fully cloud compatible or if you need to develop a cloud-native application as part of ground-up development. If the enterprise wants to fully enable a SaaS model in such scenarios, you can go for a public cloud.

  b. **Private cloud/hybrid cloud**: If the application has stricter regulatory/security and compliance requirements or if it needs specialized hardware, then you can choose a private cloud. The private cloud can also be used to satisfy any critical security or business requirement related to data.

- **Application and data consolidation analysis**: In a typical enterprise scenario consisting of multiple applications and data sources, you need to identify the opportunities to consolidate application and data. You need to identity the applications and services that are duplicate or that have overlapping features; these can be consolidated into a single application. You can create a centralized data source consolidating all databases that form a system of record.

- **Infrastructure consolidation analysis**: You can identify the infrastructure components that can be replaced in a cloud scenario. This includes server hardware, virtual software, network systems, and such.

- **Road map definition**: You can define the cloud migration road map to identify various technology components for cloud migration. You also define the migration priorities and timelines for cloud migration.

Cloud Migration Design

As part of the cloud migration design, you need to use the insights from the application audit done in the previous stage to define the appropriate migration path. The key design aspects involve the following:

- **Application migration design**: Current applications can be categorized into four main categories: remain (stays on premise), retire (de-commission/sunset the application), rewrite (redesign the application architecture/technology to be hosted on the cloud for cloud-incompatible applications), and migrate (migrate the existing application to the cloud for cloud-compatible applications).

- **Services design**: One of the best practices for cloud migration is to use containerized microservices. Microservices are a logical unit of functionality providing a nonmonolithic design and can be easily plugged into the DevOps pipeline for a quicker time to market. Hence, as part of services design, you can identify enterprise services that need to be redesigned into microservices. The core attributes of microservices are statelessness, token-based security, modularity, independent scalability, and logical independence. Containerized microservices provide resiliency, elastic scalability (x-axis and y-axis scalability), failover features, and flexibility (such as easy-to-add new interfaces and channels).

- **Data/content migration design**: Existing enterprise data and content used by the application needs to be identified for the migration. A general best practice is to consolidate data and content into a system of record if not done already. In some cases, the existing systems of record stay within enterprise data centers; in such scenarios, applications hosted on the cloud should connect to enterprise applications.

- **Security migration design**: There are three main options for security migration: the new platform can use the cloud-hosted security providers (such as cloud-based Active Directory instances), the new platform can connect to the on-premise security providers, or the on-premise security providers can be migrated to the cloud. You need

to evaluate each of these options on a case-by-case basis. For new
applications, it is best to leverage the cloud-native security providers;
for existing applications, you can migrate the user and profile
information to the cloud, but if there are strict business or regulatory
issues, then you can connect to on-premise security providers
through VPN.

- **DevOps design**: As part of cloud-based DevOps, you need to rewrite
  the DevOps pipeline scripts to enable cloud deployment. The release
  management scripts should be changed to deploy the application
  and services to the cloud ecosystem.

Cloud Migration

During this phase you perform the actual cloud migration. As a first step, you set up
the cloud environment (primary region and DR region) and develop migration scripts.
Based on the outcome of the design phase, you redesign, rewrite, or migrate the
existing application to the cloud platform. As part of application redesign, you would
do code refactoring to make it suitable for the cloud platform. Migration scripts will
be executed iteratively to migrate the application code, content, and data to the cloud
platform.

On-premise security components such as authentication providers, user
repositories, and such will also be migrated to the cloud if the application cannot use the
cloud-native security providers.

A Docker/Kubernetes-based container ecosystem is the preferred option for
deploying microservices on the cloud platform. Existing services should be migrated to
the microservices architecture for enhanced scalability.

Once the migration scripts are fully developed and tested, they can be automated
so that the migration process can be executed either in a big-bang, one-time migration
mode or in an incremental migration mode.

Cloud Operations (CloudOps) and Governance

During this phase, the cloud governance processes are set up by defining the standard
operating procedures (such as deployment process, cloud subscription management
process, and such) for a cloud-based solution.

You should set up alerts that monitor the application and services in real time and notify the system administrators if the application metrics breach the configured thresholds. You can set up alerts for performance monitoring, logging, availability monitoring, cloud metrics monitoring, and such.

CloudOps also includes configurations related to security, metrics, metering, deployment, and backup and management features such as images, containers, encryption, and such.

Cloud governance includes security, data, financial management, compliance, cloud brokerage, supplier management, and such.

Sample Cloud Deployment Architecture

I have provided a sample cloud deployment architecture highlighting the core components used for an EXP. I provide the deployment architecture for two popular cloud platforms in this section.

Note   This example of a cloud platform and its components is for education purposes only. The EXP solution architecture should be cloud agnostic so that it can be deployed to any cloud platform.

Amazon Web Services (AWS) Deployment Architecture

Figure 8-5 shows an AWS-based deployment architecture. I have depicted the secondary region as a disaster recovery (DR) region.

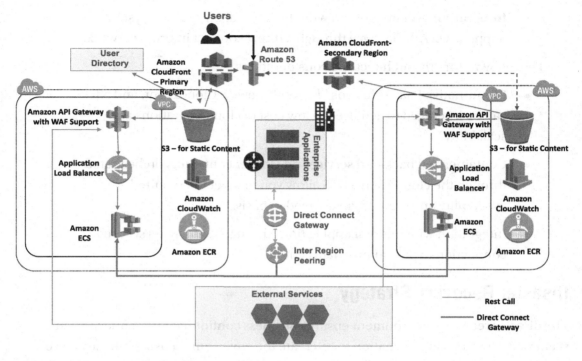

Figure 8-5. *AWS deployment architecture*

The main components in an AWS-based deployment architecture are as follows:

- **CloudFront CDN**: The CloudFront-native CDN allows you to effectively deliver the content for the consumer from different geographies.

- **Application modules**: ReactJS/Angular-based application modules can be deployed on an S3 bucket, which is integrated with AWS CloudFront. The front end is secured with Web Application Firewall (WAF). Deploying front-end static content on S3 makes it highly scalable and cost effective.

- **Custom services layer**: Back-end services that are developed using NodeJS or Spring Boot microservices can be deployed on containers using the AWS cloud-native container orchestration services, called EKS. These services are accessed through AWS API Gateway. Services that are built on NodeJS will be integrated with external services for content consumption.

- **Integration**: API integration with the internal on-premise systems happens via API Gateway through a direct connect internal network.

The following are the architectural considerations:

- Cloud-native PaaS solutions like API Gateway, CloudFront, and S3 can be leveraged to achieve the low cost of cloud operations and scalability.

- Containerized back-end services on Docker containers orchestrated through the cloud-native ECS allow you to meet the required availability and scale on an as-needed basis.

- Integration with internal applications through high-speed secured connection to on-premise data center.

Disaster Recovery Strategy

The disaster recovery environment ensures business continuity during unexpected scenarios. You can use automation to re-create the environment using infrastructure as code during the disaster scenario. I outline the core steps of disaster recovery in this section.

Preparation Phase

As preparation for a disaster situation, you need to create a one-click automation script to provision the DevOps pipeline. Here are the steps:

1. The cloud environment will be scripted using ARM templates, and the code will be checked into the code repository.

2. A DevOps pipeline needs to be created, which will pull the IaC templates from the code repository and will be able to create the environment in the secondary region.

3. A separate DevOps pipeline will deploy the application code to web app services and the back-end code to app services.

Recovery Phase

During a disaster scenario, the following steps will be executed:

1. Re-create the environment using the DevOps pipeline in the secondary region.

2. Deploy the latest code to the secondary environment using a DevOps pipeline.

3. Reconfigure the Traffic Manager endpoints to point to the secondary region.

Azure-Based Deployment Architecture

Figure 8-6 shows the Microsoft Azure–based deployment architecture.

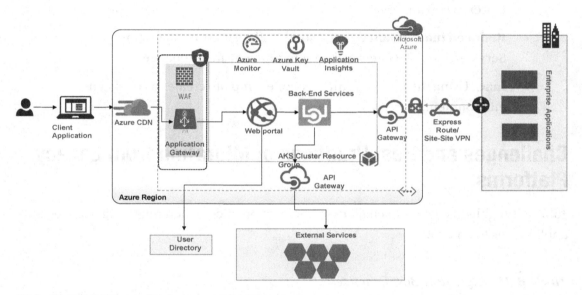

Figure 8-6. *Azure deployment architecture*

The core solution components of Azure-based services are as follows:

- **Azure CDN**: Azure CDN allows you to effectively deliver the content to the users from different geographies. Azure CDN delivers the content faster and closer to consumer regions.

- **Web App Services**: The application framework will be deployed on Azure Web App Services, front ended by an application gateway with a WAF security layer.

- **API App Services**: The application framework custom back-end services will be deployed on API App Services, which are fully managed Azure-native PaaS offerings.

- **Integration**: External services are consumed through API Gateway. On-premise applications are integrated to the cloud through Express route and communication goes through API Gateway.

The following are architecture considerations for Azure:

- **Highly scalable infrastructure**: Being purely PaaS offerings from Azure, it provides on-demand scaling.

- **Highly performance**: The CDN allows you to deliver the content closer to consumers.

- **Reduced maintenance cost**: Cloud-native solutions like App Services and API Gateway do not require any maintenance.

- **IaaC**: Using the infrastructure-as-code template creates a consistent environment.

Challenges and Best Practices of Migrating from Legacy Platforms

Table 8-1 highlights the main challenges and best practices when migrating from legacy applications to an EXP.

Table 8-1. *Migration Best Practices*

Problem Pattern	Best Practices
Distributed data sources, absence of centralized data source	Provide a single set of standardized data sources, canonical data model, standardized integration, and access through services. This avoids disparate, inconsistent (project-centric), and duplicated data with access only through prebuilt interfaces/reports.
Nonstandardized technology stack	• Select appropriate products that are best fits for the long-term business goals; central cloud-based services that contain business logic and aggregate multiple information types in an unified view. • Consolidate and standardize the technology stack.

(*continued*)

Table 8-1. (*continued*)

Problem Pattern	Best Practices
Lack of governance, absence of standard operating procedure (SOP)	• Consistency and standards ingrained across the streams such as automation, DevOps, and governance. Incorporate automation, DevOps principles, and governance as the core solution tenets of the platform/process; environments are tuned to the delivery cycles. • Define SOP for the core EXP maintenance activities such as monitoring and SLA management.
Data issues such as missing metadata, incorrect security	• Create a metadata hierarchy and associate it with data. • Create a metadata taxonomy.

Summary

This chapter covered the following:

- Legacy modernization provides a competitive advantage to the organizations by providing on-demand scalability, simplified processes, better execution speed, risk mitigation, modular architecture, technology standardization, quality of service, 360-degree view of employees, and cost optimization.

- The common challenges with legacy migration are complexity, service readiness, data integrity issues, and governance issues.

- A legacy modernization framework consists of a legacy modernization process, digital transformation blueprint, and transformation deep dive.

- In a digital transformation blueprint, you define the transformation principles, operations transformation, infrastructure transformation, and security transformation in this dimension.

- In a transformation deep dive, you provide details of the transformation related to experience transformation, process transformation, operations transformation, and data transformation.

- The legacy modernization process consists of a digital strategy definition, maturity assessment and benchmarking, modernization, and rollout.

- A transformation blueprint provides the reference point for the entire transformation process by defining the core transformation principles and key transformation elements.

- The transformation blueprint consists of transformation principles, operations transformation, infrastructure transformation, and security transformation.

- The key business drivers for cloud migration are cost optimization, quicker time to market, application scalability, and continuous availability.

- The main steps in cloud migration are cloud migration analysis, cloud migration design, cloud migration and cloud operations, and governance.

CHAPTER 9

EXP Collaboration

Employees actively collaborate for many of their daily activities. Collaboration plays a key role in improving productivity and increasing employee engagement. Figure 9-1 shows the key impacts of employee collaboration. An effective collaboration strategy should incorporate features to address these areas.

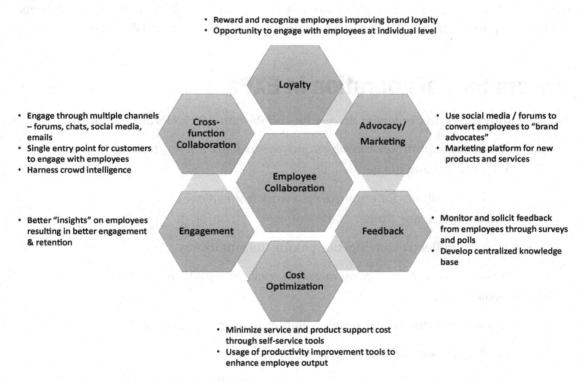

Figure 9-1. *Impact of collaboration*

Employee collaboration should recognize and reward loyal employees based on their contribution to collaborative initiatives; for instance, an employee who makes the highest contribution to the knowledge base can be rewarded with badges or loyalty

227

© Shailesh Kumar Shivakumar 2020
S. K. Shivakumar, *Build a Next-Generation Digital Workplace*, https://doi.org/10.1007/978-1-4842-5512-4_9

points. Internal and external social media channels can also be leveraged for marketing initiatives and can turn employees into brand advocates; for instance, the HR team can blog about a newly launched organization policy and request employees to rate it. Surveys and polls are effective tools to understand the employee pulse about various employee-related initiatives and organization policies. Self-service and productivity improvement tools in the collaboration platform play a vital role in the overall cost optimization. The insights gathered from polls, surveys, and analytics can be used to provide effective engagement to the employees.

The primary purpose of a collaboration platform is to provide cross-functional collaboration (provide channels to share information among people belonging to various groups, units, departments, and geographies). Cross-functional collaboration is achieved through collaborative tools such as forums, blogs, wiki, communities, chat bots, e-mail, and such. The content created by collaborative tools such as wikis and blogs are managed in a centralized content repository for easier search and discovery.

Drivers for Collaboration in EXPs

The key motivations and business drivers for collaboration in EXPs are as follows:

- Enable collaboration among employees to share and exchange information and ideas

- Provide flexibility for employees to work from anywhere and collaborate at any time

- Harness collective intelligence among the employees

- Enable co-creation of content and services to rapidly develop and deploy services

- Improve productivity through collaborative tools and services

- Enable self-service among employees

- Provide a centralized knowledge base for sharing information

- Empower employees with relevant search (such as content search and people search)

- Provide personalized and contextual information to employees in a unified view

Challenges for Collaboration in EXPs

For a successful implementation of the collaboration strategy, you need to understand the common challenges and pain points of collaboration. This helps you to devise an effective collaborative strategy.

The following are the main challenges in a typical enterprise collaboration platform:

- **Challenges in cross-functional collaboration**: Existing collaboration platforms lack features to seamlessly collaborate with people and teams from different departments, units, or geographies.

- **Multiple collaboration tools and applications**: Legacy intranet platforms have numerous collaboration tools, providing a disjointed user experience and posing integration challenges.

- **Lack of team collaboration**: Culture differences and a lack of a collaborative ecosystem get in the way of successful collaboration. Each team has different metrics and policies, posing challenges in measuring the success of the collaboration.

- **Technology ecosystem**: In some scenarios, the tools, frameworks, technology, and infrastructure components used may not be mutually compatible. This poses challenges during integration and gets in the way of setting up a standard infrastructure.

- **Organization culture**: In a few scenarios, users will be hesitant to share and collaborate because of a lack of incentives or culture differences.

Collaboration Ecosystem

An enterprise collaborative ecosystem should address the business drivers and goals and should fill the gaps/challenges in the current system. In this section, I discuss the key collaborative features and technologies that are needed to build a robust collaborative ecosystem.

Core Collaborative Features

Any collaborative system needs to support the key features necessary for implementing an effective collaboration strategy. Figure 9-2 shows the main collaborative features.

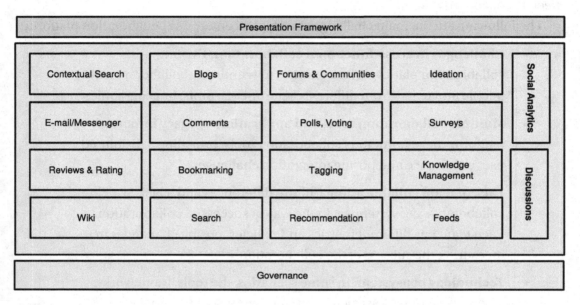

Figure 9-2. *Core collaborative features*

- **Blogs**: Personal blogs reflect a person's thoughts, opinions, point of view, or commentary about a topic of interest. Normally blogs are written in an informal style. Organizations can use blogs for various purposes such as the following:

  - Marketing team members can blog about newly launched products, services, features, or initiatives to create awareness and drive adoption.

  - Senior leaders can blog to discuss organization changes, organization vision, and insights on emerging market trends.

  - HR team members can blog about changes to organization policies and solicit feedback about HR policies.

  - Technical folks can blog about latest technology trends and the organization's adoption of them.

- Employees can also blog about their topics of interest.

- Health and wellness blogs, event-related blogs, and finance blogs are other categories of blogs that are useful to employees.

- **Wikis**: Employees can create wiki pages collaboratively to create content. Wikis are used for various purposes such as product documentation, troubleshooting guides, knowledge bases, and such.

- **Communities**: A group of like-minded people with common interests can come together to create communities. Communities provide features such as information sharing, messaging, shared calendars, event notifications, and such. Communities can be formed based on interest, skill sets, job responsibilities, project groups, organization initiatives, and such.

- **People search**: Employees use a people search feature to find colleagues based on the skill set or expertise. The people search should support following features:

  - Contact details of employees including photo, mobile number, e-mail, and such

  - Search based on skill sets and interests

  - Search based on areas of responsibility (system, business areas, and so on)

  - Search based on an employee's associations and committees

  - Search based on certifications and training

Proper governance processes should be designed to keep employee profile data information up-to-date. You should devise policies/assurances that prevent employees from sharing data in an organization with unauthorized people. The governance should also protect the sensitive private data from unauthorized access.

- **Shared calendar**: Employees can share their calendar with their colleagues so that others can view the appointments, schedule events, and share group plans. Shared calendars can be used for organizing a group event or a large meeting.

- **Polls and surveys**: Organizations can use polls and surveys to solicit feedback about matters such as organization policy, events, initiatives, and such. Polls and surveys provide vital insights into the pulse of employees. Many organizations conduct regular employee satisfaction surveys to gauge employees' job satisfaction levels.

- **Rating and review**: Employees can rate and review blogs, wiki pages, articles, forum posts, and such. The articles will ranked based on their rating value and accordingly shown in employee dashboards.

- **Recommendation**: EXPs can recommend the content and tools based on the explicit preferences and interests specified by employees.

- **Social share**: Employees can use the social share feature to share blog posts or knowledge articles through e-mail, feeds, and messages to their contacts.

- **Feeds**: Feeds are information streams about activities, news, policy updates, forum updates, and such. Generally, the employee dashboard has a feeds widget to provide the latest updates.

- **Social bookmarks**: Employees can bookmark their favorite pages using social bookmarking features. Employees can add, edit, share, and manage their bookmarks in a centralized location.

- **Idea hub**: Organizations use idea hubs to encourage employees to submit innovations and novel ideas that benefit the business based on their insights. An idea hub crowd-sources the idea generation activity. An idea hub fosters a culture of innovation by soliciting, storing, reviewing, and managing the ideas from all the employees, who can also vote for ranking the ideas. The idea hub can also collaboratively solve a complex problem.

- **Chat and instant messenger**: Employees can collaborate in real time through audio and video chat. Video chat and screen sharing tools are required for remote employees for virtual meetings and for other collaboration activities. Group chat is another popular collaborative tool used extensively in projects.

- **Knowledge management**: Employees can store, access, and manage content through a centralized knowledge management system. The knowledge management platform manages collaboration content, digital assets (images, videos, and other media files), and documents (such as Office documents) and provides a secured search feature.

- **Discussion forums**: Employees can discuss a topic through discussion forums that are also known as message boards. Generally, employees discuss the latest news, trending topics, or any organization updates.

- **Tags and metadata**: Employees can tag content with meaningful tags so that they can be easily searched and discovered. A well-defined metadata structure/taxonomy is necessary for efficient information discovery.

- **Groups**: Similar to communities, employees can form groups based on interest areas, job responsibilities, and skill sets. Groups help achieve more effective and quicker communication with all related people.

- **E-mail**: E-mails are the most popular tool for sending messages. Business e-mail serves as an official communication channel to relay information.

- **Document sharing**: Employees need to share and collaboratively edit documents such as project plans, status tracking documents, and such.

Key Collaborative Technologies

To implement the collaborative features mentioned earlier, you need corresponding technologies. The main collaborative technologies are as follows:

- **Instant messaging technology**: A next-generation collaboration tool set should provide consumer-grade real-time voice and video messenger systems. The technology is used for audio chat, video chat, file transfer, virtual conferencing, and other features.

- **Knowledge management system**: Centralized knowledge management acts as a repository for knowledge articles, documents, and other artifacts (such as blog posts, questions, best practices document, how-to documents, etc.). The artifacts in the knowledge management system should be appropriately tagged so that it is easy to discover the appropriate content.

- **Content management system**: Content management platforms are needed to design, develop, and publish content to various platforms. Content management systems manage collaboration content, web content, documents, and static assets (such as images, videos, and such).

- **Incident management**: An incident management system is needed to handle support incidents raised by employees. Normally an incident management system provides features for end-to-end incident management including incident logging, SLA management, incident workflow, status notification, feedback management, and such.

- **Search**: Enterprise search is needed to search across various information sources and help in information discovery. Search technology finds the relevant content from content management systems, web sites, database systems, systems of record (SOR) based on keyword, context, and other information.

- **Cloud**: Like EXPs, collaborative tools should be available on the cloud so that employees can use them from anywhere, anytime. You can leverage some of the popular enterprise tools such as Microsoft Teams, Slack, Microsoft SharePoint, Skype, Yammer, Google Hangouts, Fleep, Hive, Facebook Workplace, and Rocket.chat to implement the collaborative features.

Innovative Features of Collaboration Platform

The principal aim of a collaborative platform is to increase the user engagement. In this section, I cover some of the trending and innovative features of collaborative platforms.

- **Co-creation**: Use a collaboration platform to co-create the products and services with inputs and participation from all users.

- **Social innovation**: Use an idea hub and gamification features to obtain product and service ideas from employees.

- **Social marketing**: Encourage employees to blog about the products and services.

- **Communities**: Develop collaborative microsites based on themes and campaigns to better connect with employees, customers, and other shareholders. Engage and market the relevant products through interest-based microsites.

- **Collaborative sales**: Use a collaborative sales platform to share leads and opportunities among sales and partners.

- **Idea hub**: Employees can add ideas into a centralized idea repository. Organizations can develop the most popular promising idea for implementation.

- **Gamification**: To drive collaboration adoption, you can use game mechanics such as points, badges, and leader boards to engage and motivate employees to positively impact business goals and metrics. Gamification design encourages the employees, rewards their contribution, and provides a sense of achievement to the participants.

- **Automation**: Conversational tools such as chat bots and virtual assistants can be leveraged for collaboration and knowledge management. Let's briefly look at a chat bot feature.

Chat Bots in EXPs

A chat bot is program powered by artificial intelligence and natural language processing methods to provide a conversational interface. A chat bot uses predefined rules, a centralized domain-specific information store, and NLP methods to respond to user queries.

Chat bots can multitask by responding to multiple employees, and they require minimal human intervention. Once chat bots are integrated with the right information sources and defined business rules, chat bots can respond to queries with high availability and can optimize costs.

In an EXP scenario, chat bots can handle employee queries related to policies, information retrieval, process guidance, generic query handling, scheduling meetings, and search.

High-Level Assessment Framework for Enterprise Collaboration

Enterprises need to select the most appropriate collaboration platform to realize their overall vision and achieve the EXP objectives. In this section, I discuss an assessment framework and details its categorized assessment features.

Organizations can use a five-point scale to rate each of these features.

- A rating of 5 if the collaborative tool provides the complete feature set out of the box

- A rating of 4 if the collaborative tool provides the partial feature set out of the box

- A rating of 3 if the collaborative tool provides the features through configurations and extensions with minimal customization

- A rating of 2 if the collaborative tool provides minimal support through configurations and extensions requiring high degree of customization

- A rating of 1 if the collaborative tool does not provide any of the features requiring complete customization

Table 9-1 lists the essential capabilities of a robust collaborative platform in various categories. Organizations can fine-tune/customize the assessment parameters based on their business requirements and long-term collaboration strategy.

Table 9-1. *Collaboration Platform Capabilities*

	Capabilities	Requirements
Content	Content management	• Easy and intuitive to maintain and use for content owners • Ability to author and edit content easily • Ability where applicable to use editing/formatting capabilities for text, web pages • Ability where applicable to upload, store, and share different content types, including Microsoft documents, PDFs, PPT files, video and audio files, multimedia, photos • Ability to schedule content for the future and have it expire based on rules • Ability where applicable to display top-rated content, most "viewed" content • Ability to publish content in various formats • Ability for content workflows
	Localization/personalization	• Ability to deliver content/information based on user preferences, interests, and past behavior • Ability to deliver content in employee's language of choice
	Collaborative content	• Ability to manage content related to blogs, wikis, and discussion forums • Ability to secure collaborative content
	User experience	• Ability to provide minimalistic design • Ability to render uniform user experience on all devices
	Categorization	• Ability to categorize content into various folders and categories • Ability to tag and add metadata to content • Ability to support a taxonomy for content
	Knowledge Base	• Ability of system to manage the information in a centralized knowledge base system • Ability of system to search content stored in knowledge base

(continued)

Table 9-1. (*continued*)

	Capabilities	Requirements
	Search	• Ability to discover information based on keywords and context • Ability to search various types of content and assets
	Document management	• Ability to store documents of various formats • Ability to share the documents • Ability to manage simultaneous updates to the documents • Ability to archive content • Ability to manage the full lifecycle of the content
	Social recommendation	• Ability to share the content in various ways (e-mail, social post, message, etc.) • Ability of system to automatically recommend content based on employee's interest and preferences
Collaboration	Communities	• Ability to create a cross-organization collaboration spanning multiple networks • Ability to support features for discussion, sharing, and rating • Ability to provide governance for communities • Ability of system to create and manage user groups (such as employees, customers, partners) based on interests and skill sets
	Blogs, wikis, activity feeds, discussion forums, tagging	• Ability to start and maintain blogs and wikis • Ability for user to be able to control sequence of activity feed and discussion thread feed postings, from oldest to most recent, or vice versa • Ability for employees to use tagging and track which tags are used more often and display this to overall community • Ability to convert items into a knowledgebase where applicable • Enable employees to author wiki articles and manage the article lifecycle • Ability to form interest groups among employees through discussion group feature

(*continued*)

Table 9-1. (*continued*)

Capabilities	Requirements
Idea management	• Ability of the system to solicit ideas from employees along with their business impact, design, and implementation details • Ability of system to manage ideas • Ability to allow employees to vote/rate the ideas • Ability of system to use gamification concepts to drive adoption • Ability to crowd source the implementation of the selected idea
Microblogging	• Ability to enable employees to create and communicate small discussions/posts with colleagues • Ability of the platform to secure the micro posts among the group
Instant messaging	• Ability to send audio/video messages in real time • Ability to do instant messaging on all channels
Digital asset support	• Ability to support content with various file formats • Ability to ingest assets of various formats • Ability to manage the end-to-end lifecycle of various digital assets • Ability to enforce digital rights management for assets of various formats • Ability to manage the asset lifecycle through workflows
Calendars	• Ability to provide shared calendar so that colleagues can view current employee engagements • Ability to edit events on employees' calendar • Ability to schedule events on employees' calendar

(*continued*)

Table 9-1. *(continued)*

	Capabilities	**Requirements**
Governance	Content policies	• Ability to set the security for the content to enforce who can view the document • Ability to retain the content based on its sensitivity and for regulatory compliance • Ability to encrypt the content based on its sensitivity
	Compliance	• Ability to support various compliance policies related to accessibility, multilingual, omnichannel, information retention, security, and such
	Revision control	• Ability to create and manage various versions of the document
Infrastructure	Scalability	• Ability for the system to perform optimally even with increased user/content load
	Security	• Ability of the system to enforce security policies such as authentication, authorization, encryption, digital rights management, and such
	Application integration	• Ability of the system to support integration with external social media platforms • Ability of system to support flexible integration methods like services-based integration, API-based integration, and such • Ability of the system to support integration with internal applications
	Administration	• Ability of system to provide admin features such as user management, content administration, and such

Collaboration Design and Implementation

In this section, I discuss the collaboration plan, user experience, success metrics, and collaboration road map.

Devising a Collaboration Plan for the Enterprise

To define and implement an effective collaboration strategy, you can follow the steps in Figure 9-3.

	System Analysis	Collaboration Design	Collaboration Development & Improvement
Goal	• Understand collaboration needs • Understand current challenges	• Identify best collaboration tool • Design collaborative features	• Continuously improve collaboration platform • Continuous monitoring
Activities	• As-is collaboration process analysis • System audit • Employee survey • Collaboration needs analysis • Pain point analysis • Define success metrics	• Collaboration tool assessment • Collaborative Tool recommendation • Collaboration feature design • Technology standardization • Integration design • Content design • Knowledge management design • Define implementation plan & roadmap • Pilot run	• Phase wise iterative development • Communication • Enhance adoption • Monitor metrics

Figure 9-3. *Steps for implementing collaboration strategy*

System Analysis

In this phase, you need to understand the existing collaboration processes and tools. Collaboration processes include communication process, information sharing processes, and such. You conduct a system audit to understand business scenarios, gaps, and the as-is technology ecosystem. You need to understand various collaboration tools in place and the gaps and various devices used by employees during auditing. You conduct employee surveys to understand the most popular collaboration needs (such as real-time communication, information sharing, search, and such) and tools (such as messenger, video chat, etc.).

You define the specific collaboration needs based on surveys and system assessment. You also define the success metrics (discussed later) and critical success factors.

Collaboration Design

The main goal in this phase is to identify the most appropriate collaboration tools and design the key collaborative features.

Based on the understanding of the collaboration needs and requirements, you evaluate industry-leading collaboration tools using the assessment framework detailed in the previous section. Based on the outcome of the assessment framework, you select the most appropriate collaboration tool.

If the legacy applications have a diverse set of collaboration tools, you will consolidate the tools, standards, and technologies in this phase as part of the consolidation and technology standardization exercise.

You also design various aspects of collaboration platform such as user experience, integration, security, knowledge management, and content design. You plan out the UI design for a collaboration dashboard in the next section. You also define the implementation plan and collaboration road map to identify various maturity levels of the collaboration maturity. I discuss the collaboration road map in a later section of this chapter.

Finally, you do a pilot run of the collaboration features using the selected collaboration tool to understand the feasibility and performance of the collaboration tool.

Collaboration Development and Improvement

You implement the collaboration platform iteratively and improve the platform during this phase.

You implement the collaborative features as defined in the implementation plan. Project sponsors and senior leadership will communicate about the key features of the new platform to create awareness and drive adoption.

You continuously monitor the collaboration based on the definitions in the system analysis phase. The system metrics are used to continuously fine-tune the collaboration platform.

Collaboration User Experience Design

In this section, I detail the main user experience (UX) design principles for the collaboration feature. I define the key UX design principles and elaborate on them with a collaborative dashboard design.

Here are the key UX design principles that can be used while creating engaging collaboration features:

- **Mobile first and omnichannel enabled**: As the mobile channel has become the mainstream access channel, the collaborative features should work seamlessly on mobile apps and desktop browsers.

- **Responsive, interactive, and engaging user experience**: The user experience should be interactive and use responsive design concepts so that it renders optimally on all form factors and resolutions.

- **Availability of core collaborative features**: The collaborative platform should provide all the needed collaborative features such as blogs, wikis, calendar, forums, chat, etc., that are required for implementing business requirements.

- **Gamification**: The design should depict visual elements of the gamification feature to further encourage and reward employees' contributions.

- **External social platform integration**: The collaboration UI should aggregate relevant information and feeds from external social platforms.

- **Omnipresence of essential features**: A few collaborative features such as chat or feeds play a vital role in information discovery, employee engagement, and employee satisfaction. Such features should be made available in all key pages such as the home page, landing page, and such.

- **Security and personalization**: The collaboration platform should secure the information access based on the appropriate roles and privileges. Based on an employee's preferences and interests, the collaboration platform should personalize the information.

Let's look at a sample collaboration dashboard UI to understand these concepts. The collaboration dashboard provides a unified view of core collaborative features. A typical collaboration dashboard is depicted in Figure 9-4.

Figure 9-4. *Collaboration dashboard*

Let's look at how the UX design principles are implemented in the collaboration dashboard.

Mobile First and Omnichannel Enabled

The collaborative dashboard is available in the mobile app as well as for desktop browsers using responsive design. The collaborative mobile app provides push notifications to alert users about upcoming events, feed updates, and such.

Responsive, Interactive, and Engaging User Experience

As the collaborative dashboard is based on the responsive web design concept (wherein CSS3 and media queries are used), the page layout renders optimally on various mobile browsers and desktop browsers with various form factors and resolutions.

Some of the collaboration features, such as events, polls, and chat, provide an interactive user experience. Employees can click "attend" links to accept the events, employees can participate in polls directly from the dashboard, and employees can chat with colleagues using the chat feature.

Availability of Core Collaborative Features

The collaborative dashboard provides a unified view of these key collaborative features:

- **Forums/message boards**: Employees can start discussions using the post feature. Others can reply and "like" the posts. Employees can also sort the posts using filters such as most liked (sorted based on likes), most recent (sorted based on date), and most replied (sorted based on replies). Active participation in forums increases the engagement levels.

- **Questions board**: Employees can ask questions to which other employees can reply. Employees can use this feature to seek clarifications on policies or any topic.

- **Events management**: The events module on the right side of the page reminds the employees about upcoming events, and employees can accept the events. The events module is designed to increase employee participation in organization events.

- **Social media enablement**: The module aggregates feeds from external social media channels such as Twitter, LinkedIn, and such based on the tags and metadata. Employees can also share information with others.

- **Polls and surveys**: Employees can participate in polls and surveys and provide feedback. Organizations can leverage polls to understand the employee pulse and fine-tune organization policies based on the feedback.

- **Chat**: Employees can chat in real time with colleagues or support personnel. Audio and video chat facilitates real-time collaboration among employees and improves their engagement and productivity. Chat bots can also be leveraged to provide a chat feature.

- **Top contributors**: This section displays the employees who have gotten the most votes/likes.

Additionally, employees can share files and contribute to forums through the collaboration dashboard.

Gamification

The gamification concept applies the concept of game features such as points and badges to various applications. Gamification concepts are used to improve employee engagement and employee productivity. In the collaboration dashboard, when an employee replies to a question, other employees can vote on the answer. Based on the votes, the employees will be rewarded with badges (gold, silver, and bronze). A "top contributors" section features the employees who have earned top badges and recognizes them. The section is designed to motivate and encourage employee contribution.

External Social Platform Integration

The collaboration dashboard aggregates feeds from the Twitter platform based on the tagged keywords. The integration module also fetches relevant blogs and feeds.

Omnipresence of Essential Features

In the case of a collaboration dashboard, chat is an omnipresent feature that is available on all pages. Employees can initiate chat with other colleagues or support personnel from every page.

Security and Personalization

The collaborative features are secured through role-based access.

- The "events management" feature displays only the events that are applicable for the logged-in employee.

- The "social media enablement" feature shows only the feeds and blogs based on the logged-in user's preferred tags.

Collaboration Metrics

You define the collaboration success metrics in the system analysis phase. Success metrics provide quantifiable and verifiable data for evaluating the success of the collaboration platform. The following are the metrics that can be used to measure the success of collaborative tools:

- **Information shared and reused**: You can measure improvement in the information shared and reused for problem-solving.

- **Employee engagement**: Real-time online collaboration improves employees' engagement. You can measure this through the increase in employee participation in various events, forums, and discussions.

- **Productivity improvement**: You can measure the productivity improvement by understanding the improvement in average task completion time, average process improvement time, and such.

- **Cost reduction**: You can measure the overall cost reduction because of the consolidation of collaboration tools and technologies and self-service features.

- **Employee satisfaction**: You can assess the employee satisfaction levels through employee surveys and measure the improvement in satisfaction scores.

Collaboration Road Map

You can define a collaboration road map as part of the collaboration design phase to identify the collaboration implementation strategy as per the organization vision. The collaboration road map defines the short-term, medium-term, and long-term goals and implementation features for the organization based on the priorities and business impact. Organizations can use the road map to plan the budget and resources.

Figure 9-5 gives a sample collaboration road map for an enterprise.

Short term	Medium Term	Long Term
Goal		
• Core collaboration functionalities • Quick wins for business • Content management	• Business enablers • Enable platform adoption • Artificial intelligence adoption	• Knowledge management • Integration to external systems & platforms • Continuous improvement
Features		
• Community forums & posts • Message boards • Search – people, content • Blog posts, wiki, calendar • Administration capabilities • Alerts & notification • Personalization • Polls, surveys, review and rating • Content creation, publishing • Audio & video chat • Mobile apps development	• Custom profiles • Polls • Chat & messaging • Gamification • Analytics & insights • Chatbots • Self-learning • Recommendation • Predictive analytics	• Chatbots & knowledge Management platform integration • Sharing content • Integration to external systems, plug-ins, and connectors

Figure 9-5. *Collaboration road map*

The short-term stage spans one month to three months and lays the foundation for the collaboration platform. The main goals in this stage are to achieve quick wins that have significant impact for business; other goals in this stage are to implement core collaboration features as part of the foundation release and implement content management. To implement these goals, you implement the core collaboration features such as communities, forums, message boards, blogs, search, alerts, polls, and such. You also implement all the built-in collaboration features that are available out of the box in the chosen collaboration tool.

The medium term stage spans three months to six months, and you seek to provide business self-service and other business enablers. You also build other collaboration platform features on top of the foundation release and incorporate artificial intelligence (AI) features. During this phase, you implement personalization and security features on top of the foundation release. You also implement other complex features such as custom profiles, gamification concepts, and audio/video chats and virtual conferencing features. You implement the AI-powered features such as chat bots, predictive analytics, personalized recommendations, and such.

In the long term, between six months and one year, you build a robust knowledge management system that fully integrates with the internal and external systems. You also continuously improve the collaboration platform based on the collaboration metrics. During this stage you implement the most advanced features such as a chat bot using the structured knowledge from the knowledge management platform and perform integration with the various external social media platforms. Employees will be able to share the content in various formats.

Collaboration Case Study

In this section, I discuss a collaboration case study to illustrate the usage of the collaboration design and collaboration tools. I elaborate on this case study using the key steps identified in the collaboration strategy.

System Analysis

In this section, I discuss the as-is system analysis and identify the main pain points.

Background and Context

A retail organization has embarked on an intranet digital transformation because of the following challenges:

- Currently, the intranet is fragmented, lacks consistent governance, and does not offer enterprise search across all applications.

- There are vast differences in the "look and feel" between division sites and applications, so the experience for the user is very disjointed.

- There is also a significant overlap in content between applications, which makes it difficult and time-consuming for employees to determine the best place to find the information they need.

- There are no well-defined and structured content processes related to content management, content archival, content publishing, and such.

- There are no well-defined integration processes.

Business Vision

The vision is to create the next-generation digital workspace that simplifies employees' access to the information, resources, and applications needed to do their work.

By reducing the number of sites, an employee can navigate easily, and by providing a single destination from which to search and obtain relevant and consistent information, the next-generation digital workspace should help improve employees' quality of work, productivity, and engagement. The next-generation digital workplace should preserve institutional knowledge and provide a platform for trusted information. Key desired capabilities include better employee engagement, managed content creation and governance, and significantly improved information findability. The next-generation digital workspace should provide increased engagement by empowering employees ultimately improving loyalty and profitability.

In subsequent sections, I discuss design principles, the platform design, and the way in which the next-generation digital workplace addresses the challenges.

Collaboration Analysis

In this section, I discuss the as-is system analysis and identify the main pain points.

Key Design Principles of Next-Generation Digital Workplace

The key design principles of the next-generation digital workplace are as follows:

- The next-generation digital workplace must be both a platform (base of technologies or infrastructure on which additional technologies, processes, or services can be built) and a product (specific features and functions).

- The next-generation digital workplace should simplify employees' access to information, resources, and applications needed to do their work.

- The next-generation digital workplace should create an intuitive experience based on data-driven insights, analysis, and end-user feedback.

- The next-generation digital workplace must be accessible to employees from multiple devices and work locations.

- The next-generation digital workplace should provide optimized search across the entire unified site (including third-party applications wherever possible).

- The next-generation digital workplace should provide web-based on-demand analytics.

- The next-generation digital workplace should provide personalized content based on the division, department, role, and location of the user.

- The next-generation digital workplace should establish and enforce governance for content.

- The next-generation digital workplace should provide security features such as idle session timeout, single sign-on, and such.

- The next-generation digital workplace should provide a personalized experience such as custom landing page, personalized information, and functionality.

- The next-generation digital workplace should create an intuitive experience for content managers requiring minimal support resources.

- The next-generation digital workplace should provide collaborative features such as communities, forums, chat, calendar, blogs, wikis, and such.

- The next-generation digital workplace should provide faster access to relevant and contextual information,

- The next-generation digital workplace should provide consistency across various channels.

- The next-generation digital workplace should provide integration with various internal and external applications.

- The next-generation digital workplace should provide enhanced usability and simplicity.

Critical Success Factors and Value Themes

In this section you will look at critical success factors to design and build a next-generation digital workplace. Figure 9-6 shows the key success factors to address the existing challenges.

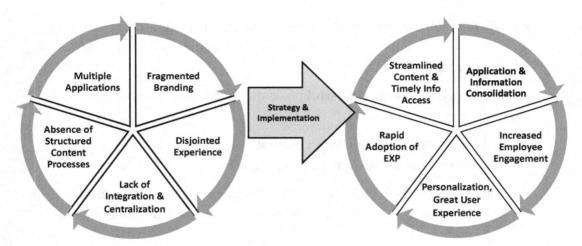

Figure 9-6. *Collaboration critical success factors*

The following are the key success factors needed for next-generation digital workplace:

- **Streamlined content processes and timely information access**: The new platform should provide easy-to-use and easy-to-manage content processes.

- **Rapid EXP adoption**: The program sponsors and senior leadership team should market and create awareness about the new platform to drive adoption. The new platform itself should inspire the employees to enhance its usage.

- **Personalization and great user experience**: The new platform should provide role-based and preferences-based personalization.

- **Increased employee engagement**: The new platform should enhance the employee engagement levels and employee satisfaction levels.

- **Application and information consolidation:** The new platform should consolidate various apps, content, and information from internal and external sources to provide a unified view.

Figure 9-7 maps the critical success factors to the value themes and value drivers.

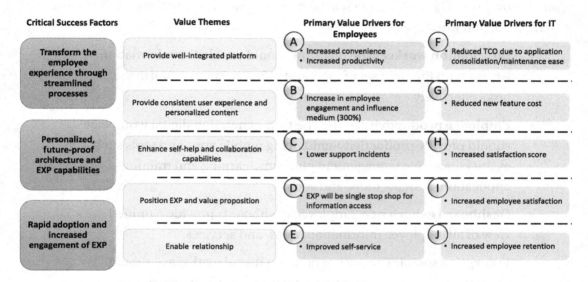

Figure 9-7. *Critical success factors mapping*

To transform the employee experience and streamline the processes, you need to provide a fully integrated platform with a consistent user experience. This digital transformation results in increased convenience, engagement, and productivity for employees and reduced total cost of ownership (TCO).

The next-generation digital workplace provides a personalized and future-proof architecture enhancing the self-service features and collaboration. This reduces the support incident volume and increases the satisfaction score.

To drive the rapid adoption of the next-generation digital workplace, you need to define the value proposition of the platform and enable the relationship levers through improved self-service. The increased adoption/engagement drives employee satisfaction and employee retention.

Forward-Looking Features of the Next-Generation Digital Workplace

The next-generation digital workplace platform should provide forward-looking features so that the platform becomes future proof and can be effectively used for future innovations. Figure 9-8 provides the main forward-looking features of the next-generation digital workplace.

- **Information worker**: The platform should enable the information worker with the right set of tools and information to perform the tasks effectively.

- **Employee productivity tools**: The next-generation digital workplace should provide productivity-enhancing mobile apps and tools such as the knowledge management platform, learning and training application, benefits tools, and such.

- **Dashboard experience**: Employee dashboards provide a unified view of all employee information, tools, and services.

- **Enterprise social**: The next-generation digital workspace should provide enterprise social features such as discussion forums, communities, and such.

- **Idea, innovation, crowdsourcing, and gamification**: The next-generation digital workspace should provide idea management through crowd-sourcing and gamification concepts.

- **Agile infrastructure**: The next-generation digital workspace should be built on an agile infrastructure to provide on-demand scaling managed by lean processes.

- **Insights and actionable notification**: Analytics tools should be leveraged to provide vital insights into employee behavior and provide actionable notification.

- **Omnichannel enabled**: The next-generation digital workspace should provide a seamless experience on all browsers and devices and implement a mobile-first strategy.

- **Cloud enabled**: The next-generation digital workspace should be cloud enabled so that the application can be accessed from anywhere at any time.

- **Digital employee engagement (news, search, webcast, communication, surveys)**: The next-generation digital workspace should provide various engagement features such as search, webcast, communication channels, surveys, and such.

- **Responsive web design**: As a part of the omnichannel design, the next-generation digital workspace should provide an interactive and responsive user interface.

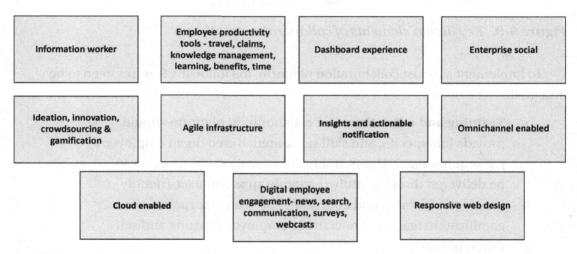

Figure 9-8. *Features of next-generation digital workplace*

Collaborative Platform Design

A robust collaborative platform is required to build a next-generation digital workplace. Figure 9-9 identifies the key design elements of the collaborative platform.

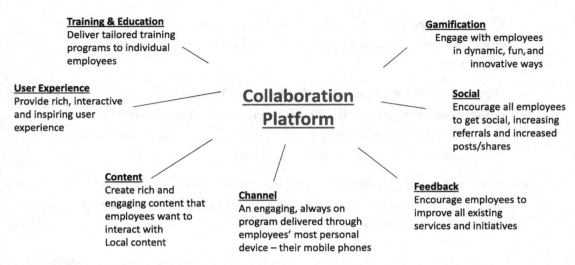

Figure 9-9. *Key design elements of collaboration platform*

To implement a robust collaboration platform, the following features need to be designed:

- **Training and education**: The collaboration platform should provide job-specific and skill set content based on an employee's job requirements. The training and education content should be delivered through intuitive mobile apps and user-friendly interfaces. Training and education apps can incorporate the gamification feature to encourage employee learning and self-development.

- **User experience**: The collaboration platform should provide an inspiring and engaging user experience across all channels.

- **Content**: The collaboration platform should provide a robust content management system to manage the collaborative content.

- **Channel**: All the collaborative features should be available on all channels such as mobile phones and desktop browsers.

- **Feedback**: The collaboration platform should use tools such as polls and surveys and encourage employees (incentivize feedback using gamification concepts) to provide feedback. Employee feedback can be used to improve the platform services.

- **Social**: It should encourage employees to contribute and share the information using social features (blogs, posts, question/answers, and such).

- **Gamification**: It should adopt the gamification concepts such as points, badges, recognition, and rewards to motivate, engage, and reward employees for their contribution.

Assessment and Pilot Phase

Once the collaboration design is completed, the assessment and pilot phase selects the most appropriate tool and executes a pilot run base. See Figure 9-10.

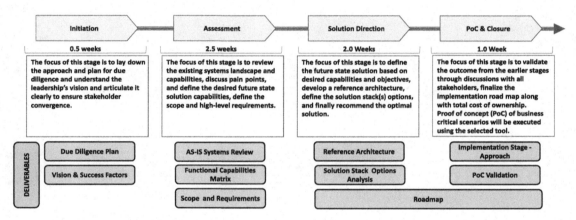

Figure 9-10. *Stages of assessment and pilot phase*

The following are the four stages of the assessment and pilot phase:

- **Initiation stage**: During this stage you define the assessment approach and understand the overall vision and define critical success factors based on the vision.

- **Assessment stage**: You do the existing system study and understand the challenges and pain points in the existing system. You also define the detailed functional requirements and capabilities for the new system.

- **Solution direction stage**: You define the high-level reference architecture and identify the technology solution stack. You do the fitment analysis to recommend the most appropriate solution stack.

- **PoC and closure stage**: During this stage you execute a proof of concept (PoC) using the selected tool, and you define the implementation road map (detailing various iterations).

Collaboration Development and Improvement

In this phase, you develop the collaboration platform and iteratively improve it.

Next-Generation Digital Workplace

Figure 9-11 shows a sample architecture of a collaboration platform.

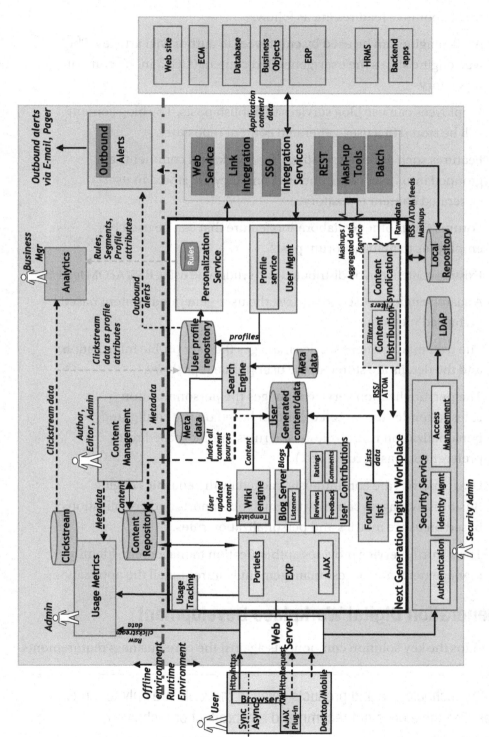

Figure 9-11. Sample architecture of collaboration platform

259

The key collaborative features are as follows:

- A wiki engine can be used by employees to author wiki articles. The wiki engine stores the user-generated content (UGC) in the content repository.

- Employees can use blog services to publish posts. The blog content will be stored in a user-generated content repository.

- Features such as reviews, ratings, feedback, and comments are grouped into "user contributions," and they are stored in user-generated content repository.

- Forums are another collaboration feature that can be used by employees to manage forum posts.

- Existing content can be distributed and syndicated using RSS/ATOM feeds.

- A search engine is used to retrieve the user-generated content based on tagged metadata.

- The user management service manages the user profile information, and the details are stored in the user profile repository.

- The personalization service manages the personalization rules to render the targeted content based on the configured personalization rules (role-based rules, profile-based rules, preferences-based rules, etc.)

- Usage metrics are continuously tracked by the analytics engine. Business managers can view the analytics reports and visualizations based on usage metrics and personalization rules.

- The security service provides authentication management, identity management, and access management features for all the applications.

Next-Generation Digital Workplace Development

Table 9-2 maps the key solution components against the core business requirements.

Note   The technologies and products given in the table are only for education purposes. The table does not recommend any product or technology.

Table 9-2. *Solution Components for EXP requirements*

Requirements	Solution components
Personalized home page view	• Users will be able to personalize their home page and subscribe to different feeds and alerts. They will be able to see the news and weather as per their preferences.
Search	• Drupal will be integrated with Apache Solr for faceted, wildcard, predictive search, and sorting. A MySQL database will also be integrated with the Solr search tool. • PDF and Office files will be loaded in Drupal, which will reside on the file system. That content will also be made searchable by using Apache Tika.
Videos viewing	• An add-on module in Drupal will provide an embedded player where externally hosted videos (including YouTube) can be viewed.
Business locations	• Integration with Google Maps for business locations. Users will be able to zoom in and see location details.
News and weather feed	• News and weather channels, which are hosting public news and weather feeds, respectively, will be integrated with Drupal to provide localized news. • News board will also be created for internal news and updates. The latest and most popular news will be shown to users on their home page.
Integration with social web sites including Facebook, Twitter, YouTube, and LinkedIn	• Drupal's social media connector add-on module will be used to integrate with Facebook, Twitter, LinkedIn, and YouTube.
Responsive interface design for desktop, mobile, and tablets	• Responsive UI design for pages and components. This will give a device-specific view to the user.
FAQ , surveys, polls, internal news, reports, e-mails, product details, departments, locations	• Drupal's CMS templates will be created to publish content. Content will go through various stages in customized workflows. On state change, the intended user will get the e-mail alerts.

(*continued*)

Table 9-2. (*continued*)

Requirements	Solution components
Workflows	• Content creation and publishing will go through custom workflows. Alerts in the form of e-mails will be delivered to the intended audience on state change, for approvals, etc.
User management	• Drupal's built-in role-based and fine-grained access controls component and granular permission model will be leveraged for this. Users will be integrated with Active Directory using Drupal's add-on module.
Multilingual support (English, French)	• Drupal's built-in multilingual feature will be used for this.

Addressing Challenges and Pain Points

The next-generation digital workplace platform addresses the challenges and pain points with legacy systems. Table 9-3 provides the best practices.

Table 9-3. *EXP Best Practices*

Pain Points and Challenges with Existing Systems	Best Practices
Multiple independent applications	Consolidate tools and content into a single digital platform with a uniform user experience.
Absence of well-defined content publishing process; duplicate outdated content	Establish publishing governance model based on a CMS. Establish the digital workspace as the primary channel of internal communication. Identify content owners and enhance content freshness. Deliver personalized and relevant content based on interests and preferences.

(*continued*)

Table 9-3. (*continued*)

Pain Points and Challenges with Existing Systems	Best Practices
Unstructured content; disjointed user experience; lack of corporate design standard	Define information architecture (IA) based on a user's mental model. Define visual design and standards and consistent design guidelines and standards.
Lack of collaboration features	Provide collaborative tools and networking opportunities for employees.

Summary

This chapter covered the following:

- Collaboration plays a key role in productivity improvements and increased employee engagement.

- The key impact areas of collaboration are loyalty, brand advocacy, feedback, cost optimization, engagement, and cross-functional collaboration.

- The main drivers for collaboration are information sharing, providing flexibility, harnessing collective intelligence, enabling co-creation, improving productivity improvement, enabling self-service, empowering employees with relevant search, providing personalized information, and providing a centralized knowledge base.

- The main challenges in enterprise collaboration are challenges in cross-functional collaboration, multiple collaboration tools and applications, lack of team collaboration, technology ecosystem, and organization culture.

- Core collaborative features are blogs, wikis, communities, people search, shared calendar, polls and surveys, rating and review, recommendation, social share, feeds, social bookmarks, idea hub, chat and instant messenger, knowledge management, discussion forums, tags, groups, e-mail, and document sharing.

- Main collaborative technologies are the instant messaging technology, knowledge management system, content management system, incident management, search, and cloud.

- Innovative features of the collaboration platform are co-creation, social innovation, social marketing, communities, collaborative sales, idea hub, and gamification.

- The key collaboration capabilities that can be used for assessment are for content (content management, localization/personalization, collaborative content, user experience, categorization, knowledge base, search, document management, social recommendation), collaboration (communities, blogs, wikis, activity feeds, discussion, forums, tagging, idea management, microblogging, instant messaging, digital asset support, calendars), governance (content policies, compliance, revision control), and infrastructure (scalability, security, application integration, administration).

- The steps for effective collaboration strategy are system analysis, collaboration design, and collaboration development and improvement.

- The key UX design principles are mobile first and omnichannel enabled, responsive, interactive and engaging user experience, availability of core collaborative features, gamification, external social platform integration, omnipresence of essential features, security, and personalization.

- The key collaboration metrics are information shared and reused, employee engagement, productivity improvement, cost reduction, and employee satisfaction.

CHAPTER 10

Digital Workplace Security Framework

Security is an important success factor for the digital workplace. As the EXP manages a lot of confidential employee information, it is imperative to ensure that the proper security standards are adopted. A comprehensive security framework covers all aspects of security such as logical security, functionality security, application security, security event tracking, and such.

In this chapter, I discuss in detail how to implement end-to-end EXP security for the digital workplace application.

Because a cloud-first design for an EXP is widely used across many implementations, we will mainly look at the security architecture of a cloud-based EXP. A comprehensive security framework consists primarily of these elements:

- **Security design**: The security design defines the comprehensive objectives and policies covering all the security areas needed for the EXP.

- **Security architecture**: The security architecture provides a detailed solution architecture to address all the requirements and policies defined in the security design.

In the next few sections, I elaborate on various components of security, security governance, and the security architecture.

265

S. K. Shivakumar, *Build a Next-Generation Digital Workplace*, https://doi.org/10.1007/978-1-4842-5512-4_10

Security Design

The rules set forth here provide a guide for adopting a set of technical, organizational, and regulatory measures that, when systematically implemented as a whole, govern logical access to and the protection of information by restricting use to only authorized people.

Information in electronic format (also defined as *logical access*) may be accessed by using *credentials*, consisting of a user ID and a private component, which may be a combination of one or more attributes regarding the following:

- Something that the user knows (e.g., password, PIN)

- Something that the user has (e.g., smartcard, token)

- A biometric characteristic of the user (e.g., fingerprints, iris)

The set of user information access rights constitutes the *access profile* assigned to the user during the profiling phase based on established rules. Logical access control includes the following phases:

- *Identification*, or the user recognition process that verifies the existence of the user ID entered

- *Authentication*, or the process that verifies the user's claimed identity by comparing the credentials provided with registered credentials

- *Authorization*, or the process of granting access to the information requested by the authenticated user

Logical access is also governed by mechanisms that record information use, which makes it possible to reconstruct past operations on information. Logical security uses information encryption techniques to protect data confidentiality and integrity and guarantee the nonrepudiation of operations on information.

General Logical Security Requirements

Data access must be permitted on the basis of requirements associated with the operating activities carried out by users. It also must be managed and controlled by the appropriate instruments or processes that guarantee that authorized individuals can access only the information required for their work.

Basic Elements to Be Considered for Access Control

Procedures must be established to define access credentials and assign them to users, as well as manage the appropriate access profiles to ensure that access is only allowed the information required for operating activities.

The objectives and policies are defined as follows:

- Ensuring that logical access to nonpublic information is permitted only after the completion of the identification, authentication, and authorization phases

- Defining a process for the creation, long-term management, and cancellation of authentication credentials

- Assigning a personal, unique ID to each information system user within the company, which should not be reassigned to other users, even in the future

- Establishing processes and instruments to define, create, and manage access profiles and the relative user assignment rules based on the profiling model adopted

- Updating credentials and user profiles any time operating requirements change

- Repeatedly verifying in a structured manner the validity of credentials and access profiles in line with applicable legal provisions, also with respect to the assignee's roles and tasks

- If access profile management is outsourced, ensuring that the contract includes appropriate clauses to guarantee that the defined access profile management rules are applied and that it is possible to verify the operating procedures in use

- Keeping track of operations on information based on the information classification level

Identification and Authentication

Procedures must be established for the definition, long-term management, and cancellation of user IDs.

Management of User IDs

Procedures must be established for the definition, long-term management, and cancellation of user IDs.

The objectives and policies are defined as follows:

- Defining unique user IDs over time

- Assigning user IDs in such a way so as to ensure unambiguous association with the user

- Defining user IDs at the company level based on a specific nomenclature standard

- Ensuring that user IDs cannot be traced back to their associated access rights

- Defining protection measures and procedures for authorizing new users in order to prevent any improper use

- Fulfilling requests to reactivate deactivated user IDs only after conducting requester recognition controls and verifying the permissibility of the request

Management of Private Components of User Credentials

Processes, procedures, and mechanisms must be established to define, distribute, protect, and recover the private components of user access credentials. The objectives and policies are defined as follows:

- Defining a process to manage and distribute logical and physical private components, which guarantees their confidentiality, integrity, and availability to ensure that authentication procedures function properly

- Defining measures to protect newly created private components

- Implementing the identification and authentication techniques identified in line with legal and regulatory provisions on security and privacy

- Establishing systems for the management of private components of access credentials, which, for passwords, require at least the following: change on first login, independent replacement by the user (after verifying the user's identity), a composition standard, a minimum length, an expiry, and saving in encrypted form

- Defining a process that guarantees the availability of private user credentials while also ensuring that they remain secret and identifying beforehand in writing the parties responsible for custody of such credentials for cases in which it is necessary to immediately intervene exclusively for system operations and security reasons, in the case of the user's prolonged absence

Network Access Paths

Mechanisms must be defined to protect network connections. The objectives and policies are defined as follows:

- Ensuring that any logical access to the network is protected via authentication mechanisms

- Identifying specific network paths from the workstation to the destination system to limit the possibility that users use paths on networks other than those defined

- Defining and regulating appropriate methods that provide external network access to personnel or third parties, also on the basis of current regulatory requirements

Personnel Authentication via Remote Connections

Appropriate authentication processes and procedures must be defined for remote connections to the company network. The objectives and policies are defined as follows:

- Establishing procedures and mechanisms that enable remote connections in line with access control rules and in relation to operating requirements, limiting access to only the necessary functions and using strong authentication when required under current regulations

- Preventing remote connections through independently installed and unauthorized instruments (e.g., external modems and wireless access points).

Network Traffic Control

Technical security solutions must be defined to filter and control network traffic. The objectives and policies are defined as follows:

- Controlling network traffic and user connections to limit the use of specific services or functions depending on actual operating requirements (e.g., outgoing file transfer, e-mail attachment size limits, etc.).

User Access Procedures

System and application logon procedures must be defined to prevent unauthorized access.

The objectives and policies are defined as follows:

- Informing users that systems and applications must be used exclusively for work purposes

- Avoiding showing system and application identifiers until the access procedure has been completed successfully

- Validating access information only after it has been entered in full, without indicating which data is incorrect if any errors are made

- Limiting the number of possible consecutive failed access attempts, after which time the user ID will be blocked

- Defining criteria to limit the maximum number of simultaneous accesses by the same user ID to the same application or system, ensuring that it does not exceed actual operating requirements and that the operations carried out can be definitively linked to the user ID

Automatic Locking of Workstations and Limitation of Connection Times

Mechanisms must be activated to automatically lock workstations and, when possible, automatically disconnect sessions after a certain period of user inactivity, as well as limit system connection times. The objectives and policies are defined as follows:

- When workstations are temporarily not in use, activating automatic lock mechanisms that require authentication to access the user's work session

- Defining criteria for restricting system connection times

- When possible, locking work sessions after a certain period of user inactivity

Working Remotely

For users who work remotely or telecommute, dedicated processes must be formalized to authorize the remote use of IT equipment. Appropriate protection measures and user rules must also be defined to prevent the unauthorized theft and disclosure of information.

Authorization

Procedures must be established to define and assign to users the appropriate profiles, enabling access to only the information they need for their operating activities.

Definition of Information Access Profiles

User information access profiles must be defined and assigned so as to prevent any unauthorized changes to or the improper use of information or services. The objectives and policies are defined as follows:

- Defining access profiles that analytically list the permitted areas of operations based on operating requirements and the classification level of the information accessed, with the aim of fulfilling data confidentiality, integrity, and availability requirements

- Authorizing operations on information based on the "separation of duties," which makes it possible to distinguish actions on information depending on the activities carried out

- When it is necessary to increase security levels, requiring the use of joint authorizations by separate users

- Applying the need-to-know and least privilege principles, so as to enable access to only essential information for carrying out the assigned tasks

- Setting forth criteria for identifying and processing information to be considered confidential pursuant to sector legal and regulatory provisions

- Defining access profiles so as to guarantee that information to be considered confidential pursuant to sector legal and regulatory provisions is processed properly

- Separating access profile management responsibilities from application, system, and network management responsibilities

- Separating system development, test, and production environment management functions and responsibilities in order to prevent unwanted changes to software and data deriving from activities connected to the various environments

Security Event Tracking

User activities on systems, applications, and data must be tracked.

Event Tracking

Suitable event and activity tracking methods must be defined, particularly with respect to the actions of users with special privileges. The objectives and policies are defined as follows:

- Defining the appropriate responsibilities for logging activities

- Identifying and documenting the list of events that must be logged for each system and application, also on the basis of current regulations

- Creating a system and application event log, in compliance with any legal obligations, which does not make it possible to immediately identify users and which only allows the operator or the process responsible for a specific event to be identified subsequent to more detailed analyses, for the purpose of forensic investigations to protect the company before the court

- Configuring or designing systems, services, and applications in a manner that ensures that logging functions are activated and run properly

- Configuring network devices (e.g., switches, routers, firewalls) to log the necessary data, particularly failed access attempts, access by users with administrator privileges, and configuration modifications

Log Storage

Information about user access and activities must be saved, stored, and protected to make it possible to analyze operations in the event of actions that do not comply with defined rules or following security incidents. The objectives and policies are defined as follows:

- Protecting and storing event logs in compliance with applicable legal provisions and business requirements by establishing suitable policies and procedures

- Adequately protecting event log files, particularly by limiting access to authorized personnel, ensuring that log content cannot be altered and complying with storage time requirements, and logging access to and modifications of such files

- Backing up log files in accordance with established procedures

Encryption, Hashing, and Digital Signatures

Encryption and hashing techniques must be established to ensure the confidentiality, integrity, and nonrepudiation of the information saved or transmitted. Procedures must also be established for the management of encryption keys.

Fundamental Elements for the Use of Encryption Controls and Hashing

The proper use of specific encryption and hashing techniques for information protection must be evaluated. The objectives and policies are defined as follows:

- Defining criteria for the use of encryption and hashing techniques to protect information based on a security risk analysis and obligations established by current regulations

Encryption

Encryption techniques must be managed and used to protect data confidentiality and integrity on the basis of information classification levels. The objectives and policies are defined as follows:

- Identifying the characteristics of encryption keys (e.g., length) and the quality of algorithms to be used based on information classification levels

- Using encryption techniques to protect data confidentiality and integrity on the basis of information classification levels

Digital Signature

Digital signature mechanisms must be used on the basis of information classification levels to protect information integrity, guarantee the sender's authenticity, and avoid repudiation. The objectives and policies are defined as follows:

- Using encryption techniques based on a pair of public and private keys and defining the appropriate measures to protect private key confidentiality

- Defining criteria for the use of nonrepudiation techniques based on qualified digital signature mechanisms, in compliance with legal, regulatory, and contractual provisions

Key and Certificate Management

The keys used in encryption techniques must be properly managed and adequately protected. The objectives and policies are defined as follows:

- Securely managing encryption keys and certificates based on defined responsibilities, procedures, methods, and rules, as well as establishing methods for promptly replacing compromised keys or expired certificates

Network Management

The appropriate countermeasures must be adopted to secure the network and supporting devices and to guarantee that information is properly and securely distributed. Network and device management responsibilities must also be identified so that they are separated from operating system management responsibilities.

The network, along with its components and services provided, must be protected from unauthorized access, including remote access, by properly configuring the devices, evaluating the possibility of partitioning the networks, and controlling network traffic.

Network Separation

Technical security solutions must be defined to separate the networks. The objectives and policies are defined as follows:

- Defining and updating logical network partitioning criteria in line with network service access profiles

- Creating independent network perimeters and partitioning the network at least logically using the appropriate instruments (e.g., gateways or firewalls)

- Configuring instruments so as to filter communication between network partitions and block any unauthorized traffic

Definition of Network Countermeasures

A process must be defined to identify and implement appropriate security countermeasures, including organizational, to protect the *internal network* and network services, also by using techniques to check for vulnerabilities and possible intrusions. The objectives and policies are defined as follows:

- Defining network management responsibilities so as to keep responsibilities for operations carried out on network devices separate from responsibilities for operations carried out on the associated systems

- Designing the network in consideration of security aspects that ensure information confidentiality, integrity, and availability, as well as the use of instruments and solutions to filter and control network traffic

- Protecting network access points, particularly those located in public areas

- Guaranteeing the security of data transmissions to outside networks to protect data confidentiality, integrity, and availability

- Documenting and submitting for approval all phases for the implementation of new network services, from design to testing to release in production

- Identifying the critical events to be logged

- Periodically reviewing and updating network device security settings and rules

- Recording each network device configuration change

- Protecting information on network addresses and configurations from unauthorized access

- Installing intrusion detection and prevention systems and, more generally, network monitoring systems

- Requiring the use of appropriate security mechanisms (e.g., encryption, backup, digital signature) to guarantee data confidentiality, integrity, and nonrepudiation

- Defining suitable countermeasures to ensure network availability on the basis of business process requirements

- Ensuring that events are logged and considering the possibilities provided by the various network devices

- Periodically, or when any significant change is made, conducting intrusion and control tests to identify vulnerabilities that could potentially threaten network and system integrity, as specifically required under current regulations

- When expressly required under current regulations, adopting network device configuration standards

System and Network Security

Adequate responsibilities and procedures must be established for the design, development, and modification of systems and networks, including criteria for accepting solutions.

Security Requirements

The security requirements of new systems and networks must be analyzed to choose security solutions that protect the information managed. The objectives and policies are defined as follows:

- Identifying and documenting the security requirements of systems and networks to guarantee the confidentiality, integrity, and availability of the information processed

- On the basis of the security requirements identified, defining the solutions needed in line with the security measures of the associated IT environment

- Identifying the organizational unit that verifies the accuracy and comprehensiveness of the defined solution on the basis of defined security requirements, as well as its consistency with the existing security infrastructure

Application Security Controls

Applications must be configured to limit access to only authorized individuals via identification, authentication, and authorization instruments that are external to the application. Verification, validation, and logging mechanisms relating to activities carried out on data must be established in line with current laws. The appropriate code control (secure code) methodologies and countermeasures to guarantee availability and nonrepudiation must also be set forth.

Protection of Data in Transit

Mechanisms must be used to protect the integrity and confidentiality of data in transit.
   The objectives and policies are defined as follows:

- Taking the appropriate countermeasures to prevent unauthorized interceptions or modifications of the content of transmitted information

Use of Encryption Techniques

The use of encryption techniques must be evaluated on the basis of the classification levels of the information managed by the applications.
   The objectives and policies are defined as follows:

- Evaluating the use of encryption techniques on the basis of the value of the information managed by the applications and specific application or legal requirements to guarantee confidentiality, integrity, and nonrepudiation

Application Development Process Security

Security aspects must be adequately controlled and documented during application implementation and modification phases to ensure that applications function properly. In particular, responsibilities must be assigned to ensure that the development process, carried out either internally or by third parties, is managed in a controlled and verifiable manner via the appropriate authorization procedure.

Internal Development of New Applications

Specific protection measures must be defined for the controlled, secure, and verifiable management of the application development phase. The objectives and policies are defined as follows:

- Ensuring that all software development and maintenance activities are controlled, tracked, and logged

- Carrying out application development activities within a separate IT environment, at least aligned with the production environment in terms of version and updates

- Adopting protection measures that ensure that personal data is not associated with production data and that the remaining critical data remains confidential

- Fulfilling the security requirements defined and validated during the security requirement analysis phase

- Documenting the security solutions implemented to meet established requirements

- Protecting the source code from any unauthorized modification

- Using data not associated with production data in development and testing activities

- Preparing technical and operating documentation of the development phase inclusive of functional testing

Acquisition of Packages from Third Parties

Dedicated procedures must be defined for the selection and acquisition of application packages from third parties. The objectives and policies are defined as follows:

- Governing the selection and acquisition of application software and hardware so as to verify content and product installation and management security requirements

- Defining dedicated contractual clauses to ensure that the package complies with security and service provision rules and legal or regulatory security requirements and that it is compatible with the security management and control instruments adopted

- Using copyrighted application software based on the provisions established in the associated license agreements

- Verifying that the operational and security functions of acquired software comply with defined contractual clauses

Information Classification

Information is classified on the basis of confidentiality, integrity, and availability.

Information classification is fundamental to assess risk, i.e., the potential damage that the improper use of such information may cause to the group's data assets. This process also makes it possible to define IT asset protection requirements.

The classification must cover all types of information as well as the documents that contain information and the programs that process it (basic software, application software, and office suites), regardless of the type of media on which it is saved.

Information, regardless of type, format, and the media on which it is saved and recorded or the instruments used to exchange it, must be classified based on confidentiality, integrity, and availability using dedicated methodologies to identify the appropriate level of protection.

Information Classification Model

A unique group information classification model must be defined to adopt countermeasures suited to the classification assigned.

The objectives and policies are defined as follows:

- Defining and formalizing within a document the asset or information classification model based on information confidentiality, integrity, and availability requirements

- Defining and formalizing within a document the responsibilities, processes, methods, and instruments for the long-term management of asset or information classification levels

- Defining and formalizing within a document the criteria for identifying the appropriate methods to protect IT assets or information based on the classification level assigned

- Based on the classification level assigned, defining and formalizing information management methods in accordance with requirements set forth in current regulations

Assignment of Classification Levels

IT assets must be marked with the classification level assigned in order to ensure that they are properly managed. The objectives and policies are defined as follows:

- Unambiguously marking (physically or logically) IT assets with their classification level assigned on the basis of defined criteria

- Identifying suitable methods for the management of electronic and hard copy documents based on the classification of the information they contain in order to ensure confidentiality, integrity, and availability

Security Incident Management

Information security management requires an effective system to monitor and control suspicious situations and security incidents. These topics must be continuously monitored. A management model must also be prepared to recognize, combat, and resolve situations that pose the risk of loss of information confidentiality, integrity, and availability.

Event Reporting

The appropriate communication channels and methods must be established to promptly report incidents and suspicious situations in order to minimize the damage generated and prevent the recurrence of improper conduct.

Reporting of Information Security Incidents

Procedures must be defined to report security incidents and suspicious situations.

The objectives and policies are defined as follows:

- Defining procedures and instruments for reporting security incidents and suspicious situations, as well as the organizational units that should be involved

- Preparing templates to report and define the information needed to resolve incidents and suspicious situations

- Defining user rules and training plans regarding security events and the resulting actions to be taken

Incident Management

Procedures and responsibilities must be established to ensure a rapid, effective, and orderly response to security incidents. Management procedures, based on the severity of the disruption generated, must include different escalation levels in accordance with the provisions of the emergency and crisis management plan.

The objectives and policies are defined as follows:

- Identifying the organizational units responsible for the management of system attacks and security incidents and assigning the appropriate responsibilities for coordination, intervention, damage containment, and data collection

- Defining and classifying incident types, severity levels, and impacts depending on severity, as well as criteria for transition between the various levels and maximum intervention times

- Establishing different escalation levels based on incident severity

- Defining processes for incident detection, the activation of incident management units, the limitation of impacts, and interaction between group entities involved and with the competent authorities, ensuring the prompt involvement of the responsible departments and the integrity of proof

- Defining methods and instruments for reporting, sending the competent departments and the company's top management, storing and making available incident documentation

- Preparing incident management reporting templates

- Identifying procedures, rules, and standards for users concerning the appropriate conduct before, during and after a security incident is detected, and formalizing all appropriate recovery procedures

- Defining the information to be recorded, report submission timing, and report storage requirements for the various types of incidents, in compliance with the requirements of the competent authorities and in accordance with legal provisions, also in order to use such information as evidence in disputes

- Analyzing and processing the information collected to produce periodic reports for the assessment of incident evolution

- Formalizing, testing, and periodically reviewing an emergency and crisis management plan in line with regulatory requirements

- Adopting suitable measures to ensure that data access is recovered if data or electronic instruments are damaged

Learning from Security Incidents

Incidents must be analyzed to identify those that are recurring or have the greatest impact to take adequate countermeasures, including organizational measures and training.

The objectives and policies are defined as follows:

- Analyzing the most frequent incidents by quantifying and monitoring types, volumes, and impacts in order to define and plan the appropriate corrective actions, including to improve prevention capabilities

- Updating training activities as required with elements regarding the most frequent risks and the suitable conduct for preventing or managing security incidents

Collection of Proof

Proof must be collected in a manner that ensures that it can be used in legal disputes.

The objectives and policies are defined as follows:

- Assigning responsibilities and defining appropriate processes to govern the collection and storage of proof beginning with the first phases of the investigation

- Collecting proof, also on the basis of forensic computer techniques, that is admissible, complete, and enforceable in disputes against people or other organizations, in both civil and criminal cases

Security in Relations with Third Parties

Information security management requires data to be processed appropriately in relation with third parties, to comply with the law and ensure information security.

Therefore, it is important to pay attention to contractual requirements concerning security in relations with third parties that require access to company resources to provide the agreed services.

Exchange of Information with Third Parties

Responsibilities, processes, instruments, and methods must be formalized for the exchange of information with third parties. The possibility of using nonrepudiation techniques must also be evaluated.

Information Exchange Methods

The exchange of information and software with third parties must be formalized in a contract that establishes the responsibilities, processes, and methods for sending, transmitting, and receiving them. The objectives and policies are defined as follows:

- Defining specific contractual clauses regarding the confidentiality, protection, and destruction of information to be sent outside the company

- Defining responsibilities in agreements in the case of loss of information and software integrity, confidentiality, or availability

- Defining and agreeing upon the methods to be used to transmit information and software

- Evaluating whether it is necessary to transfer information externally and defining appropriate measures to protect confidentiality, integrity, and availability, to be included in agreements between the parties

- Ensuring that information and software are exchanged in line with legal, regulatory, and contractual provisions on security

- Defining rules for the protection of the property rights of the bank or third parties relating to software, files, and documentation exchanged with third parties

- Evaluating the use of nonrepudiation techniques for the transfer of information

Security Checks and Compliance

For countermeasures to remain adequate over time, they must be continuously controlled and verified so as to improve the level of protection they provide as well as identify new risks or any violations of rules and procedures.

All activities associated with information protection must comply with legal and regulatory provisions on information security as well as supervisory body directives.

Security Checks

Controls must be in place to verify that information systems comply with internal security provisions and to identify any nonconformities. The instruments used to carry out the checks and controls on systems and applications must be protected and must not interfere with the systems being controlled. Lastly, the adequacy of the protection measures activated must also be checked over time.

Control of the Application of Security Regulations

Compliance with internal security regulations by the various company departments must be checked periodically.

The objectives and policies are defined as follows:

- Assigning responsibilities for the correct execution of internal control phases

- Planning and carrying out internal controls in agreement with the individual departments involved

- Documenting the results of checks and reviewing them with the managers of the departments subject to internal controls in order to define actions to resolve any nonconformities

- Planning periodic internal controls to prevent security risks

- Verifying at established frequencies the proper implementation of actions addressing any nonconformities detected

Technical Controls

Systems and applications must be checked periodically to verify their adequacy with respect to issued security regulations and to detect any vulnerabilities. The objectives and policies are defined as follows:

- Identifying and assigning responsibilities for the implementation of a security control system in line with the group's current organizational model in order to maintain information system reliability

- Verifying the proper application by personnel and third parties of the rules defined for the proper use of the group's IT assets

- Ensuring that checks are carried out at pre-established frequencies by specialists using methodologies and standardized controls, under the supervision of authorized personnel

Information System Controls

System, application, and network control activities must be planned so as to limit impact on normal user operation to a minimum. The objectives and policies are defined as follows:

- Ensuring that personnel dedicated to control activities are allowed only the access required for their activities

- Identifying and making available the personnel required for controls

- Documenting all control requirements and procedures before the controls are conducted

- Tracking and monitoring access during control activities

- Guaranteeing that control activities interfere as little as possible with ordinary company activities

- Identifying specific areas for analysis to be certified/accredited periodically by independent third parties

User Security Rules

For protection measures to be effective, it is necessary to cultivate a feasible "culture of security" in addition to developing suitable information and training plans, by preparing user rules that guide daily activities to ensure that information is managed properly.

User Rules

Rules must be defined that make users, employees, and third parties responsible for the proper use of credentials. The IT equipment provided, in addition to other devices such as fax machines, photocopiers, telephones, videoconference equipment, etc., must also be protected by applying the appropriate rules for usage, storage, and protection during the user's temporary or permanent absence.

Use of IT Assets

User rules must establish how to correctly use the company's IT assets to protect the information they contain. The objectives and policies are defined as follows:

- Defining user rules that identify suitable methods for the management of electronic and hard copy documents based on the classification of the information they contain, also avoiding unnecessary duplications

- Defining user rules that establish how to correctly use the group's IT assets to protect the information they contain

- Defining user rules that prohibit the use of equipment that has not been assigned by the company to process company information without specific authorization, as well as unauthorized connection methods

- Defining rules for the physical and logical protection and safekeeping of instruments, equipment, and IT assets, when used outside the company offices, which are at least equivalent to those adopted for internal use and take into consideration specific risks

- Defining user rules regarding the management of any removable storage devices used

- Defining the appropriate user rules relating to prevention and protection from maligned code

- Defining user rules on the use of e-mail and Internet services, which state the associated risks

- Defining user rules to check the reliability, authenticity, and integrity of information coming from outside the company, if received by telephone, fax, or e-mail

- Defining user rules to protect the integrity and confidentiality of information exchanged verbally (directly, by telephone, via video conference, etc.)

- Defining rules for the use and placement of collective verbal and visual communications systems (e.g., videoconference) to protect the integrity and confidentiality of information exchanged

- Defining rules to protect the group's or third party's property rights in relation to the software, files, and documentation exchanged

- Informing personnel and third parties of the rules defined and the controls that may be carried out

Security Architecture

A comprehensive security architecture implements a three-tier architecture to protect the confidentiality, integrity, and availability of information systems. Three-tier architecture and security components at every layer will ensure the defense-in-depth principle is met and will reduce or eliminate the risks related to modern-day threats.

In this section, I cover the various solution components needed to incorporate comprehensive security for an EXP. The security architecture elements are designed to implement the security governance and objectives covered in the previous sections.

Security Overview of a Cloud-Based EXP

It is imperative that the security in an EXP solution prevents any unauthorized access and maintains confidentiality of the information. In a multitenant cloud-hosted scenario, the importance of a highly scalable and robust security architecture becomes much more significant, but at the same time, it is important that the proposed security architecture doesn't add unwarranted complexity and maintenance overhead.

Successful security strategies employ the concept of "defense in depth," which uses multiple layers and complementary functions to mitigate threats throughout the network.

The security responsibilities leverage the shared responsibility model provided by cloud vendors. The infrastructure provider/cloud provider provides the required perimeter layer of security, as well as network-level intrusion prevention and infrastructure security, physical and environmental security, business continuity management, and network security. In addition to the security layer provided by the cloud provider, it will provide a set of security controls configured, managed, and maintained as part of the EXP solution as a service offering.

Table 10-1 lists the security controls to be implemented.

Table 10-1. *EXP Security Controls*

Security Area	Subarea	Rationale for the Requirement
Application security	Web Application Firewall (WAF)	• To provide protection against web-based attacks. WAF provides an additional layer of protection by analyzing the layer 7 application logic.
Data security	TLS/SSL	• To provide secure communication from client machines to target machines.

(continued)

Table 10-1. (*continued*)

Security Area	Subarea	Rationale for the Requirement
Security management	Identity and access management (IAM)	• To provide secure access control (authentication, authorization) to the application users.
	Vulnerability management and patch management	• To ensure vulnerabilities present in the platform are identified and remediated proactively before they are exploited by the threat. • To ensure the platform receives patches in a timely manner.
Network security	Virtual private cloud (VPC)	• To provide a secure isolated network with a private IP range.
	Security groups	• To provide outbound and inbound firewall capabilities at the host level.
	Access control list (ACL)	• To provide a secondary layer of defense by blacklisting the types of access.
Endpoint security	Antivirus	• To prevent, detect, and remove malicious viruses from virtualized and nonvirtualized environments.
	Intrusion detection system	• To examine all incoming and outgoing traffic for protocol deviations, policy violations, or content that signals an attack.

The security controls for providing comprehensive security are as follows:

- Identity and access management
- Web Application Firewall
- Antivirus/malware protection
- Vulnerability management
- Host intrusion prevention system
- AWS security groups

- AWS access control lists

- TLS/SSL and VPN

I will go through each one of these in the following sections.

Identity and Access Management

The identity and access management system for an EXP infrastructure is comprised of the following elements:

- Identity manager

- Active Directory domain

- Integration layer

- Single sign-on (SSO)

Identity Management

Identity management (IDM) is achieved through an identity manager. The identity manager provides self-services, provisioning, and identity synchronization functionality. The identity manager is used to manage the user accounts. This includes managing user credentials, groups, and roles throughout the user lifecycle. Identity management also provides web service endpoints for identity management.

The major components of an identity manager are as follows:

- **Identity management portal**: The identity management portal is a UI component that can be accessed using a browser. The user operations such as create, update, enable, disable, and password reset can be done in the portal.

- **Identity management services**: Identity management services process all requests received from the identity management portal. They enforce authentication and authorization before processing the request.

- **Provisioning engine**: The provisioning engine component triggers provisioning to a target based on rules.

- **Policy engine**: This component is used to manage all the policies and control permissions to the portal and can run the workflows that make things happen.

- **Workflow and approval**: This component manages the user approval and access approvals needed for the system access.

Access Management (Single Sign-On and Federation)

Access management services provide authentication, authorization, and single sign-on functionality. The access management services will authenticate EXP users based on their credentials, authorize users based on their roles, and allow users to log in once and gain access to all the systems that a user is authorized to access without prompting for the credentials again at each of the systems within the same session.

The identity management system will be used as an identity store. Authentication and single sign-on are based on a federation model.

- An identity management service can be used as the identity store that provides authentication.

- The SAML plug-in provides the federation service and acts as an identity provider (IDP).

- EXP SSO provides the login page.

The identity management service will be used as a user store in the EXP security implementation and will be used to authenticate users. The identity is asserted in the form of claims to the EXP SSO. This mechanism is based on the SAML 2.0 protocol. EXP SSO provides the login page and also performs (coarse-grained) role-based access management to the EXP user for access to the various applications and other EXP apps (Figure 10-1).

1. User accesses an EXP portal using a browser.

2. The login page is directed to the user.

3. Credentials passed for authentication, and post-authentication attributes passed back to the EXP portal.

4.   Once the user clicks any of the applications (application 1, application 2, or application 3) on the EXP landing page after authentication, the SAML plug-in will fetch information from the identity management and generate a SAML token on the back end.

5.   The SAML token generated by the SSO plug-in in step 4 is passed to any of the admin applications that the user has selected in step 4. (The SAML token will have user data called *claims* and will be used for authorization.)

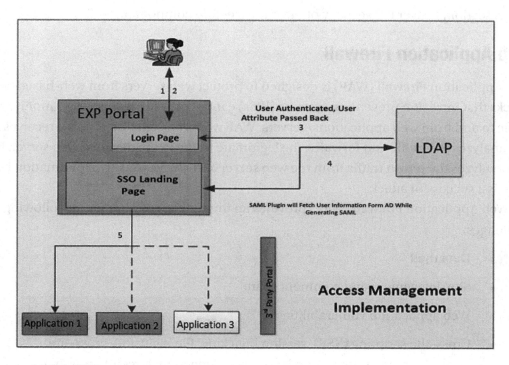

Figure 10-1. *EXP access management*

The solution implements the following standard best practices for user access management:

•   Use of encrypted passwords

•   Password complexity along with multifactor authentication

User Provisioning Solution

The user lifecycle will be managed via the identity management service. Any user created in other applications will be created in the identity management system as an identity and then will get autoprovisioned to the user repository.

Changes in user details in other applications will be populated in the identity management system, and the updated attribute will get synced with the user repository.

Infrastructure Security

In this section, I cover the security of the infrastructure components.

Web Application Firewall

Web Application Firewall (WAF) is designed to protect web servers from web-based attacks that intrusion prevention systems (IPSs) cannot prevent against. WAF monitors traffic to and from web applications/servers. WAF works on signatures, and it receives and analyzes the traffic and forwards the legitimate traffic to the destined web server. It also analyzes the return traffic from the web server and blocks sensitive information if there is a successful attack.

Web Application Firewall (WAP) provides an immediate solution for the following challenges:

- Data theft

- Site defacement and comment spam

- Web application vulnerabilities

- Cross-site scripting (XSS), session hijacking, file inclusion, cross-site request forgery, information leakage and injection, forceful browsing, cookie poisoning, and invalid input

- SQL injection and XSS attacks

- Traffic bottlenecks and single points of failure

WAF features centralized logging, analysis, statistics, version history and rollback support and built-in log analyzer, flexible filters, and easily export filtered logs.

WAF can be used to apply business rules to online traffic, inspecting and blocking attacks such as SQL injection and cross-site scripting (XSS).

Antivirus (AV) Software/Anti-malware

Antivirus and anti-malware software can be used to protect systems and files from malware, spyware, viruses, and other security risks. It detects and removes malware and configures antivirus policies to manage quarantined items. Virus scan enterprises offer easily scalable protection, fast performance, and a mobile design to protect the user systems from the following threats:

- Virus, worms, and Trojans

- Access point violations and exploited buffer overflows

- Potentially unwanted code and programs

The anti virus and anti-malware software detects threats present in the systems and then takes the remediation measure to counter them as configured by the administrator. Antivirus software is deployed on all the systems in the environment. Antivirus software enables a centralized security management software, which provides flexible, automated management capabilities so you identify, manage, and respond to security issues and threats.

Vulnerability Management

A vulnerability management solution scans passively, nonstop, or actively to discover, assess, remediate, and report on various assets. It uncovers devices hidden on the network as well as smartphones, tablets, and laptops that come and go between scheduled scans. A vulnerability management solution helps you to identify and protect the systems on the network. This allows you to monitor and respond to changing risks in your environment.

A vulnerability scan searches selected systems on the network for known vulnerabilities, such as whether a service pack is installed. A vulnerability scan can return all scanned data (vulnerable, not vulnerable, or indeterminate) or only vulnerable data in a report. A vulnerability management solution provides some preconfigured scan templates and scan configurations.

Host-Based Intrusion Prevention System (HIPS)

A host-based intrusion prevention system protects the system resources and applications from external and internal attacks and prevents zero-day attacks. Zero-day attacks are exploits that take advantage of software vulnerabilities unknown to security professionals. Because it's an unknown bug, no virus and spyware signature updates have been issued yet to thwart the malware. Zero-day attacks can penetrate deep into the enterprise, causing damage for days, if not weeks, before a fix is available.

A HIPS can protect information and prevent the compromise of system and network resources and applications that store and deliver information. The IPS feature has monthly content updates, which reduce the urgency of patches for new threats.

HIPS comes with dashboards that are a collection of monitors that are an essential tool for managing the environment. IPS policies turn host intrusion prevention protection on and off, set the reaction level to events, and provide protection through the application of exceptions, signatures, and application protection rules. IPS protection is kept up-to-date with monthly content updates that contain new and revised signatures and application protection rules.

Network Security

In this section, I discuss the key aspects of network security such as security groups, access control lists, and communications security.

Security Groups and Segregation

Security groups are planned to segregate environments in a web server tier, application server tier, and database tier. A security group restricts access from instance to instance and user to instance based on IP address, subnet, and port.

Communication Security

The communication channel to the cloud over the Internet can be secured using an IPSec VPN. The communication will be done only through secured protocols such as HTTPS, SFTP, and such. The enterprise communication channel will be secured using SSL certificates. There will be no plain-text data transferred over the network. All in-bound/out-bound operations work on SSL, and the data transfer between the two systems will be encrypted in transit using these certificates. Other than that, all the users will access the portal and application over the Internet using the SSL channel. Other security controls are outlined here:

- The firewall will ensure access controls are configured for users and EXP administrators/developers.

- Virtual private connectivity is ensured for identified credit institution users. Access to systems will be monitored by firewalls such as internal firewalls and Web Application Firewall.

- A system administrator's access permissions to manage the systems are implemented at the internal firewall.

Access Control Lists

Network access control lists (ACLs) provide an additional layer of defense to the security groups. They provide firewall functionality for controlling traffic. An ACL operates at the subnet level, whereas the security group operates at the instance level.

- All external connections will be protected by a firewall and will be the first line of defense for the entire EXP solution.

- The EXP solution network is segmented into five logical zones, as given in Table 10-2.

Table 10-2. EXP Network Security Zones

Zone Name	Description
DMZ zone	All components that require access from external network will be hosted from this zone.
	• Perimeter network protection components such as DDoS prevention, IPSs, spam protection gateways, and DLP gateways will be implemented to inspect all the ingress/egress traffic.
	• A VPN concentrator will be hosted to receive external inbound traffic from the Internet.
	• Load balancers and web servers that will receive inbound connections will be hosted from this zone.
	• An SFTP server will be hosted from this zone.

(continued)

Table 10-2. (*continued*)

Zone Name	Description
Production zone	All EXP solution components will be hosted from this zone. This also includes supporting components such as HSMs, domain controllers, antivirus servers, patch management servers, load balancers, and so on.
Dev/test zone	All the development and test systems will be hosted in this zone.
User zone	All users who have the requirement to be part of EXP solution development and support activities will be operating from this zone.
VPN zone	EXP services requiring exposure to institutions that are connected through a VPN will be hosted from this zone.

Application Security

The main application security measures are as follows:

- Captcha and dynamic session token/keys protect against reply attacks.

- Use AES 256 standard cryptographic keys for all user-related authentication requirements.

- Implement inactivity session timeouts.

- Use security parameters to expire cookie parameters and applicable HTTPS flags.

- Header parameters will have parameters/flags configured to guard against session fixation and cross-site scripting.

- All components that interact with web portals will access APIs over HTTPS.

Data Security

The following security measures will be used to protect against data theft/leakage:

- All sensitive data at rest including the data that will be stored in tapes will be encrypted using the cryptographic keys.

- Data in transit will only be sent over a secure channel that uses HTTPS or TLS.

- A tokenization solution will be implemented to ensure data tokenization is supporting all data access requirements.

- A data leakage prevention (DLP) solution will be implemented to monitor the occurrences that can lead to information leakage. The DLP solution will cover channels such as HTTP/HTTPS, FTP, and e-mail.

- All cryptographic key material will be stored in the HSM, and the key material will comply with the AES 256 standard. The HSM will have sufficient controls against key tampering or deletion.

- Database monitoring is implemented to monitor the database access.

- Direct access to database administration is not permitted. Database admins will be able to use a console or go through program interfaces to manage the databases. Administration activities such as database changes will be delivered in accordance with an IT security policy.

- The SFTP server will provide a service to ingest data. Each credit institution will have separate folder to ingest their corresponding data set.

End-User Security

End-user computing will have standard IT security controls that will be enforced through a centralized group policy. Those controls include but are not limited to the following:

- Laptop storage will be encrypted and will be implemented with a boot password.

- Users will be authenticated by the domain controllers before logging into the system.

- All user logon events will be logged and reported.

- Internet access will be permitted through proxy servers to control and identify malicious traffic at the gateway.

- CD-ROM/USB mass storage access is revoked by default, and endpoint protection controls will be configured to enforce the policies.

- Users will have no access to install any unauthorized system software. Only approved software will be provisioned.

- Group policies will ensure password management for endpoints.

- User access governance best practices will be implemented to ensure that:

  - User accounts will be created after successful onboarding into EXP delivery.

  - All accounts are disabled/deleted for those who are not part of the support and delivery.

- Any assets that get damaged or lost will be tracked, and necessary audit trails will be put in place.

- Employee declarations demonstrating the user responsibilities will be documented, and acceptance will be obtained.

Summary

This chapter covered the following:

- A comprehensive security framework consists of security design, security architecture, and security governance.

- The security design defines the comprehensive objectives and policies covering all security areas needed for EXPs.

- The security architecture provides a detailed solution architecture to address all requirements and policies defined in the security design.

- The governance defines roles and responsibilities needed for security management.

- Security design defines logical security requirements, identification and authentication, authorization, security event tracking, encryption, hashing and digital signatures, network management, system and network security, information classification, security incident management, exchange of information with third parties, security checks and compliance, and user security rules.

- A comprehensive security architecture implements a three-tier architecture to protect the confidentiality, integrity, and availability of information systems.

- The security architecture covers identity and access management, infrastructure security, network security, application security, data security, and end-user security.

- Security governance defines the processes for maintaining the security standards and security policies elaborated on in the security design.

CHAPTER 11

Digital Workplace Maintenance and Governance

Maintenance and governance are essential for digital workplaces during the post-production phase. Efficient maintenance/governance is necessary for the continued success of the digital workplace.

Maintenance includes activities such as enhancements, automation, and patching that are part of the day-to-day activities of an EXP. Governance includes standard operating procedures (SOP), roles, and responsibilities for managing EXP operations.

This chapter covers the EXP maintenance and governance-related topics.

EXP Maintenance Framework

EXP maintenance includes the regular maintenance activities to keep the platform running and performing optimally.

The following are the key pillars of an EXP maintenance framework:

- **Automation**: This includes automating the routine management activities such as backups, data synchronization, and such.

- **Monitoring**: This includes monitoring the EXP systems and applications in real time and notifying users in case of an SLA violation.

© Shailesh Kumar Shivakumar 2020
S. K. Shivakumar, *Build a Next-Generation Digital Workplace*, https://doi.org/10.1007/978-1-4842-5512-4_11

- **Core maintenance:** This includes performing activities such as patch management, log management, and such.

- **Incident management:** This includes handling system enhancements and handling application-related incidents.

- **Operations KPIs and focus areas:** This includes defining the KPIs and metrics to measure and quantify the effectiveness of the maintenance/operations framework. Here you define the core KPIs and the focus areas for the KPIs and metrics.

Next I will cover the common challenges in operations and maintenance of an EXP.

Common Challenges in EXP Maintenance

Table 11-1 describes the common issues related to EXP maintenance.

Table 11-1. *EXP Maintenance Challenges*

Maintenance Issue Category	Brief Issue Details	Best Practices
Responsiveness/ compatibility/omnichannel experience	If the EXP UI is not responsive, the UI will not be usable across various devices and browsers. Disparate user experience across various channels.	• Using responsive UI leveraging CSS 3, media queries, adaptive images • Providing mobile apps for popular sites
Identity management and SSO	Varied identity across affiliate and partner sites. Absence of identity management system.	• Centrally managed identity management • SSO across all affiliate and partner sites

(*continued*)

Table 11-1. (*continued*)

Maintenance Issue Category	Brief Issue Details	Best Practices
Usability (localization, information discovery, information architecture)	Difficult to use the site. Difficult to find relevant information quickly. Unfriendly navigation. Suboptimal content strategy. Challenges in the user journey. Challenges in using the digital platform on all channels and mobile devices.	• Contextual menus • Chat bots/virtual assistants • Guiding hints • User segmentation • User journey mapping • Personalization and contextual information delivery • Search as key information discovery tool • Rich metadata and tagging with well-defined taxonomy • Intuitive information architecture • Persona-based design and user-centric approach • Decision-making tools such as product comparators, various sorting options, various filters
Security	Data breach, identity theft, absence of authorization, absence of encryption of sensitive data.	• Addressing OWASP top 10 security issues. • Robust security testing • White-box, black-box testing • Penetration testing/ethical hacking

(*continued*)

Table 11-1. (*continued*)

Maintenance Issue Category	Brief Issue Details	Best Practices
Performance	Site is slow or not responding, request times out, page response time is high, images load slowly.	• Performance-based design • Multilayer caching • Real user monitoring • Robust performance testing • Containerization • Proper infrastructure sizing
Availability	Site/service availability, frequent outages, absence of monitoring infrastructure, absence of real-time application monitoring.	• Multinode cluster/cloud deployment • Real-time availability monitoring and notification • Disaster recovery (DR) setup • Business continuity planning (BCP) • Cloud deployment
Images/videos	Heavy images, numerous images on landing pages, using nonstandard video formats.	Using adaptive images and responsive images
Heavy registration forms	Too many fields and pages, multiple steps for form completion	• One-click registration/ onboarding • Minimal field form
Heavy landing pages	Too much content. Too many images on landing pages impacting performance. Cluttered user interface.	• Minimalistic design • Light-weight landing pages • CSS at top, JS at bottom • Minimal JS includes • Usage of merged/minified files

(*continued*)

Table 11-1. (*continued*)

Maintenance Issue Category	Brief Issue Details	Best Practices
Search engine optimization (SEO)	Suboptimal SEO strategy impacting site traffic, absence of content tags, absence of metadata, absence of information architecture.	• Friendly URLs • Proper, meaningful page metadata • Properly labeled ALT tags for images • Intuitive site map, information architecture
Suboptimal content	Generic non-personalized content. Duplicate content. Absence of metadata. Broken links/images.	• Robust content strategy • Targeted content delivery • Properly tagged content • Searchable content • Personalization • Content marketing strategy
User engagement	Minimal user engagement, absence of contextual information, absence of collaboration, absence of self-service.	• User-centric design • Chat bots • Information architecture • Omnichannel • Self-service features • Collaboration features • Personalization
Integration issues	Timeouts, errors, integration performance.	• Fully tested integrations • Graceful error handling

In the subsequent sections, I discuss the key pillars of the EXP maintenance framework.

Automation and Process Optimization

Automation and process optimization are used primarily for productivity improvement and cost optimization. In this section, I discuss the key methods for automation and process optimization.

Automation

Repeatable maintenance activities are ideal candidates for automation. You can create machine-learning bots and automation scripts for such activities. An AI-first approach can be used for the activities such as automated issue analysis, ticket triaging, reactive maintenance, preventive maintenance, and adaptive maintenance.

The following are the automation opportunities in maintenance, which can use bots or automated scripts:

- Reporting requirements that generate predefined reports and dashboards on a periodic or on-demand basis.

- Monitoring requirements such as infrastructure monitoring, service monitoring, application monitoring.

- Data reconciliation requirements.

- Access management such as defining, adding, creating, updating and deleting user permissions.

- Account creation/activation/deactivation requirements.

- Forgotten password/updating password requirements.

- Machine Learning (ML)-based incident pattern analysis and feeding the insights back to users or the service management team.

- Chat bot services for handling user queries and triggering automated tasks.

- Building machine learning models to predict volume, which allows the support team to do proactive maintenance during holiday seasons and other business-critical days.

- Intelligent operations, which involves predictive and knowledge-driven automation.

  - Self-learning bot for ticket analysis and categorization

  - Conversational AI for descriptive user training

- Robotic operations, which effectively involves "codifying standard operating procedure" for resolving the specific subcategory of tickets.

  - End-to-end automation for data manipulation related tickets using the bots

- Automating job schedule failures (back-office data issues) and user management issues (reset password) to eliminate manual intervention. The automation opportunities should be able to automatically rerun jobs, alert users, and take the right actions.

- Adopting intelligent automation to learn from human actions to imitate some of the corrective actions adopted by the support team.

- User training based on the knowledge base and application know-how.

- Providing access to systems through a bot operating in batch mode or real-time mode.

- Monitoring batches and raising alerts through a bot. This can evolve into auto-remediates wherever possible based on the use case identified.

- Using a bot to generate periodic or on-demand dashboard.

Process Optimization

Process optimization involves identifying the business processes that can be optimized based on insights from analytics and based on user satisfaction surveys. During process optimization, you identify opportunities to optimize the existing operation processes for productivity improvement and cost optimization. The following are the main process optimization opportunities:

- Standard Operating Procedure (SOP)-based shift-left (process to move and automate the activities to L1/L2 support) for high-volume issues and automation of SOP-based left-shifted issues.

- Focused enrichment of logs to expedite root-cause analysis.

- Self-service portal for user management, account management, access management, password management, report generation, dashboard customization, and such. You can develop a self-service portal for business managers.

- Auto-diagnosing incidents for faster resolution and self-service through assisted operations.

  - Self-service portal for user management

- Deployment process optimization through consolidating the deployment items and deploying only affected artifacts.

- Knowledge management by capturing the process documents, troubleshooting details, FAQs, root-cause analysis documents, and such.

- Through shift-left, enhancing SOP/knowledge base of data issues for the L1 team.

- Training and cross-skilling resources to handle incidents related to multiple technologies.

- Productivity improvement through continuous improvement and automation.

Core Maintenance and Operations

Core maintenance and operations activities are used for the regular and ongoing maintenance tasks of an EXP. In this section, I discuss the main activities of maintenance and operations.

Patch Management

You need to design a centralized patch management solution to monitor the progress of patches. Security patch implementations and the scope will be governed in accordance with the defined IT security policy.

The best practices to implement security patches are as follows:

- **Security patches with zero-day mitigation**: Provide 100 percent coverage within three days.

- **Other security patches**: Provide 100 percent coverage within 30 days for all critical system, and provide 100 percent coverage within 45 days for non-business-critical systems.

- **Other**: All other patch types can follow standard implementation cycles.

As part of the security function, you will collaborate with other teams such as server admins, end users, and the help desk to ensure that an ongoing patch management program is implemented for all the stakeholders. The security function will track and publish weekly and monthly reports. Any critical unattended events will follow an incident management process.

Log Management

The EXP system will be configured to maintain audit logs, event logs, and error logs in a centralized log management system for all monitoring and events according to the security governance policy and will provide information upon request. These audit logs will be secured and stored as per the defined retention policy.

The logging standard controls will be designed to handle the following:

- Log sources are verified where feasible.

- Log sources are authenticated and sent over a secure communication channel.

- Logs are categorized and available in the system.

- Logs does not contain any personal or sensitive information.

- Log normalization is within the permissible limit.

- Security audit logs are segregated from other log types.

- Direct viewing of logs in human-readable format will not be permitted.

- Log collectors or aggregators are secured from any misuse or sabotage.

- Log rotation and archival will be in accordance with a retention policy.

- Log parsing or extraction is performed from approved sources only.

With these guiding principles, the centralized log management system will receive security logs from the following systems and more:

- Domain controllers

- Firewalls

- IPS/HIDS

- Antivirus gateway

- Application servers

- Web Application Firewall

- DLP servers

A security incident and event management (SIEM) solution can be leveraged to monitor and detect anomalies as they happen. SIEM alerts and logs will be configured for reporting.

Monitoring

The monitoring infrastructure plays a key role in ensuring high availability and faster responses. In this section, I discuss various aspects of monitoring. Figure 11-1 shows an example machine-led automated operations model.

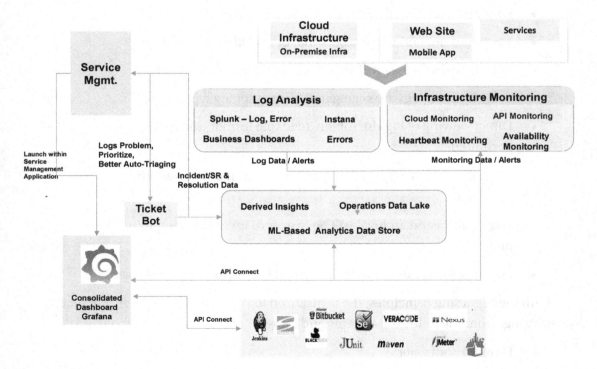

Figure 11-1. *Machine-led EXP operations model*

The automated operations setup is designed to automatically monitor the systems, services, applications, mobile apps, and infrastructure. The operation model automates the following activities:

- **Infrastructure monitoring**: The monitoring setup includes components such as heartbeat monitoring (for checking the service availability), API monitoring (for checking the API performance), cloud monitoring (for checking the cloud component availability), and availability monitoring (for checking the service and system availability). The infrastructure monitoring components monitor the on-premise infrastructure, services, applications, and cloud applications in real time. Resources such as CPU, memory, storage, network elements, and traffic are monitored in infrastructure monitoring. The following are monitored as part of application monitoring:

  - APIs to understand the response times, error rate, availability and performance of APIs.

  - Service availability to understand the availability % of services.

  - Third-party services to understand their performance, availability

  - Response time (90th, 95th, and 99th percentiles) of application and services

  - Error rates and top ten exceptions

  - Page response time, average throughput, total throughput, average hits, total hits

  - Count of transactions passed and failed

- **Log analysis**: These components continuously monitor the application logs and system logs for system errors and application errors. The data obtained from the log analysis and infrastructure monitoring is fed into the machine learning models for further analysis.

- **Dashboard**: A consolidated dashboard provides information about the log issues, monitoring issues, code quality issues, testing reports, build issues, and such.

- **Service management**: Based on the analysis of the log errors and infrastructure monitoring by machine learning models, a ticket bot will automatically raise the tickets. Additionally, alerts are sent to notify the admin in case of threshold violations.

Early Warning System for Proactive Maintenance

An early warning system (EWS) is a set of systems that proactively and continuously monitors the key systems with defined parameters. Once the specified SLA is violated, it should trigger an e-mail notification to the configured admins. I recommend the use of an EWS for proactively monitoring the following parameters:

- System availability to monitor the availability % of all the involved systems and applications.

- Service availability to monitor the availability % of all services.

- CPU usage to continuously monitor the CPU utilization %

- Memory usage to continuously monitor the memory utilization %

- Disk usage to continuously monitor the disk utilization %

EWS Implementation

A comprehensive monitoring solution involves application and services health check monitoring and real user monitoring/synthetic monitoring through Nagios.

Application/Services Health Check Monitoring

As part of best practices, you need to monitor your servers and applications for performance. You need to monitor the infrastructure and applications from a 360-degree perspective. The advantages of monitoring the systems and applications are as follows:

- Continuous monitoring for vulnerabilities and threshold configurations

- Instant alerts and notifications when a downtime incident is reported

- Faster root-cause analysis

- Reduced cost of ownership

- Improved productivity and accelerated turnaround

- Health dashboards with in-depth reporting features such as a summary report, busy hours report, trend report, downtime report, and so on provide holistic view of performance, health of all involved systems.

- Improved customer satisfaction

You can leverage application monitoring tools to build the health check/heartbeat monitoring of the services and systems. You can create health rules for key performance metrics that you want to monitor. You can create notification alerts for serious health rule violations. For instance, you could create a health rule to detect errors for HTTP response code 404 (not found), 500 (Internal server error), or 502 (not available), and send out an e-mail notification to the system administration team.

Synthetic Monitoring

Synthetic monitoring tools such as Nagios can be used for real-time application monitoring. For real-time monitoring of the EXP application, you can use these steps:

1. Configure the production URL for the EXP application. You can configure the core EXP pages for this.

2. Configure Nagios to monitor the performance of the servers.

3. Configure e-mail addresses in Nagios to send the alert notifications.

Log Monitoring

Log monitoring tools such as Splunk, ELK, Kibana can be configured to monitor the critical errors in the application log files. You can configure Splunk to alert for HTTP 500 errors. You can create a search query for key errors and configure real-time alerts for notification.

AI-Led Operation Model

You can leverage bots to handle the initial response to the incidents. Figure 11-2 shows the machine-led operations for monitoring and incident management.

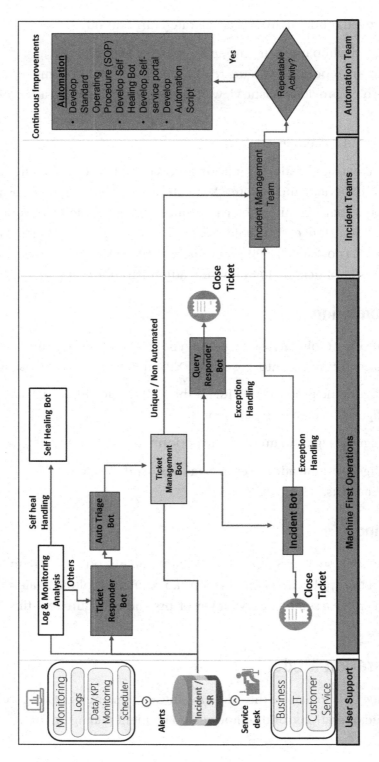

Figure 11-2. Machine-led operations and incident management

The machine-first operations model uses bots for expediting the response and ticket resolution. An incident or service request is logged by customer service representatives or through automated monitoring agents when the agents detect KPI/SLA violations. Based on the analysis of the error logs, a self-healing bot can address the issue for simple/predefined issues. For example, a self-healing bot can be trained on certain errors and the resolution steps:

- If the server is down, restart the server.

- If the service is down, redeploy or restart the service.

The ticket responder bot and auto-triaging bot can identify false positives and forward the details to a ticket management bot. If the logged incident is not a real issue, the ticket management bot can route the request to an incident bot, which closes the incident with a proper response.

If the logged incident can be responded to with details from an existing knowledge base, the ticket management bot forwards the request to the query responder bot, which provides the relevant response and closes the incident.

If the ticket is complex and needs manual intervention, the ticket is forwarded to the incident management team. The automation team analyzes the historical data of incidents and does the root-cause analysis and resolution analysis. All repeatable activities will be taken up for the following given automation initiatives:

- Development of self-service features

- Development of self-healing bots based on the repeatable activities

- Development of standard operating procedures (SOPs) to implement the shift-left policy

- Development of automation scripts

- Development of batch jobs and synchronization jobs for data-related activities

Proactive Log/Event Monitoring and Predictive Maintenance

Figure 11-3 shows a sample proactive log/event monitoring and predictive maintenance model. The figure depicts the open source tools for implementing the monitoring ecosystem.

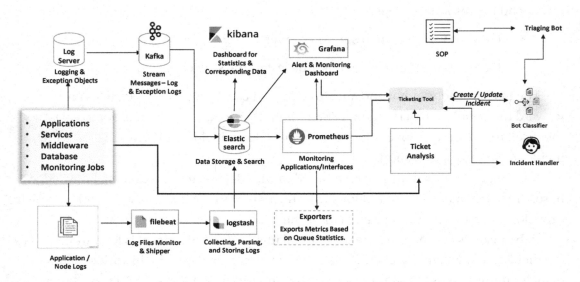

Figure 11-3. *Proactive log and event monitoring*

Components such as applications, services, middleware (ESB, API Gateway), and databases are continuously monitored, and the monitoring events and errors are logged in centralized log files. Apache Kafka is used for processing the log stream and feeding the inputs to Elasticsearch. Filebeat also manages the logs and feeds the data to Logstash for parsing and analyzing the log entries. Kibana provides the unified dashboard depicting all the events and data. Elasticsearch, Logstash, and Kibana (ELK) act in unison to provide robust log monitoring, log analysis, and visualization capabilities.

Prometheus can monitor the applications/interfaces, and Grafana can be used for visualizations. Based on the application monitoring, Prometheus can feed the data to a ticketing tool that can create tickets.

The ticketing tool can leverage the bot classifier to forward the ticket request to an appropriate bot or to an incident handler. The root-cause analysis (RCA) can further be used for automating the activities and creating a standard operating procedure.

Incident Management

In this section, I cover the AI-led approach for incident management.

AI-First Approach

Conversational AI can be used for user training using the NLP and conversational interface modules. Conversational AI such as chat bots can also be used to implement the bot-first ticket handling. Figure 11-4 shows a sample setup of automated ticket handling.

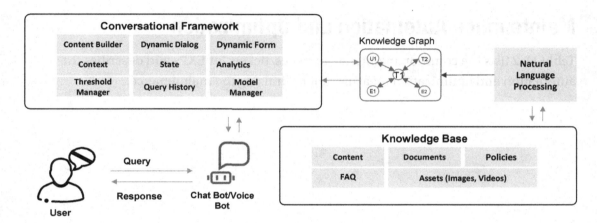

Figure 11-4. *Sample ticket handling process*

The following are the high-level steps of a bot-first service request/incident management flow:

- The user inputs the query to the chat bot. Alternatively, the user can ask the query to a voice bot in natural language.

- The bot is built using a conversational framework that handles the query. The conversational framework extracts the main entities, keywords, and intent from the user query.

- The conversational framework leverage the knowledge graph that stores the entities and relationships.

- Natural language processing (NLP) is used to build the knowledge graph from the knowledge base. The NLP module extracts the entities from various knowledge artifacts such as documents, policies, FAQs, and web content.

In this model, the bot can handle the bulk of user queries, and for complex/unknown queries, the bot can log the incident to be handled by a human support analyst.

Maintenance Automation and Optimization

Table 11-2 lists the common maintenance issues/tickets for EXPs and describes the automation and optimization measures for optimizing the maintenance.

Table 11-2. *Automation Opportunities for EXP Maintenance Issues*

Category	Brief Details	Intervention Type	Intervention Details
System/application/ service configuration	• Request for changing application configuration with well-defined steps/SOPs • Request for changing server configuration with well-defined steps/SOPs • Fixing account lockout issues • Fixing password reset issues	Automation	• Provide self-service portal with automated workflows to do the repetitive tasks such as password reset, unlocking account • Develop and use how-to document providing detailed instructions on making configuration changes • Develop automated scripts to unlock account and reset password
System/application/ service access	• Providing access/permissions to applications • Creating new accounts	Automation	• Provide self-service portal with automated workflows to do the repetitive tasks of granting access permissions and creating accounts • Develop automated scripts for new account creation and reset password

(continued)

Table 11-2. (*continued*)

Category	Brief Details	Intervention Type	Intervention Details
System/application/ service error	• Web application errors such as HTTP 500, 502, and 404 • Generic application error message	Automation, problem management, shift left	**Automation** • Set up an automated monitoring and alerting mechanism • Configure thresholds to automatically send alerts on errors • Automatically monitor for 50x and 40x errors in the server logs and splunk logs and notify the administrators automatically **Problem Management** • Perform root-cause analysis of recurring problem patterns • Document the solutions/workarounds/ configuration changes/best practices/SOPs needed to address the errors • Store the document in a searchable centralized knowledge base • Create a mapping document of common application error messages to remediation steps **Shift Left** • L1 can use the documented workarounds, best practices, and SOPs to address the most common error scenarios

System/application/ service availability	• System/service/application is down • System/service/application gives HTTP 404/service unavailable exception • System/service/application access times out	Automation, problem management	**Automation** • Set up an automated system/service/availability monitoring and alerting mechanism • Set up real automated user monitoring to monitor the sites in real time • Configure the thresholds to report the performance issues • Set up automation scripts to monitor the system performance (CPU, memory, disk usage network usage) and do the heartbeat monitoring (such as pings, HTTP endpoint invocation) for the key systems and services **Problem Management** • Constantly monitor the growth of user traffic/content growth and accordingly revisit the infrastructure sizing, application memory/CPU requirements • Conduct thorough availability testing to test the system behavior • Set up disaster recovery environment and business continuity process

(continued)

323

Table 11-2. *(continued)*

Category	Brief Details	Intervention Type	Intervention Details
System/application/ service performance	• System/service/application takes a lot of time to respond • System/service/application hangs or times out	Automation, problem management	**Automation** • Set up an automated performance monitoring and alerting mechanism • Set up real automated user monitoring to monitor the sites in real time • Configure the thresholds to report the performance issues **Problem Management** • Perform root-cause analysis of all performance issues and document the solutions, best practices, and SOPs • Conduct robust performance testing (such as endurance testing to identify memory leaks, stress/peak load testing to test system behavior and system breakpoints) for each of the releases to uncover the performance early
System/application/ service security	Injection attacks, identity theft	Problem management	• Perform various forms of security testing such as penetration testing, black-box testing, white-box testing • Perform security testing for each release/sprint
Data backup and data synchronization	Request for data backup and data synchronization	Automation	Create automated script for data backup

Automation-Led Operations Road Map

Figure 11-5 shows a sample two-year road map for automation interventions and machine-led operations management. It shows the prioritized list of optimization interventions such as shift left and the timelines for implementing the optimizations in that category.

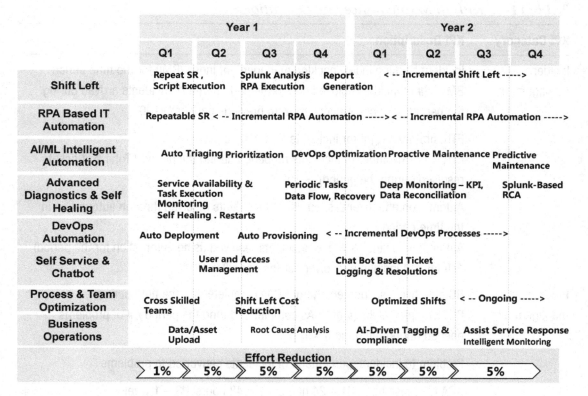

Figure 11-5. Prioritized list of optimization interventions

Operations KPIs and Focus Areas

In this section, I cover the key performance indicators (KPIs) for EXP operations and maintenance, as well as the focus areas to achieve the KPIs.

Operations and Maintenance KPIs

The main categories in operations and maintenance are incident management, problem management, service request management, configuration and release management, and knowledge management. Table 11-3 depicts the KPIs that are mainly used in maintenance and operations.

Table 11-3. *KPIs in Maintenance and Operations*

KPI Category	KPI Description
Incident management	Incident backlog index: backlog management index (BMI) for the time period BMI = (# of incidents closed during the period) / ((# of incidents arrived during the period) + (# of incidents c/f from previous periods))∗100
	FTR: first time right for incidents for the time period FTR = (1 - (Number of incidents reopened during the period / Total # of tickets resolved during the period)) ∗ 100
	Automation effectiveness: number of incidents resolved through automation in the time period Automation usage % = (# of incidents resolved using automation for the period) / (Total # of Incidents resolved for the period) ∗ 100
Problem management	RC effectiveness: percentage of RCAs completed for the time period RCA completion %: (# of RCAs completed during the period / # of problems opened during the period) ∗ 100
	Problem to incident: percentage of incidents converted to problems
	RCA response time: P1 – 24 hours, P2 – 48 hours, P3 – 1 week
	Percentage of preventive fixes rolled into production (subject to development commitment / L3)
	Incidents reduction rate for the period ((# of incidents reported in previous period - # of incidents reported in current period) / # of incidents reported in previous period ∗ 100) ∗ (Year of engagement), period = quarterly (12-month rolling basis), where L3 is in scope
	First time right for problems for the time period: FTR = (1 - (Number of problems reopened during the period / Total # of problems during the period)) ∗ 100

(continued)

Table 11-3. (*continued*)

KPI Category	KPI Description
Service request fulfilment	SR backlog management index for the time period (BMI) = (# of incidents closed during the period) / ((# of incidents arrived during the period) + (# of incidents c/f from previous periods)) * 100
Configuration and release management	Percentage of errors contributed due to configuration issues in the time period: Configuration error index = (# of incidents attributed to configuration issues in the defined period) / (Total # of incidents reported in the defined period) * 100 (L3 in scope)
	Release accuracy percentage for the time period: Release accuracy % = 1 - ((# of actual releases in the defined period - # of planned releases in the defined period) / 100) (L3 in scope)
	Rollback percentage for failed releases in the time period: Rollback % = (# of rollbacks in the defined period) / (# of Releases made in the defined period) * 100 (L3 in scope)
Knowledge management	Percentage of resources onboarded through the agreed knowledge management process: Onboarding effectiveness % = (# of people onboarded through the process in the defined period) / (Total # of people onboarded in the defined period) * 100
	Percentage increase in knowledge articles during the time period: % increase in knowledge articles = (# of new knowledge articles) / (Total number of knowledge articles) * 100
	Percentage of articles converted to self-help during the time period: (Number of self-help articles created in the time period / Total number of articles created in the time period) * 100

Focus Areas for Operations and Maintenance

The focus areas to achieve the KPIs for incident management, problem management, service request management, configuration and release management, and knowledge management are depicted in Tables 11-4, 11-5, 11-6, 11-7, 11-8, and 11-9.

Table 11-4. *Incident Management*

Incident Management		
Focus Areas	**Levers**	**Expected Outcomes**
Major incidents	On-time actions: speedy response and actions, SLA adherence Preventive maintenance: monitoring and operations management	Better business alignment, better service availability, reduction of high-priority incidents
Knowledge reuse	Leverage standard operating procedures (SOP), application playbooks, leverage knowledge management	Faster response times, right first-time improvements, enhanced productivity
Operational performance reporting	Statistical analysis of various operational and ticket attributes and performance measures, derive patterns, trends for continual improvements	Enhanced proactive and predictive maintenance multilayered performance management reporting
Automation	Leverage KM: standard operating procedures (SOP), event correlations, tool integrations	Machine-first operations, productivity enhancements

Table 11-5. *Configuration Management*

Configuration Management		
Focus Areas	**Levers**	**Expected Outcomes**
Version management	Synchronized environments for better build and test effectiveness	Right first-time builds
Service introduction	Cohesive ways of working between dev and operations teams for better defect control and effective root-cause analysis	Minimum impact to service operations and better customer experience and faster and effective solution efforts
Integration and interfaces	Critical continuous integration, continuous integration dependencies and interfaces	Comprehensive landscape management, better impact analysis of changes
Automation	Versioning, license management, asset tracking and reporting	Automated configuration reporting

Table 11-6. *Maintenance Governance*

Maintenance Governance

Focus Areas	Levers	Expected Outcomes
Avoidance	Well-defined RACI: ownership assignment	Well-defined roles and responsibilities
	System performance management: preventive and predictive operations, periodic housekeeping, health checks	Schedule and track operational health checks and heat-map observations
	Service introduction: efficient traceability of business requirements to application changes to operational runbooks better handshake between dev and ops, better business alignment	Address knowledge gaps, defect prevention and on-time redressal, operational ownership (PGLS)
Management	Robust governance: communication channels for various processes such as major incidents, outage communications	Expectations setting, proactive communications, on-time actions
	Centralized and up-to-date RAID trackers	Transparent and open reviews

Table 11-7. *Capacity and Performance Management*

Capacity and Performance Management

Focus Areas	Levers	Expected Outcomes
Monitor, measure, manage	Platform-driven dashboards	Transparent service and performance management
Continuous service improvements	Platform-driven service improvements	Drive overall productivity and performance improvements
Automation	Machine-first operations: RPA and ML-based automation	

(*continued*)

Table 11-7. (*continued*)

Capacity and Performance Management

Focus Areas	Levers	Expected Outcomes
Capacity utilization/workload distribution	Review against benchmarks/ thresholds to assess performance on monthly basis	Team composition optimization
Demand management/business volume indicators (BVI)	Analyze trends, rolling forecast to plan and manage capacity	Proactive and seamless ramp-up initiation as per changes to BVI

Table 11-8. *Monitoring and Alerting*

Event Management (Including Monitoring and Alerting)

Focus areas	Levers	Expected Outcomes
Automation	Tool integration for auto-ticketing and SOP integration for self-healing, retrospective analysis of correlation of events and incidents and SLA impacts	Reduction of false positives, incident resolution effectiveness
Elimination of false positives	Leverage machine learning capabilities to build false positive correlations with system behavior	Quantitative predictive maintenance
Predictive maintenance	Alignment with runbooks, periodic health checks	

Table 11-9. *Operations Continuity*

Operations Continuity Management

Focus Areas	Levers	Expected Outcomes
Align service continuity strategy with overall BCP	The operations continuity should be aligned with overall business continuity plan (BCP).	Zero business impact, operational support continuity, higher service availability, risk-mitigated services delivery
Regular business impact analysis	The business continuity process should be continuously updated to ensure that it is in sync with the business processes.	
Risk assessment	Recognize the vulnerabilities and risks associated	
Service continuity strategy	Recovery plans, standby arrangements, risk reduction measures	
Test	Test the implemented solution with updates to SOPs and risk trackers	

Governance

Because cloud-first designs for EXPs are widely used across many implementations, in this section I cover the security governance that defines the roles and responsibilities needed for security management.

Security Governance

Security governance defines the processes for maintaining the security standards and security policies covered in the security design. The security governance includes roles and responsibilities, iterative testing, patch management, and ongoing security compliance. I discuss these topics in this section.

Security Roles and Responsibilities

The security organizational model must identify the required data protection activities and the departments concerned and their interaction and assign them the responsibilities of ensuring implementation, verifying activities over time, and supporting the top management in making security policy decisions.

Information security management roles and responsibilities must be assigned to ensure that a standard approach is taken across groups involved in protecting the company's data integrity in the various operating phases.

The following are the key objectives and policies for defining security roles and responsibilities:

- Providing an overview by identifying strategic guidelines and managing security initiatives (e.g., correctly assigning roles and responsibilities and defining risk management policies), in addition to assigning these tasks to an interdepartmental body representing the top management, made up of members with specific skills in this area

- Assigning specific responsibilities in compliance with current regulations to provide oversight over security policy-making and governance, risk management and control, and the design, implementation, application, and control of countermeasures to protect the company's data

- Defining and managing over time the relationships among the departments (ensuring that the controller and the controlled are independent of each other), operating processes, autonomies and budget responsibilities, and establishing delegations and procedures for managing security risks

- Assigning precise responsibilities for the management of security aspects, including those set forth in specific regulations on the topic, to the organizational departments that develop and manage information systems

- Assigning responsibilities to ensure that internal rules and legal or regulatory provisions on security are applied

- Defining responsibilities and mechanisms to manage abnormal security events and crisis situations, in line with regulatory requirements

Security Compliance

Complying with various standards and policies is a key to achieving the set business goals. The solution implements the following items, to meet the compliance requirements

- Audit compliance reports and closure plan.

- Security plan.

- Security components uptime.

- Penetration testing reports.

- System configuration review reports.

- Remediation agreement and road map for vulnerability closures and patch management.

- Adherence to GDPR, ISO 27001, DSCI, OWASP, and ISO 22301.

Summary

This chapter covered the following:

- Maintenance and governance are essential for digital workplaces during the post-production phase.

- The key pillars of EXP maintenance framework are automation, monitoring, core maintenance, enhancements, and incident management and operations KPIs and focus areas.

- Common issues related to EXP maintenance are responsiveness/ compatibility/omnichannel experience, identity management and SSO, usability (localization, Information discovery, information architecture), security, performance, availability, images/videos, heavy forms, heavy landing pages, search engine optimization (SEO), nonoptimal content, user engagement, and integration issues.

- An AI-first approach can be used for the activities such as automated issue analysis, ticket triaging, reactive maintenance, preventive maintenance, and adaptive maintenance.

- Process optimization involves identifying the business processes that can be optimized based on insights from analytics and based on user satisfaction surveys.

- The machine-led automated operations model includes infrastructure monitoring, log analysis, dashboard, and service management.

- Early warning system and proactive maintenance includes application/services health check monitoring, synthetic monitoring, log monitoring, and the AI-led operation model.

- An early warning system is a set of systems that proactively and continuously monitor the key systems with defined parameters.

- Security governance elaborates on the security roles and responsibilities, log management, patch management, security testing, and security compliance.

CHAPTER 12

EXP Case Studies

Case studies elaborate on real-world business scenarios and provide insights into proven methods and best practices that could be adopted. In this chapter, you will look at some real-world scenarios related to digital workplaces. I will use the proven patterns and methods discussed in earlier chapters for these case studies.

Development of a Next-Generation Digital Workplace

In this case study, I cover the various methods and activities for developing a modern digital workplace. I start with the case study background and then discuss the challenges of the current system. Finally, I explain the specific digital transformation process.

As part of the digital transformation process, I detail the various activities of an execution methodology by covering the activities in phases such as project management and governance, requirements elaboration, detailed design, iterative development, iterative testing, functional testing, performance testing, security, and accessibility testing.

Background and Business Context

A globally distributed services organization wants to build a next-generation digital workplace. The primary business goal is to develop a next-generation workplace that improves employee engagement through the following features:

- Enhanced collaboration among employees

- Improved information access for employees

- Improved two-way communication between the organization and the employees

335

© Shailesh Kumar Shivakumar 2020
S. K. Shivakumar, *Build a Next-Generation Digital Workplace*, https://doi.org/10.1007/978-1-4842-5512-4_12

- Friendlier user interface with high usability and high information discoverability

- Ability to rapidly onboard new capabilities

- Ability to scale and manage high-volume transactions

- A single point for accessing information with a unified user interface

- Improved search capabilities resulting in finding relevant and contextual information

Challenges

The main challenges of the existing intranet platform are as follows:

- The existing platforms do not provide a unified employee experience.

- The only collaboration feature is text-based chat.

- The existing systems need a lot of maintenance to add new features.

- The existing platforms are not able to scale to an increased employee load.

- The existing platform provides a basic and primitive search feature that does not provide relevant search results.

Digital Transformation

In this section, I cover the various aspects of the digital transformation. I discuss the core attributes of the digital transformation, the road map for digital transformation, and a detailed execution methodology.

Attributes of Digital Transformation

Figure 12-1 shows the key attributes of a next-generation digital workplace.

Figure 12-1. *Attributes of digital transformation*

In this case study, a digital transformation of the next-generation digital workplace focuses on these core attributes:

- **User experience**: The next-generation employee platform should provide an omnichannel-enabled, easy-to-use, and easy-to-find-information user experience.

- **Content**: The content should be designed to effectively communicate the organizational updates.

- **Collaboration**: The platform should provide collaboration features to share information and enable interpersonal collaboration.

- **Security**: The platform should provide secured and role-based content and functionality.

- **Mobility**: At a minimum, mobile apps should be made available for core features of the platform.

- **Governance**: Governance needs to continuously maintain, update, and improve the platform.

- **Alerts and notification**: The platform should provide on-demand alerts and notifications to employees.

- **Services**: The platform should provide services that can be used by other internal applications and mobile apps.

- **Reports and dashboard**: The platform should provide an aggregated single view of employee details and interaction through dashboard reports.

- **Feeds**: The platform should be able to consume and publish feeds.

- **Integration**: The platform should provide a flexible and scalable integration methodology with internal and external applications.

- **Search**: The platform should provide relevant search functionality to enable faster and relevant information discovery.

- **Self-service**: The platform should provide automation and self-service features for employees to improve the task completion time and process completion time.

- **Personalization**: The platform should provide personalized information and services based on employee roles, job responsibilities, and preferences.

- **Analytics**: The platform should provide analytics features to gather insights about platform usage, employee actions, and such.

- **Workflows**: The platform should model the employee flows (related to content, claims, leaves, etc.) through workflows.

Road Map for a Next-Generation Digital Workplace

The road map for a next-generation digital workplace defines various implementation phases and detailed activities for each of the phases.

Figure 12-2 shows the implementation road map, which identifies the key milestones.

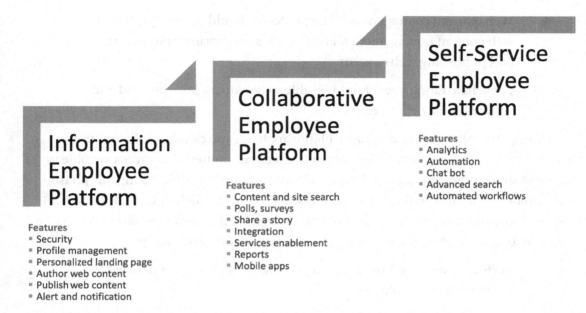

Figure 12-2. *Road map for next-generation digital workplace*

As shown, there are three implementation stages for the development of the next-generation digital workplace: the information employee platform, the collaborative employee platform, and the self-service employee platform. During the information employee platform phase, you develop the core platform features such as security, profile management, and personalization. Basic content management features such as content authoring and content publishing are developed during this phase. The main employee scenarios for the first iteration of the revamp are as follows:

- **Personalized home page**: The intranet home page should provide personalized information and functionality.

- **Alert and notification**: The platform should provide alerts and notifications for upcoming events.

- **Profile management**: Employees should be able to manage their profile attributes and manage passwords and security questions.

- **Search**: The platform should support a search feature for content search, people search, skill search, and document search.

- **Web content management**: The platform should be able to provide web content management features such as authoring web content and publishing web content.

- **Favorites**: Employees should be able to bookmark favorites and add a favorites list of articles.

During the collaborative employee platform phase, you develop collaboration features such as polls, surveys, chat, forums, and communities. Employees are able to blog and share their experiences through a "Share a story" feature. During this phase, the employee platform is integrated with upstream systems such as CRM, ERP, web applications, and services. Reports and mobile apps are developed as part of this phase. Detailed features such as the following are developed during this stage:

- **Polls and surveys**: The platform provides polls and surveys to get feedback from employees.

- **Communities**: The platform provides community support for employees. The other collaboration features provided are blogs and wikis.

During the self-service employee platform stage, you develop features such as analytics, automation, and chat bots to enable self-service and productivity improvement. Automation is introduced into a few workflow steps such as the leave system, space allocation system, asset allocation system, and such. Advanced search features such as faceted navigation, search filters, suggestions, and search-driven recommendations are introduced.

Execution Methodology

The execution methodology for implementing a next-generation digital workplace is elaborated on in this section. Figure 12-3 identifies the key activities and deliverables for each of the activities.

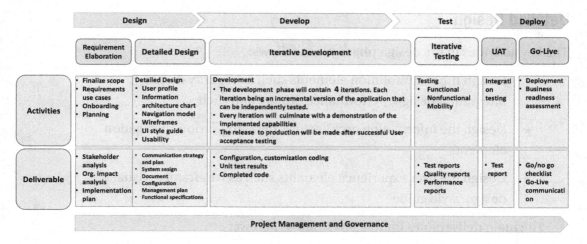

Figure 12-3. *Execution methodology for next-generation digital workplace*

Requirements Elaboration

The key activities in the requirements elaboration are as follows:

- Finalizing the scope for each of the iterations

- Developing requirements use cases

- Doing a requirement gap analysis

- Gathering the as-is security architecture and details of external applications

- Finalizing business rules and model business processes

- Finalizing integration points with other applications

- Finalizing the software products and source control systems

- Onboarding project resources

- Developing a project plan for the entire project

The main deliverables for this phase are as follows:

- Stakeholder analysis document detailing the needs and priorities for each of the stakeholders

- Impact analysis document detailing the impact of the project on various ecosystem elements

- Detailed project plan for the project execution

Detailed Design

The key activities in the design phase are as follows:

- Design the main solution elements such as security design, integration design, performance design, and such

- Design the information architecture, detailing various navigation elements

- Design the user experience elements such as wireframes, visual design, style guide

The main deliverables for this phase are as follows:

- Detailed design documents for overall solution

- Analysis and flow diagrams for each of the business processes

- Communication plan document detailing the communication strategy for all stakeholders

- Information architecture document detailing various elements such as menus, site hierarchy, and other navigational elements

- Training plans for training the onboarded resources

- Functional specifications document to detail the specification for integrations

- Configuration management to detail the version control and source control management

One of the key activities in the design phase is the user experience design. Figure 12-4 shows the main steps in the user experience design.

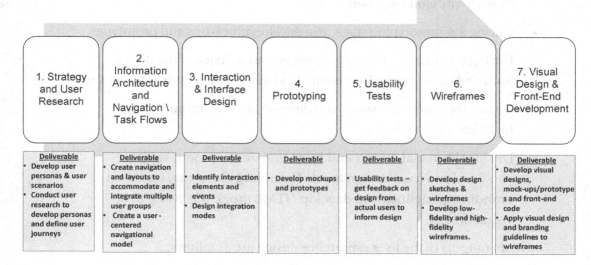

Figure 12-4. *User experience design for next-generation digital workplace*

For each of the stages, here are the activities and corresponding deliverables:

- The first step in the user experience design is to do strategy development and user research. During this initial stage, you develop distinct employee personas based on common user needs, interests, and goals. You also model user journeys for each of the identified personas. The main activities in the user research stage are as follows:

  - Stakeholder interviews to understand business goals, user profiles, needs, and pain points

  - Working sessions with actual users as identified by business stakeholders

  - Prioritization of user scenarios and user profiles

- In the second stage, you identify key navigational elements (such as menus, breadcrumbs, site hierarchy) and develop a user-centered information architecture. You also model the navigation flows and task flows closely based on the users' mental models.

- In the interaction and interface design stage, you define the interaction elements such as event handlers, action buttons, interactivity elements, and such.

- During the prototyping stage, you develop mock-ups and prototypes.

- During the usability test stage, you get the feedback of the design from end users during beta testing and iteratively improve the design.

- During the wireframe stage, you develop low-fidelity and high-fidelity wireframes.

- During the visual design and front-end development stage, you develop visual design assets (branding elements) based on branding guidelines and develop HTML mock-ups using the visual design.

The main outputs of the user experience design are as follows:

- User personas identifying the main employee personas

- Information architecture defining the key navigational elements

- Wireframes for all platform pages

- Static JPEG images of visual design for unique page types

- UI style guide document defining the color scheme, font specifications, image specifications, and such

- Prototypes and mock-ups for the pages

The next stage in execution is the actual system development that happens iteratively.

Iterative Development

You develop the system in iterations. Each iteration is an incremental update over the previous iteration. The main activities in this phase are as follows:

- Coding and development of modules

- Configuration of the application servers and web servers

- Integration of the system with upstream systems

- Content creation (static contents, templates, workflows)

- Unit testing of the developed code artifacts

The main deliverables from this stage are unit-tested code, code review reports, test coverage reports, and code quality reports.

Iterative Testing

During the iterative testing phase, you validate the quality of code artifacts iteratively. Detailed use cases and business rules are used to develop test cases and test plans.

Functional Testing

Functional testing involves the validation of core application functionality. The following are key activities in this category:

- Creating functional test cases based on requirement scenarios and user stories.

- Requirement traceability matrix that maps the requirements to their corresponding test cases

- Identifying and creating test data needed for testing

- Test execution to run all the test cases

- Defect management to prioritize and close the defects

- Status report detailing the test coverage, SLA compliance, defect age, code quality, and such

Nonfunctional Testing

Nonfunctional testing validates the quality attributes of the application such as performance, security, scalability, availability, modularity, accessibility, and such. During the requirements elaboration phase, the business users specify the scope and SLAs for nonfunctional requirements, which will be validated during this testing.

- Performance testing includes workload modeling, performance test script development, validation of response time SLAs, and such.

- Security testing includes development of a security test plan based on threat assessment and security requirements and execution of various security vulnerability scenarios.

- Accessibility testing validates the accessibility standards such as WCAG standards.

The entire project needs proper governance and project management. The project management track spans all stages, as detailed in the following sections.

Project Management and Governance

The key activities in this stage are as follows:

- Launch project initiation activities

  - Document project objectives and scope

  - Initiate project governance, establishing project steering committee and core team

  - Confirm detailed project plan

  - Establish project schedule management, risk/issue management, change control, quality management plan

- Drive deliverable release scheduling

- Work with business area representatives across the application portfolio to prioritize and schedule the project releases

- Execute ongoing project management activities

- Track project schedule, risk/issue management, change control, budget, and project teams

- Conduct project closure/lessons learned

The key deliverables in this phase are as follows:

- Program plan that defines various releases, milestones, and deliverables

- Issues and risk register to track the known risks along with their priority, impact, and mitigation plans

- Change control tracker to manage all change requests

- Resource plan for onboarding and managing project resources

- Status reports detailing various project activities

Benefits

The next-generation digital workplace for this case study provides these benefits:

- Provides a platform for unified collaboration and personalized platform

- Provides seamless omnichannel experience with employee mobile apps

- Scalable modular platform that can manage high-volume transactions

- Enhanced search with improved information discovery

- Provides a single-stop-shop experience for all employee communications

Legacy Intranet Transformation

In this case study, I discuss the digital transformation of a corporate intranet platform developed on legacy technologies to a next-generation employee experience platform.

Background and Business Context

A global manufacturing organization has been running an intranet built on older web technologies for more than two decades. The legacy intranet has more than 50 independent web sites each with different brand identity. Each web site has a distinct set of user role definitions.

Challenges

The following are the challenges of the legacy intranet platform:

- There is a diverse and inconsistent user experience across multiple intranet applications. Users often get confused in the navigation because of the diverse look and feel.

- The legacy intranet web site has an inconsistent information architecture.

- There is no single source of truth of information.

- There are no collaboration features to encourage employee interaction.

- The legacy intranet has poor information findability and communication.

- There are no governance processes related to content publishing.

Digital Transformation

In this section, I discuss the process for digital transformation.

Migration

- The data of all 50+ intranet applications were migrated to a single centralized database. During the migration, the duplicate and outdated information was removed.

User Experience

- The next-generation digital workplace was built on a responsive design leveraging web-oriented technologies (ReactJS and microservices).

- A user-centric design was created, and information architecture depicted the mental model of the employees.

- The landing page was personalized for employees with benefits information and news content.

- The employee-centered information architecture was designed based on the employee's mental model.

- Omnichannel was enabled on the new platform using mobile apps and a responsive design.

- The new platform provides personalization and customization features for employees.

Governance

- The content publishing process was streamlined, and roles were defined for content authoring, content approval, and content publishing.

Collaboration

- The new employee experience platform supports user-generated content (UGC) such as blogs, review comments, wiki articles, and such.

- Employee productivity and self-service tools such as a benefits calculator, knowledge base search, ticketing application, and leave application were developed to help employees.

Benefits

The following are the benefits:

- Since the rollout of the employee experience platform, the employee platform is the primary channel for organization communication.

- The new employee experience platform is the one-stop shop for policy information, applications, and collaboration.

- Employee satisfaction increased by more than 30 percent, and employee productivity increased by more than 20 percent.

Employee Platform for Retail Organization

In this case study, I discuss the employee platform of a retail organization that has been growing through acquisitions.

Background and Business Context

The retail organization had acquired multiple companies in the recent past. As a result of these acquisitions, there were multiple intranet platforms. Management of employee communications was challenging, and the organization was forced to use the e-mail channel.

Challenges

The following are the current challenges for this case study:

- There is a lack of a common communication channel for employees, leading to a heavy reliance on e-mails.

- There is no centralized repository to maintain skills and knowledge.

- There are no governance processes related to content publishing.

Digital Transformation

In this section, I will discuss the process for digital transformation.

Consolidation

- Four different intranet platforms were consolidated into a single platform to create a uniform design.

- Interviews were conducted with all stakeholders and employees to understand the holistic requirements for the employee platform.

- A uniform URL/link structure was created for all user groups with localization support.

Content

- A content evaluation was conducted to understand the pain points and challenges of the existing content.

- Content processes were created to streamline the content creation and content publishing process.

- A centralized knowledge management was created for storing the content centrally and using it for learning.

<u>Integration</u>

- The new employee platform was integrated with partner channels.

- The new employee platform was integrated with enterprise search for content search, people search, and site search capabilities.

<u>User Experience</u>

- Various aspects of user experience such as user research UI design, visual design, content design, governance, taxonomy, and style guide were redesigned.

- Based on the user requirements and needs, user personas were created.

- Newly revamped wireframes and visual designs were created to visualize the future intranet platform.

Benefits

A unified corporate communication and collaboration platform was created.

- Four road map tracks helped to improve communication, collaboration, productivity, metrics, and governance.

- The employee satisfaction increased by more than 50 percent.

Employee Portal for Unified Information

In this case study, I discuss the employee platform of a technology organization that faces challenges with information management.

Background and Business Context

The organization wants to create an "employee portal" to streamline information availability, enable higher employee collaboration, and improve productivity through integrated tools and content. The core requirements are given in Figure 12-5.

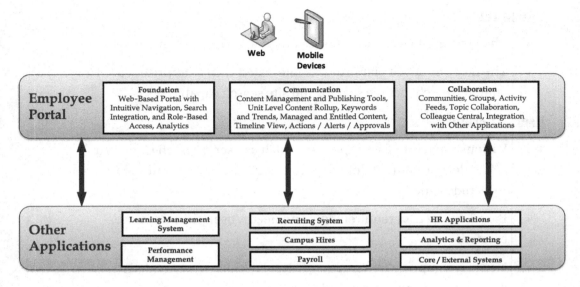

Figure 12-5. *Employee portal requirements*

Challenges

The following are the current challenges:

- There is no employee collaboration in the existing intranet.

- There are no defined processes for information management.

- Many of the employee tasks are done manually, leading to higher turnaround times.

Digital Transformation

In this section, I discuss the process for digital transformation.

Transformation Themes

Figure 12-6 shows the core digital transformation themes.

Employee Empowerment	Work flexibility	Rewards & Recognition	Information Management
• Collaboration • Self-service • Automation • Useful applications	• Flexible schedule • Work from anywhere • Work-life balance	• Continuous feedback • Instant recognition • Gamification	• Document management • Insights and analytics • Search & knowledge base • Content sharing

Figure 12-6. *Digital transformation themes*

The primary transformation principle is employee empowerment. Using collaboration tools and self-service and automation methods, employees can perform tasks faster and achieve higher productivity levels. Many of the employee functions have digital applications that further enable the employees' productivity.

Providing work flexibility is another key transformation principle for employees. This includes providing flexible work schedules and remote work enablers to provide a work-life balance.

Millennials who form a major portion of the workforce are motivated by instant recognition. Hence, the employee platform should provide tools for continuous feedback and recognition. The platform should also leverage gamification concepts to recognize and reward the employees.

The information management category includes efficiently managing the content, documents, and overall information so that the information is easily accessible by employees. As a part of this, the company enabled knowledge-based search functionality.

Employee Portal Architecture

The employee portal architecture was created to implement the key transformation themes, as shown in Figure 12-7.

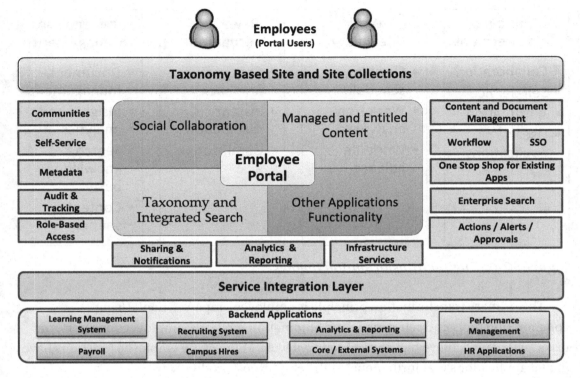

Figure 12-7. *Employee portal architecture*

The main building blocks of the employee portal are collaboration, content management, and information management using taxonomy and search and supporting applications. The social collaboration category includes communities, forums, chat, blogs, and a wiki for improved collaboration. The content management category provides improved content and document management, workflows, content archival, and content publishing. For the information management capability, you implement a taxonomy, metadata, and integrated search. Using a centralized knowledge base, you can use search to provide the right information. You should enable employees with applications to improve the overall productivity of the employee. Employee dashboards should provide a one-stop-shop experience and provide secured access to content and functionality.

Other features such as analytics and reporting, alerts, and notification provide insights into employee actions.

A service integration layer is leveraged to communicate with the system of records such as the learning management system (LMS), recruiting system, payroll system, HR systems, and such.

Benefits

The following are the benefits:

- A seamless and secured information management was provided by the employee platform using content management, search, and knowledge base.

- Using metadata, taxonomy, and search provided enhanced information discovery.

- Using analytics, audit, and reporting provided vital employee insights.

- A scalable and extensible integration platform was developed using services-based integration.

Summary

This chapter covered the following:

- The development of a next-generation digital workplace had challenges related to collaboration, information access, communication, scalability, and availability.

  - The key attributes used in digital transformation were user experience, content, collaboration, security, mobility, governance, alerts and notification, services, reports and dashboard, feeds, personalization, integration, search, analytics, self-service, and workflows.

  - The main road map stages of digital transformation were information employee platform, collaborative employee platform, and self-service employee platform.

  - The execution methodology for the next-generation digital workplace included requirement elaboration, detailed design, iterative development, iterative testing, UAT, and go-live.

- For a legacy intranet transformation, the main challenges were inconsistent user experience, inconsistent information architecture, absence of collaboration features, and lack of governance.

  - The digital transformation process involved user experience transformation, migration, governance, and collaboration.

- In an employee platform for a retail organization case study, the main challenges were lack of common communication channel, absence of centralized repository, and absence of governance process.

  - The digital transformation process included consolidation, content, integration, and user experience.

Index

Printed in the United States
By Bookmasters